Valley of Heart's Delight

The publisher and the University of California Press Foundation gratefully acknowledge the generous support of the Ralph and Shirley Shapiro Endowment Fund in Environmental Studies.

Valley of Heart's Delight

ENVIRONMENT AND SENSE OF PLACE
IN THE SANTA CLARA VALLEY

Anne Marie Todd

UNIVERSITY OF CALIFORNIA PRESS

University of California Press
Oakland, California

© 2023 by Anne Marie Todd

Library of Congress Cataloging-in-Publication Data

Names: Todd, Anne Marie, author.
Title: Valley of heart's delight : environment and sense of place in the Santa
    Clara Valley / Anne Marie Todd.
Description: Oakland, California : University of California Press, [2023] |
    Includes bibliographical references and index.
Identifiers: LCCN 2022018545 (print) | LCCN 2022018546 (ebook) |
    ISBN 9780520389571 (cloth) | ISBN 9780520389588 (paperback) |
    ISBN 9780520389601 (epub)
Subjects: LCSH: Agriculture and state—California—Santa Clara Valley
    (Santa Clara County) | High technology industries—Environmental
    aspects—California—Santa Clara Valley (Santa Clara County) | Santa
    Clara Valley (Santa Clara County, Calif.)—History.
Classification: LCC F868.S25 T63 2023 (print) | LCC F868.S25 (ebook) |
    DDC 979.4/73—dc23/eng/20220518
LC record available at https://lccn.loc.gov/2022018545
LC ebook record available at https://lccn.loc.gov/2022018546

31 30 29 28 27 26 25 24 23 22
10 9 8 7 6 5 4 3 2 1

For Louis

CONTENTS

ACKNOWLEDGMENTS

This research was supported by grants from San José State University and the College of Social Sciences at SJSU. I am indebted to the librarians and archivists who supported my research: Cate Mills, History San José; Lisa Christiansen, California History Center; Charlene Duval, Sourisseau Academy, and Rebecca Kohn and Shane Curtin, Special Collections, Martin Luther King Library, San José State University.

My deepest appreciation to Stacy Eisenstark at UC Press for seeing the possibility of this project and shepherding it through multiple revisions with encouragement and support. Thank you to Naja Pulliam Collins for detailed and responsive editorial support.

My gratitude to my colleagues at San José State, including Kate Davis for suggesting pathways for publication, Glen Gendzel for sharing his love of California history, Alan Leventhal for background and context regarding the Ohlone indigenous people, and Rona T. Halualani for ongoing support and motivation.

A very special thank you to David Mariani for sharing his own family research, additional historical resources, providing editorial feedback, and for numerous conversations including lunch! I am immensely grateful for Jennifer Wool for her extraordinary efforts in facilitating multiple delightful visits with the Wool family, and for sharing family archives. Thank you to April Halberstadt for a series of conversations, for sharing resources, and for her National Heritage Area efforts.

Thank you to Cayce Hill, Bill Morrison, Kate Shuster, Emily Schwing, and Thomas R. Todd Jr. for reading drafts of the manuscript and providing edits and helpful suggestions.

Thank you to the reviewers, including two anonymous reviewers and Richard Besel for their helpful critique and comments that strengthened the manuscript and contribution. Particular thanks to Samantha Senda-Cook for her extensive feedback in the review process and her additional advice and support with several aspects of this project.

Finally, I am indebted to the following people who took the time to share their recollections and understanding of the Valley of Heart's Delight: Vicky Bosworth, Robin Chapman, Terry Christensen, David Cortese, Chris Costanzo, Eric Goodrich, April Halberstadt, Mac Hamilton, Tori Hamilton, Mike Kutilek, Joanne Larsen, Andy Mariani, David Mariani, Mark Mariani, Patty MacDonald, Mike MacDonald, Jean McCorquodale, Joe Melehan, Betty Nygren, Charlie Olson, Deborah Olson, Barbara Pyle, John Pyle, Chad Raphael, Xavier Regli, Audrey Rust, Ruth Savage, Ted Smith, Brad Stapleton, Sam Thorp, Peter Coe Verbica, Bruce Wool, Deb Wool, Jennifer Wool, Jim Zetterquist.

Introduction

CHARLIE OLSON WATCHED as the bulldozer started its engine and slowly steered toward the cherry trees. He hugged a family friend whose face crumpled in tears. The gathered crowd held its collective breath, mouths agape, as the excavator arm extended toward the trees, jaws open. One man held his hat over his heart in a reverent gesture. The sky flashed, and a bolt of lightning startled onlookers. Undeterred, the bulldozer tore the first trees from their roots. Many in the crowd blinked back tears at the "loud cracking of the aged cherry wood."[1] The bulldozer made quick work. By the end of the day, sixteen acres of 100-year-old cherry trees were gone. Charlie's sister, Yvonne Jacobson, lamented, "it took about 100 years of cultivation to get them all in place, but it takes them less than two minutes to pull out one of those trees."[2] In the orchard's place? Three hundred apartments and a sixty-thousand-square-foot shopping center.[3] The dramatic destruction of the Olsons' orchard was a high-profile moment in the transformation of the Santa Clara Valley, a stark example of urban and suburban development of agricultural land in America.

Charlie Olson shakes his head as he remembers that day: "It was the crime of the century: paving over the best soil in the world."[4] Olson is one of the last orchardists still working in the Santa Clara Valley—tending a piece of the orchard his grandparents bought in 1901: ten acres of apricot trees and three acres of cherry trees on the heritage orchard in Sunnyvale. His office is covered in family photos, birthday cards, news clippings, State Fair ribbons, and dozens of plaques for civic awards. Sunnyvale's housing developments and strip malls surround the Olsons' shrinking acreage. "The orchard, once part of a living sea of trees carpeting the valley floor, is now a miniscule oasis in the midst of concrete, condos and freeways."[5] Charlie Olson still tends his acres. "I don't really know why I'm the last one here. . . . It's just that farming is special to me, and I love my job."[6]

The Olsons have grown fruit for more than a century, witnessing the rise and fall of the fruit industry in the Santa Clara Valley, once known as the Valley of Heart's Delight. The phrase "Valley of Heart's Delight" was likely coined in 1905 when the *San José Mercury Herald* held a competition to find an appropriate name to market the valley's fruit.[7] Also known as the "Garden of the World," the Santa Clara Valley, about fifty miles south of San Francisco, was the premier fruit-producing region in the United States from 1860 to 1960. It was the largest orchard the world had ever seen, with eight million fruit trees blooming each spring.[8] Although the decline of the fruit industry in this area began shortly after World War II, the bulldozing of the Olsons' orchard in 1999 signaled the end of an era in a region the world now knows as Silicon Valley.

THE VALLEY OF HEART'S DELIGHT

In 1856, Louis and Pierre Pellier brought cuttings of the *petit d'Agen* prune from their native France to farmers in the Santa Clara Valley, and in doing so launched an industry. Fruit grows exceptionally well in the Santa Clara Valley. Its temperate climate, protective foothills, and ten feet of alluvial soil create premium growing conditions for outstanding fruit. When news of the prune's success spread, would-be orchardists came to the Santa Clara Valley in droves. Many of these were gold-seekers who found mixed success in the Sierra Nevada mountains and turned to cities and agricultural land as their next prospect.[9] The pastoral land offered money to be made in agriculture and cattle and thus began an era of growth and development in the valley unparalleled anywhere in the country.[10]

By 1920, seventy years after Louis Pellier brought the prune to California, Santa Clara County grew one-third of the prunes in the world.[11] The growth was exponential. Three hundred acres of prunes in 1870 grew to ninety thousand in 1900. Apricots, cherries, peaches, pears, and almonds also grew in abundance. Between 1880 and 1890, the number of fruit trees in the valley doubled to 4.5 million.[12] Canneries proliferated: San José Fruit Packing Company opened in 1873, Golden Gate Canning in 1875, J.M. Dawson Packing Company in 1879, and California Packing Company in 1885.[13] These canneries employed more than one thousand workers during the 1887 season, producing one million dollars of canned goods and four million pounds of dried fruit.[14] After the valley produced a record twenty-two million pounds of prunes in 1892, the California Board of Horticulture declared Santa Clara County the preeminent horticultural county of the State.[15] In 1893, the San José Fruit Packing plant was the largest cannery in the world.[16] At this time, the Santa Clara Valley produced 90 percent of California's fruits and vegetables.[17]

To understand the importance of Santa Clara Valley's fruit production for the rest of the country, consider the story of the rains of 1918 when the federal government called in the Army to help save the prune crop. The first week of September 1918 was dry and sunny as usual. The valley was covered in acres of fruit trays: millions of purple prunes lay on eight-foot wooden trays drying in the sun. During the weeks after the prune harvest, rain "was dreaded, never even mentioned."[18] All farmers had contingency plans: "If it rained or even looked like rain, all of the fruit would be stacked in piles of about twenty-five trays high, empty trays placed on top to try to keep the rain from getting to the drying fruit."[19] On Wednesday afternoon, September 11, it began to rain almost without warning; nearly half an inch of rain fell that night. The rain continued: on Thursday, 4.32 inches of rain fell, on Friday, 1.43 more inches.[20] The *Mercury Herald* reported that by 5 p.m. on Friday, 6.5 inches of rain had fallen in San José—more than three times the precipitation ever recorded in an entire September.[21]

As the storm passed over the valley, all contingency plans were useless. On Friday, the *Mercury* reported "damage to tomatoes, prunes and peaches, hay and grain so enormous that ranchers and canners refuse to even try to estimate the loss." One woeful grower estimated "fully one-half the prune crop is ruined."[22] A subsequent heavy fog held moisture in the air, preventing the prunes from drying.[23] The California Prune and Apricot Growers surveyed the damage and found much of the fruit on trays and on the ground had started rotting. "Trays were floating in water, and no effort could save those that had rotted. The whole valley smelled like fermented prunes."[24]

A large portion of the prune crop was destined for soldiers mobilized for World War I. The Food Service Administration proclaimed it to be the "patriotic duty" of every prune grower to save as much fruit as possible, and came to the valley to tour the losses.[25] The *San José Mercury* urged growers to "Save Fruit for Our Boys!" advising growers to turn their prunes to avoid decay or mold, which would render them "unfit" for soldiers.[26] The War Work Council dispatched one thousand soldiers from Camp Fremont, a military base in Palo Alto, to help save the crop. Volunteers from across the county helped soldiers pick prunes from the ground, carry out trays in the morning and back in at night, and turn the prunes on the trays.[27] Despite the community's valiant efforts, on Tuesday the *Mercury* reported, "Prune loss is near total."[28] The 1918 crop was estimated to be seventy million pounds, already only 65 percent of a normal crop. According to the *San José Mercury Herald*, it devastated every family in the valley.[29] This episode demonstrates the precarious nature of an agricultural economy susceptible to weather events, particularly for a community devoted to a single crop. That the federal government would deploy soldiers to help save the prunes also reveals the national importance of the agricultural production of the Santa Clara Valley.

The valley would recover, and continue to be known for its fruit. At the valley's productive peak in the 1920s, 7,000 farms grew 130,000 acres of orchards.[30] That is nearly ten million trees: including 7,652,000 prune trees, 665,000 apricot trees, 482,000 peaches and 380,000 cherry trees, producing 250 million pounds of fruit per year.[31] By 1922, of 867,200 land acres in Santa Clara County, 743,822 acres had nearly 24,000 farms.[32] That statistic is staggering: 86 percent of the land in the valley was agriculture. Santa Clara Valley and California were humming toward a billion-dollar annual agricultural production.[33]

The stock market crash of 1929 and subsequent economic woes almost immediately affected the Santa Clara Valley fruit industry. In 1929, growers were paid 10 cents a pound; by 1930, they received 5 cents. Between 1929 and 1932, annual farm income in the United States plummeted from twelve billion dollars to less than five billion dollars.[34] Santa Clara Valley growers faced particular challenges due to what would later become known as the Great Depression. Prices dropped as consumers cut out specialty fruit like prunes, apricots, and pears.[35] Associations like Cal-Pak and the Prune and Apricot Growers fought to maintain price stability and to protect growers and packers. Beleaguered growers suffered, while canners fared a bit better because they could diversify.[36] The Depression would have long-lasting effects on labor in fruit growing and packing in the Santa Clara Valley.[37] Mechanization of agriculture and increasing integration and incorporation of food processing systems amplified the pressure on workers. While the valley's productivity remained strong, the Great Depression profoundly affected farmers in the Santa Clara Valley. It "changed the nature of the local economy and consequently of the landscape itself."[38] Toward the end of the

1930s, growers were uprooting fruit trees. More than 4,500 acres of prunes were leveled by 1941.[39]

World War II was a "catalyzing event."[40] The valley's transition from agricultural productivity can be "directly traced to wartime electronic research."[41] World War II opened up industrial opportunities as defense-related industries moved in, laying the framework for post-war development of Silicon Valley.[42] World War II also introduced the Santa Clara Valley to thousands of military and civilian personnel stationed in the Pacific Theater.[43] Soldiers remembered the temperate weather, expansive open space, and beautiful fruit trees as they passed through the valley on their way to the Pacific front.[44] "For the first time, the quiet, peaceful agricultural valley was exposed to intense public view."[45]

World War II sparked an industrial rush aided by government officials and developers eager for business. Fruit trees were torn up and canneries shuttered, replaced by houses, roads, and office parks—the infrastructure to support the bourgeoning electronics and computing industry. Between 1945 and 1964, 17,000 agricultural acres were bulldozed per year, 340,000 acres of farmland gone in twenty years.[46] Acres devoted to fruit in Santa Clara County dropped by more than 90 percent between 1960 and 1992, from 64,453 acres to 5,325.[47] The latter half of the twentieth century saw the decline of the fruit capital in a swiftly changing economy instigated by the rapid growth of the computer era.

The story of the Santa Clara Valley is an American story of the development of agricultural lands and transformation of rural regions. The United States has been consistently urbanizing since the 1920s. American farms declined from nearly seven million parcels in the 1930s to about two million in 2000.[48] Technological developments in "manufacturing, agriculture, mining, fishing, and forestry accelerated migration from rural to urban areas."[49] The urbanization continues: between 1992 and 2012, the United States converted more than thirty million acres of agricultural land to other uses.[50] However, rural regions continue to be of critical importance to "the country's economic and social well-being" by preserving essential natural resources that provide the rest of the country with "food, energy, water, forests, recreation, national character, and quality of life."[51]

The history of the Santa Clara Valley brings the impact of rural change into stark relief because of the wholesale transformation of a region completely dedicated to fruit to one entirely devoted to computers. The advent of computing sparked an industrial rush and subsequent housing boom that priced out the orchards and canneries. The Santa Clara Valley story is particularly significant because of the ecological and agricultural value of the land that was developed for housing and office parks. The urbanization of the Santa Clara Valley "cannot be neatly explained by the old clichés of suburban sprawl. . . . The valley floor was not empty, low-priced land before the developers arrived; it was one of the most productive agricultural regions in the nation, filled with highly profitable orchards and small businesses where the trees' fruit was processed."[52] As new industries moved in, the land that was once valued for its ecological character and agricultural productivity was now valued simply as a space to build, with no connection or commitment to the particular local environment.

The decline of the fruit industry in the Santa Clara Valley is just one example of the global economic restructuring that affected the agricultural industry across America.[53] The story of the Valley of Heart's Delight is the story of the decline of American agriculture on a grand scale. The acres of trees and the volume of exported fruit of extraordinary quality demonstrate the significance of the Santa Clara Valley's agricultural economy to the nation and the world. However, the statistics and accolades for the valley's productivity do not adequately convey the significance of the valley as a place. To understand the history of the Santa Clara Valley, it is important to consider a sense of place in the valley: what it was like to live and work in the fruit capital of the world.

PURPOSE OF THIS BOOK

This is a history of place: a rhetorical and environmental history of the Santa Clara Valley. I explore an environmental sense of place in this elapsed agricultural community and consider the implications of Santa Clara Valley's wholesale transition from a regional economy devoted to fruit to one focused on technology. Applying a multifaceted theoretical framework for studying place, I examine rhetorical expressions of place in multiple genres of discourse to articulate a sense of place in the Valley of Heart's Delight. In doing so, I hope to offer insight into how place-based connections in agricultural regions change in response to urbanization and other environmental exigencies.

In this rhetorical history of place, I approach "historical narratives as rhetorical discourses, instances of purposeful communication, written in narrative form and loaded with interpretation."[54] I examine the evolution of the Valley of Heart's Delight into Silicon Valley, drawing from historical artifacts of that time as well as the personal experiences of people who lived the Santa Clara Valley's agricultural history. The interplay of public history and personal narratives reveals a relationship between individuals, the community, and the environment. This review of a broad array of historical discourse reveals a complex history of the Valley of Heart's Delight: a powerful narrative of changing environment that invites us to reflect on the meaning of place in Silicon Valley.

The purpose of this study is to understand how a sense of place emerges and changes in an evolving agricultural community. This research reveals three substantive changes in the community's sense of place in the rise and fall of the fruit industry in the Santa Clara Valley. First with the rise of fruit cultivation, an aesthetic sense of place emerged that promoted caretaking and stewardship of the environment. The valley's environmental aesthetic emphasized the link between the valley's ecological health and its abundance. The sense of place in the valley relied on a profound emotional attachment to the land to cultivate a strong ethical commitment to preserve the valley's beauty and bounty. Second, agricultural work engendered a dynamic, material sense of place. The daily and seasonal practices of fruit work in the valley fostered a sense of place through embodied practices that cultivated an intense connection with the land. As agricultural practices mechanized, technology separated workers from the environment, and changed the communal nature of agricultural work, emphasizing economic interests rather than community vitality. Third, exponential population and industrial growth after World War II disrupted the aesthetic and agricultural sense of place. As political and economic leaders promoted urban development at the expense of fruit cultivation, land became valued as space to build rather than for its extraordinarily fertile soil. This shift disrupted place-based meaning, as the valley became "undifferentiated" and "abstract" space without values or meaning attributed to place.[55] The development of orchards into housing tracts and office parks signaled a shift away from consideration of the valley's environmental characteristics and the vital role of the orchards in community health and economic independence.

THE SEASON

Fruit defined the economy and also the community and identity of Santa Clara Valley. Yvonne Jacobson explains the integration of fruit work with the rhythm and cycle of life as "work punctuated by family gatherings and by friends coming and going, the children being bathed on Saturday night, the Sunday dinner after church, the community meetings, the occasional picnics, the coming of the gasoline motor and the automobile, the trips to San José for supplies, the crops coming in and being sold, the money being put aside for the future, the births and christenings, deaths and funerals."[56] Fruit work influenced the daily practices of living in the valley, fostering a sense of community as residents worked together, participating in the yearly rituals of the Season.

Summertime was simply called "the Season" because from May to September, nearly everyone in the valley was working on the harvest or the pack or supporting the fruit industry in some way.[57] The canneries were the valley's biggest employers.[58] During the Season, canneries operated around the clock, typically employing three shifts of workers.[59] The sights, sounds, and smells were visceral reminders of the importance of the harvest and pack to the economic vitality of the valley and its residents. At the start of the Season, canneries blew steam whistles, calling thousands of valley fruit workers to the packing plants. "You'd hear one long blast on the whistle and everybody would then head for canneries. When the season ended there'd be another long blast and everybody would go home and wait for summer."[60] Robin Chapman, whose family harvested apricots each summer from trees on their property, remembers hearing the noon whistle as a child, knowing that it was lunchtime at the canneries."[61] During packing season, the smell of cooked fruit infused the valley. Deborah Olson remembers the dense smell of cooked fruit near Libby's Cannery in Sunnyvale: "The smell would permeate the air. It's very distinct and it's running twenty-four hours a day."[62] At times the smell of stewed tomatoes was so strong "it was like driving through someone's kitchen."[63] The rhythm of the Season influenced the visceral sense of place—the smells and sounds of fruit production were identifying markers of place that fostered a strong connection to the land and community.

During the Season, life in the Santa Clara Valley coalesced around the harvest and the pack. The fruit bloomed in waves: first cherries, then apricots, then prunes; fruit harvesting drove the valley's "rhythm of life."[64] Apricots were packed in July, peaches and pears in August, prunes in September, and tomatoes in September and October.[65] For a generation of cannery workers, the cannery defined their summer. Frances Sanchez, a long-time F. G. Wool cannery employee remembered: "Summertime in the cannery, it's a fact of life, a part of you."[66] The prune harvest started in mid-August, and usually took a month, but sometimes went into October.[67] "Prune season would encroach on the beginning of school in those days," California State Senator David Cortese remembers.[68] School didn't start until the prunes were picked.

Weaving together community and the land itself, entire families worked in the canneries and the orchards. For fruit families, farming "was a way of life in which the smallest child participated."[69] Summers were spent in the orchards. Vince S. Garrod, whose family had an apricot orchard in Saratoga, remembers, "The apricots started the 1st of July, sometimes the 30th of June It always screwed up your 4th of July. It went for about 14 days. Once they were ripe it was a hustle."[70] His daughter, Vicky Bosworth, recalls, "In our family, vacations were around the fruit season. There was a week between the end of apricots and the beginning of prunes that we could take off and go someplace."[71] Deborah Olson remembers: "Everyone went to the beach during the summer. They'd say and can't you go? No, I can't. I've got to work. I had to work every summer my whole life."[72] She remembers, "I was just always in the fruit stand in the summer time. . . . I worked side by side with my grandmother and sold, packed, and sorted cherries."[73] Cannery families couldn't take a vacation either. Sisters Ruth Savage and Betty Nygren (née Wool), whose grandfather founded F. G. Wool Cannery, remember their friends vacationing on the Russian River: "We were envious of them, because they were having fun as we were having fun with the cherry machine."[74]

Even for families not directly involved in the fruit industry, the Season framed the year.[75] Those who didn't work in the orchards or the canneries worked in a business that supported the fruit industry. Jim Zetterquist, whose father worked in the canning industry for forty years, and who himself worked at several canneries including: F. G. Wool Canning Co., San José Canning, Richmond Chase, Filice and Perrelli, and Schuckl canneries, remembers: "Everybody was connected one way or another to food products, whether it was packers or canners. If you were the barber, you were cutting the plant manager's hair. . . . My PE teacher and my sixth-grade teacher both worked with me later in the cannery during the summer [to] supplement their incomes."[76] Restaurants, hardware stores, and banks all supported the cannery workers. Warehouses stored raw fruit until processing, and again before shipping. Trucking companies hauled fruit. Local companies such as Muirson Label and American Can Company provided materials, and Anderson Barngrover supplied machinery.[77]

Fruit drove the valley's economy. The health of the agricultural industry determined the strength of the local economy. Dollars made on the farm and in the cannery were "recycled through the economy several times."[78] Farmer Ray Benech remembers:

Everybody knew the price of prunes—because if the price of prunes was good, farmers made money, and if farmers made money, they paid the bank back, they paid their gas bills, they went to the hardware store and bought a new shovel, they went to the dry good store and bought a new pair of shoes—everybody benefited. If the price of prunes went down, farmers hunched in and nobody got paid—everybody was in trouble. It was a one-industry area here, and when that industry got hurt, everybody got hurt.[79]

The fruit industry determined employment and income; the region's "economic vitality" was tied to the seasonal fluctuations of fruit growing.[80] The valley was "a textbook example of a fully integrated agricultural community."[81]

After World War II, the foundations of Silicon Valley began to uproot the agricultural industry. As the computer industry transformed the valley, the personal and community rituals that centered around agriculture changed. Just as the rapid planting of the orchards significantly altered the valley's landscape in the late 1800s, the development of the valley in the second half of the twentieth century brought about sweeping change to the physical landscape of the valley as houses and office parks replaced orchards and farms. With these material changes, the industrial transition transmuted the community's relationship to the Santa Clara Valley's natural environment. In this stunning example of industrialization of rural land, we see a dramatic change in the region's economy and community, and with that, a changing sense of place.

This introduction outlines the framework for this rhetorical history of place. First, I articulate a four-part theoretical framework of place as an environmental concept: highlighting material, dynamic, aesthetic, and collective senses of place. Second, I outline the methodological approach of this research: analyzing narratives of place. I explicate the method of rhetorical history and articulate the process of artifact analysis: detailing the types of artifacts I consider and outlining the specific procedures I engage in to analyze and synthesize the meaning of these artifacts into the three case study chapters. Finally, I discuss the importance of critical analysis of historical narratives: acknowledging hegemonic spaces and emphasizing marginalized voices to articulate a diverse, nuanced history of place.

To understand the transformation of the Santa Clara Valley, this book examines the history of the Valley of Heart's Delight as a *place*. In general terms, place is a location with physical or geographical parameters. For instance, we might ask "your place or mine?" when discussing plans with a friend. Place is also a state of mind or an emotion: we might hear someone describe a situation that provides comfort or relaxation as their "happy place." Place, generally, is a physical site in which we engage in activities, that has situational context, and has deep meaning. "We all were born, live and will die in towns, neighborhoods, villages or cities that have names and which are filled with memories, associations and meanings."[82] Place provides the daily context of life, in our homes, in our cities, in parks, at work, on our commutes, on vacation, and so on.

Place is how we learn who we are, through "concrete and contingent circumstances which serve as the grounds of our existence, our experiences and lives."[83] Place is thus existential; it "serves as the *condition* of all existing things. . . . Place belongs to the very concept of existence."[84] Where we live provides perspective, "a way of seeing, knowing, and understanding the world."[85] Our relationship with place is "expressed in different dimensions of human life: emotions, biographies, imagination, stories, and personal experiences."[86] Thus, place is rhetorical: the way we "discursively invoke images or memories of a place"[87] reflects our "attitudes and aspirations."[88]

This study draws upon an interdisciplinary understanding of place as "territories of meanings" cultivated by daily practices in physical settings and landscapes.[89] Three integrated and interdependent facets of place are location, locale, and sense of place. Location is the "where of a place": a particular point in space "with a specific set of coordinates and measurable distances from other locations." Locale is the physical element of place: the "material setting for social relations—the way a place looks. Locale includes the buildings, streets, parks, and other visible and tangible aspects of a place."[90] The third aspect of place underscores the way that place creates meaning: through "feelings and emotions" in what is known as a *sense of place.*[91]

Places are significant because we "come to know them and invest them with meanings, ideas, and sensibilities." Our sense of place and attachment to place is distinct from the location or material conditions of a place, it includes knowledge and ideas about a place and deep, emotional symbolic connections to place.[92] Our sense of place is an identification with a particular area that includes our understanding of location and locale, and our developing connections to the land and community. These connections foster an attachment to place that may have negative or positive connotations based on our experiences.

Sense of place evolves through personal experiences, and defines how people view, interpret and interact with their world.[93] Our experiences give place meaning as we develop a sense of belonging and identity shaped by our surroundings.[94] Sense of place includes both a "sense of the character or identity that belongs to certain places or locales, as well as to a sense of our own identity as shaped in relation to those places—to a sense of 'belonging to' those places."[95] For example, how we describe where we live, and relate the importance of home provides an "affective connection" to our home place.[96] Whether we have an affinity for or aversion to our home place, our intimate connection fosters a strong identification with that place that influences our values, our sense of community and our sense of ourselves, and a sense of our environment.[97]

Place Is Environmental

Place refers to a specific geographical place with particular environmental features. Environmental communication scholars study the way we communicate with and about the rest of the natural world and how this affects our attitudes and actions. Donal Carbaugh and Tovar Ceruli note, "Environmental communication is, inevitably, a place-based form of communication."[98] Environmental places are not simply physical settings on which environmental issues play out, as the places themselves influence communication about environmental issues.[99] Carbaugh and Ceruli remind us that communication is an "emplaced practice" that plays "a formative, constitute role in creating our sense of place."[100] Samantha Senda-Cook articulates this constitutive function of environmental rhetoric and place: "Landscapes are not only material parts of our world but also politically and rhetorically powerful spaces."[101] Thus, our sense of place is rhetorical: we articulate our response to the environment, convey our location-based knowledge, and frame our individual and community identity in relation to place. James G. Cantrill and Susan Senecah expound a "sense of self-in-place" that is "socially constructed upon an edifice of the environmental self that, in itself, is a product of discourse and experience."[102] Our sense of place and environmental self is rhetorically constructed, based on how we communicate our experience in that environment.[103] Through our relationship to place, we gain perspective of the world that influences our sense of self within our community and surrounding environment.

Considering place as environmental means that "a place is not a mere patch of ground, a bare stretch of earth, a sedentary set of stones."[104] Our everyday practices cultivate our sense of place. "Place-based practices profoundly influence human-nature relationships."[105] Embodied practices are emplacing practices, those that define and nurture our relationship with the environment and with others. We organize our lives "within the context of environmental conditions and natural resources of that place . . . the *history* of residents' shared experiences in and with that place."[106] Places are environmental because the ecological features are resources and conditions that influence our individual and collective identity. This history of place reviews the environmental transformation of the Santa Clara Valley from fruit-growing region to technology capital.

Place Is Material

Of the integrated aspects of place: location, locale, and sense of place, location is the most immediately obvious: our physical surroundings. Geographer David Harvey outlines a materialist framework that integrates space, place, and environment into social process and practical politics.[107] The topography of a place—its natural features—and its built environment—humanmade structures such as buildings or bridges—are the scaffolding for our social interactions and our relationship with the rest of nature.

Material features impact the daily practice of place-making. "Everyday signifying practices are influenced by historically situated material conditions."[108] Danielle Endres and Samantha Senda-Cook note, "Materiality includes physicality and social conditions, but it also includes embodied experiences in place."[109] Individuals and communities develop specific "practices of place that reflect embodied relationships with local landscapes."[110] The way that we move through and relate to a place is material. Our lived experience is embodied and material, and thus we engage in place-making practices as a part of our everyday life.[111] Sense of place is cultivated through practice. "Places are practiced. People do things in place. What they do, in part, is responsible for the meanings that a place might have."[112] Thus, "places are embodied rhetorical performances" whose meaning is accrued over the daily actions of living.[113] We come to know a place through mundane experiences that offer "a unique blend of sights, sounds, and smells, a unique harmony of natural and artificial rhythms such as times of sunrise and sunset, of work and play."[114]

Places are environments made significant through "discursive activity, filled with symbolic and representational meanings."[115] We infuse our physical surroundings with meaning through emotional attachments such as hope and fear. Material features represent our aspirations—tall buildings reaching for the sky are signs of human potential, while grand mountains remind us of the scope of geologic time. Our commute into a city may affirm that we are part of a bustling society, while a walk in the woods reminds us of the rejuvenating power of nature. Place gains significance through lived experience in material conditions of the environment through embodied, cultural practices that cultivate relationships with people and the environment.

Place Is Aesthetic

Places are environments in which we experience daily life and see the world. Thus, place is aesthetic. Aesthetics, conceived broadly, is the philosophy of art: the study of perceptions of beauty and taste.[116] Environmental aesthetics encompass a broad sense of the world at large, help us to consider the role of place in how we interpret experience, and rest on the assumption that the world's environments offer much to appreciate.[117] Aesthetic terms evoke an emotional reaction—we feel pleasure, optimism, or other sentimentality toward a concept represented in words or images. Environmental aesthetics necessarily involve an ethical sense of beauty: a sense that one must act to preserve the value of the environment.

Environmental aesthetics begets an environmental exceptionalism that rests on the concept of the sublime. The sublime is a particular perspective of the environment that rests on a "sentiment to the physical beauty of the landscape."[118] This may range from what Christine Oravec terms the "pastoralized picturesque" to a more "abstract" wilderness aesthetic.[119] The sublime response combines "visual, narrative, personal, and moral connotations" in an emotional reaction to place.[120] The concept of the sublime is central to how we rhetorically construct nature. Sublime rhetoric employs three strategies to cultivate appeal of place, and convey exceptionalism: exaggerated features, emotional aesthetics, and self-reflexivity.

The first aspect of the sublime is the exaggeration of characteristics of a place for the purpose of representing a landscape in a certain way. Emotional reactions to sublime representations afford a distance from the object itself. "The sublime had always signified a general lack of verisimilitude [or] realism because of its distortion of the facts of the scene and its use of hyperbole for effect."[121] In exaggeration, sublime rhetoric confronts human vulnerability and fears of irrelevance by representing land as landscapes and imbuing them with rhetorical significance for human observers.

The second aspect of the sublime is the emphasis on an emotional aesthetics: written descriptions and visual representation of the natural world designed to cultivate emotional attachment to particular places. Sublime rhetoric is intended to "evoke emotional responses toward nature, to confirm aesthetic or ethical beliefs about nature, and to call attention to particular landscapes for settlement, tourism, or preservation.[122] Our sense of place cultivates "emotional resonance" with the natural world through personal and community activities that create place attachment—intense emotional bonding with the environment.[123]

The third aspect of sublime rhetoric is self-reflexivity, a rhetorical positioning that leaves "the observer feeling both within a scene and also outside of it, viewing the scene (and reflexively, the self) from a higher or more distant (and morally outstanding) perspective."[124] The sublime offers not only a perspective on the environment, but also a mirror into a speaker's sense of self and what it means to be human. How we represent our surrounding environment is powerful, "affecting the actions, the choices and the consciousness of people, shaping our image of the world and with it, reality."[125] Frequently deployed in nature writing and tourist propaganda, the sublime aesthetic offers a view of human aspiration and cultivates an aesthetic-based sense of place.

Place Is Dynamic

Our sense of place embraces the materiality of an environment and through everyday practices cultivates "social rootedness and landscape continuity."[126] Our rituals of place provide constant and ongoing practice that imbues places with dynamism. "Place lies at the center of human experience as both a process and a perspective."[127] Places are moving, growing, and improving: we see this in changes of the season or in new buildings altering a city skyline. Though we might think of places as rooted by geographical location and thus having continuity, places are "actively constituted by mobility— particularly the movement of people but also commodities and ideas."[128]

While our maps are defined by city limits, county jurisdictions, and state lines, places are "not clearly bounded, rooted in place, or connected to single homogeneous identities but produced through connections to the rest of the world and therefore are more about routes than roots."[129] Our sense of place evolves as our place-based identities produce and reproduce attachment and meaning—this is the dynamic of place. Sense of place reflects tension between rootedness and change, and is a negotiation between static physical location and movement of people, processes, and flow.[130] Place is dynamic: our sense of place evolves as we respond to cultural, social, and environmental change through a "constant reiterative process."[131]

The dynamics of place bring about questions of power. We encounter and respond to exercises of power in everyday practice and discourse, engaging social and cultural structures. As we engage in different experiences and changes over time, our sense of place shifts. In this way, places are not confined by geographic boundaries, "they are also fluid, changeable, dynamic contexts of social interaction and memory."[132] Place changes, due to ecological processes, human development, or individual perspective, and thus, our place-based identities are fluid. "Because place is many things and speaks in many voices—individual biography, shared history, meaningful memory, and moral lesson, as well as euphemism—it is constantly shifting, emerging or receding, being accentuated or veiled."[133] Our rhetoric of place reflects this: we use words and images to convey our changing perception of and relationship with place. The dynamic rhetoric of place reflects the ongoing search for meaning to understand the world and ourselves.

Place Is Collective

We have already established that place is existential and ontological; it is the source of how we define ourselves and our community, and thus it is at the center of the human experience.[134] A sense of place can be deeply personal, while individual activities contribute to a broader, collective relationship to place. We experience place through social interactions that form the context for cultural community. "Places are symbolic contexts [that] emerge and evolve through ongoing interaction with others and the environment [and] are reflections of cultural and individual identity."[135] We engage place rhetorically; when we express our sense of place, we are cultivating place-based community identity.

Regional identity emerges from collective awareness and shared consciousness of a common environment. "A sense of place, a consciousness of one's physical surroundings, is a fundamental human experience. It seems to be especially strong where people . . . possess a collective awareness of place."[136] Regional identity demonstrates how place situates us in a common world. This sense of place is both personal and social and is thus collective.[137] Regions acquire deep meaning through "accrual of sentiment."[138] Our experiences over time shape our sense of place in a regional community. Geographic places are "symbolically transformed into meaningful places through processes of human interaction across time."[139] Our sense of place reflects our historical and experiential knowledge of a particular location.[140] Place has "a history and meaning, incarnating the experiences and aspirations of a people."[141] Collective identity emerges through experience over time as we develop collective memory in an "imaginary of belonging."[142] Place is a lens through which to tell regional history, a repository of meaning and experiences. A history of a particular region must engage a sense of place to capture how a community lives, works, and plays in a specific environment.

The nature of places as dynamic and collective affects power structures and relationships. It is vital that historical and rhetorical scholars acknowledge how structural inequalities influence the production of public discourse and how power and privilege affect interpretations of history and thus public memory. "Issues of contested space, social networks, and landscape imprint reveal identity and explore how spaces have become places charged with meaning" in different ways for different social and cultural groups.[143] A shared sense of place engenders negotiation of meaning. It is "only in holding open the gaps and tensions in cultural representation itself that we can glimpse an 'other' mode of cultural critique that speaks from a 'place' of contingency, vulnerability and felt impact."[144] To enfranchise multiple ways of speaking and knowing, studies of place must acknowledge diversity of experiences. "Only through analysis of the collective, constructed potential of place will social and cultural power be made manifest."[145] A rhetorical sense of place emerges in "local narrative history and socially managed symbolic forms, which are shaped at least partly by the work of local culture."[146] Examining the interconnectedness of power and place in local narrative history is the task of the rhetorical historian.

Our experiences of place are told through stories. The stories we tell help to amplify and animate place. Geographer Yi-Fu Tuan notes that, "Places become vividly real through dramatization. Identity of place is achieved by dramatizing the aspirations, needs, and functional rhythms of personal and group life."[147] Material, cultural, and identity-based meanings highlight different situational contexts in which we interpret and express our sense of place. We make sense of the meaning of place in multiple stories of overlapping experiences and contexts to create a history of place. A history of place seeks to understand historical events and trends within a context of particular locations or regions.

Historical narratives are "explanatory schemes on which we humans rely to make sense of our experience."[148] Historical discourse creates an understanding of the past. Put another way, "history is the archives of human experiences and of the thoughts of past generations; history is our collective memory."[149] Telling stories of change in a place, explaining its growth and development, is at the heart of local history. As we examine the local history of Santa Clara Valley, we must consider how to understand history of place as both public and personal. This research investigates the story of the Santa Clara Valley through consideration of historical knowledge of public discourse and experiential knowledge of personal narratives. I argue that place is fundamentally rhetorical, and articulate a methodological framework for analyzing narratives of place, outlining a general method of rhetorical history, and detailing the specific process of this research.

Rhetorical History

Our sense of place is "deeply entangled with the words and images and ideas we use."[150] We relate to place through "what we hear and say" about it.[151] When we explain where we live, or how we feel about our neighborhood, we communicate a sense of place.[152] Communication plays a "formative, constitutive role in creating our sense of place.... People actively create meaningful places through conversation and interaction with others. . . . The reality of place emerges and is confirmed in the common symbolic languages and discourses of people."[153] Sense of place is discursive because the stories that we tell about a place give it meaning. Our social relationships, community building, and sense of self all emerge from our relationship with place: our sense of place.

More specifically, our sense of place is rhetorical in that we use symbolic, persuasive language to convey knowledge of place and express our identity in relation to place.[154] "Place affiliations are sustained by rhetorical (i.e., in the classic sense: persuasive) uses of language, with participants using stylistic devices such as icons, imagery, argumentation, symbols, and metaphors, among others. The derived symbols of place are formalized through use into coherent language structures and appear to people as narratives, myths, fables, and the like."[155] To engage place as rhetorical is to read descriptions of a place as a location and as activities within that location. Endres and Senda-Cook explain, "Place is not just a discursive resource but is itself rhetorical. That is, the confluence of physical structures, bodies, and symbols in particular locations construct the meaning and consequences of a place."[156] A history of place can be understood through the rhetorical articulation of a community's relationship with the environment.

Rhetorical history tells the story of a place through the discourse of its time. History is "a collection of stories and arguments about some set of events."[157] Throughout history, we use stories to create meaning in particular situations, and thus shape and reshape, politics, culture and identity.[158] History is the story of humanity, told in "symbols created by people about people, places, and events. It is the very capacity that we possess as symbol-making beings that enables us to create the languages that cross the boundaries of time and space to recreate those significant images that constitute "history."[159] Rhetorical history examines discourse or rhetoric in context.[160] I approach rhetorical history as what David Zarefsky calls the rhetorical study of historical events.[161] In this method, "one uses the critical tools cultivated by one's rhetorical sensibility to understand history itself, conceiving of people, event and situations as *rhetorical problems* for which responses must continually be formulated, reformulated and negotiated."[162] Rhetorical artifacts are a public record, an "index or mirror of history."[163] The public discourse of the Santa Clara Valley tells the story of how an agricultural community responded to historical exigencies. Rhetorical history is the critical examination of public discourse to form an illuminating narrative of a place or period of time.

History of place must go beyond public discourse to incorporate personal history. "Places are complex constructions of social histories, personal and interpersonal experiences, and selective memory."[164] Because place is embodied, practiced, and dynamic, a "sense of place also represents a culling of experience."[165] The experience of place is "shaped at every turn by the personal and social biography of the one who sustains it."[166] Thus it is "impossible to talk about place, or to talk about how people talk about place, without encountering biography."[167] Historical, personal narrative is a crucial way to access the nuance of a region. We develop a sense of place and communicate it in "a stream of symbolically drawn particulars—the visible particulars of local topographies, the personal particulars of biographical associations and the national particulars of socially given systems of thought."[168] Thus, narratives of place draw upon visual description, autobiographical context, and broader social influences. We can understand "the past, the relation of past to present and the lives of others through time" by examining individuals' communication "about the events and experiences through which they have lived."[169]

Place narratives represent and convey the meanings of place to individuals and communities. Through these stories, "social and cultural values of place, then, become sustained in the language, culture, and history collectively experienced, imagined, and remembered across groups and communities of people."[170] Understanding narrative as part of how we write history is "predicated upon the centrality of the individual life as the most powerful lens through which may be revealed the complex social contexts within which lives are lived."[171]

Stories of a place emerge through the words of individuals who make up its community: "memories and personal commentaries of historical significance."[172] Family stories, the ones told at the kitchen table, are the ingredients of community history. "Embedded in the daily lives of ordinary and extraordinary people, storytelling flourishes. People make sense of their experiences, claim identities, interact with each other, and participate in cultural conversations through storytelling."[173] Life narratives, the autobiographical entries in a rhetoric of place, are situated in time and place and offer meaningful insight into a community's experiences and relationships. Personal narratives of place "are culturally and historically specific. They are rhetorical in the broadest sense of the word. That is, they are addressed to an audience/reader; they are engaged in an argument about identity; and they are inevitably fractured by the play of meaning."[174] Stories are how we make sense of the public history of a place or time and offer "insight into the complexity of experiences and interpretations of historical phenomena."[175] Historical narratives are embedded in both public and personal discourse, offering stories of a region and community that describe the meaning of a place in a period of time. "The power of such stories and images as symbolic constructions of reality for their publics is precisely the stuff of the rhetorical historian."[176]

Artifact Analysis

Archival research is the process of discovering examples of historical rhetoric and piecing together interpretations of events to construct a narrative of the valley. We are advised to "view historical texts as incomplete and fraught with the weight of opinion and perspective."[177] Considering public discourse as inherently fragmented led me to consider personal discourse to amplify our understanding of history of the valley. This addresses the "rhetorical problem of embedding a multiplicity of local voices in the more insular and synthetic voice of anthropological authorship."[178] Considering the region of the Santa Clara Valley to be a "discursively constructed setting,"[179] I incorporate personal stories into this rhetorical history to "augment the written historical record with the inclusion of vernacular, traditionally excluded, and ordinary people who experienced the historical phenomenon in question."[180] There is not one singular story that encapsulates the fruit worker experience in Santa Clara Valley, rather the situational contexts of narrative of place highlight distinct and divergent experiences in the region.

Rhetorical history begins with the critical approach. "The rhetorical perspective affects not only the questions we ask of history, but also what we consider to be "evidence" and how we interrogate that evidence."[181] Thus, artifact analysis involves evaluating different types of artifacts and considering the specific context and purpose of each type of artifact as well as what we know about that genre of discourse. I examine artifacts in four general categories: public discourse, tourist discourse, corporate discourse, and personal discourse.

Public Discourse. Rhetorical studies traditionally focus on public discourse. Public discourse refers to "rhetorical processes and products articulated, circulated or performed, deliberated, and rearticulated in the public sphere by private people come together as publics or movements."[182] Public discourse involves general civic and political rhetoric as well as "vernacular public discourse [through which] we create public opinion about particular issues and at the same time . . . we create and sustain our conceptions of identity and community."[183] Public discourse may be considered as both expressing public opinion and community identity and thus also creating, influencing, and responding to public discourse.[184]

I examine public communication including news articles, political speeches, editorials, government meeting minutes, planning reports, and more. From these primary sources, a historical narrative of the Santa Clara Valley emerges, revealing trends across historical periods. Newspaper articles provide public accounts of events: written and visual records of the changing valley with scenic details such as weather and material conditions. Political speeches, meeting minutes, and government reports provide details and rationale for policy decisions. City and county planning reports offer insight into policies that have profound effects on the environment and people. I examine hundreds of news articles from local newspapers, primarily the *San José Mercury News*, and its previous iterations, the *San José Mercury*, and the *San José Mercury Herald*, from the 1870s to 2000s, and nearly thirty public reports, government documents, and other civic publications regarding agriculture, the fruit industry, and business and land development. This public discourse offers details of historic events and outlines a historical narrative of the valley. I apply a critical lens to this public discourse to emphasize the economic and social structures that produced it, and draw upon personal narratives of place that are differently situated in terms of socioeconomic class, migration period, and racialized positionality.

Tourist Discourse. Tourist texts articulate cultural meaning through representation of specific places.[185] Tourist discourse consists of visual and textual representations of place produced for our consumption, inscribing dreams and myths onto places, spatializing social meaning through images.[186] Tourist discourse can serve as a "mediating force of human-nature relations in burgeoning sites of intersecting cultures and natures."[187] Tourist texts generally incorporate descriptions of a physical place and of the feeling of what it is like to be in that place, promoting civilized expectations of nature.[188] The landscape is an essential element to descriptions and images of tourist discourse. Written descriptions and visual images of tourist discourse animate a particular place, amplifying its significance for an audience.

Tourist discourse may be considered place propaganda. Brochures, pamphlets, and promotional packets directly appeal to a reader's sense of place. Magazine articles, travelogues, postcards, and other ephemera also contribute to place propaganda, historically called booster literature. I examine brochures, pamphlets, and small books produced by chambers of commerce, improvement clubs, and industry groups to sell the Santa Clara Valley spanning 1873–1930. These articles range from one page to one hundred pages. Shorter pamphlets might simply list facts about the valley or quote from famous travelers describing its beauty. Longer booklets would reprint "scholarly" articles about the climatology of the region and factual economic assessments. All told, I examine more than fifty pieces of propaganda designed to entice tourists and would-be orchardists to prosper in the beautiful Santa Clara Valley.

Industry Discourse. Organizations have a clear role in civil society.[189] Corporate discourse influences the public sphere and participates in public dialogue.[190] "Corporations shape conceptions of nature through affective, sensuous, and culturally specific appeals at places and spaces."[191] Corporate rhetoric includes internal and external advocacy, with distinct messages defining organizations for their members and the public. Internal rhetoric conveys nuance and complexities, defining expectations or goal-setting.[192] External rhetoric includes storytelling to boost a company's public image. Branding and advertising are the most direct ways that companies convey identity through the power of naming.[193]

Trade journals and annual reports from industry groups offer a look at internal communication. Published corporate histories and advertisements are outward facing rhetoric designed to burnish the image of the company in the eyes of the public. I examine dozens of issues of fruit industry publications such as *Orchard and Farmer, Canning Age,* and *Western Canner and Packer.* I analyze nine reports published 1930–1984 by industry groups such as California Canners and Growers and California Prune and Apricot Growers; twenty-four bulletins from the Santa Clara County Fruit Exchange published 1893–1901; and six published bylaws and convention proceedings from various fruit organizations. I analyze seven corporate histories published by fruit corporations, more than two dozen published advertisements for fruit products, and more than two hundred fruit crate and can labels from the Santa Clara Valley.

Personal Discourse. Personal narratives offer "social truths" that add depth of perspective to public narrative.[194] In examining personal stories, we can explore memory as a heritage device that produces collective history. Examining first person accounts is particularly useful, because "autobiographical truth resides in the intersubjective exchanges between narrator and reader aimed at producing a shared understanding of the meaning of life."[195] Memoirs make history, commemorate a community, convey cultural nuance, and highlight aspirations. Autobiographical texts reveal "narrative tropes, sociocultural contexts, rhetorical aims, and narratives shifts within the historical or chronological trajectory of the text [with] ethical, political and cultural dimensions."[196]

Examination of narrative discourse to understand history must be done with care, to both acknowledge the fallibility of memory, and also to account for the tendency for the past to take on a rosy glow in recollection. Stephanie Coontz, in her research on the history of the American family, refers to this as the "nostalgia trap": one that denies a diversity of experiences and "leads to false generalizations about the past as well as wildly exaggerated claims about the present and the future."[197] Mythical concepts of place based on "abstract nostalgia" can neglect the complex relationships and experiences in a given place.[198] As Lauret Savoy notes, "How a society remembers can't be separated from how it wants to be remembered or from what it wishes it was. . . . The past is remembered and told by desire."[199] In this way, personal accounts of history have something to offer; the way people remember a place tells us what that place meant to them. Our individual, diverse experiences with place inform a nuanced and dynamic place-based community.

Memoirs, interviews, and other personal discourse serve an important role in preserving history. I examine fifteen memoirs concerned with the agricultural history of the Santa Clara Valley from a variety of perspectives including second- and third-generation immigrants from China, Europe, Japan, and Vietnam, as well as seasonal migrant workers who traveled from Mexico. I also draw on interviews with fruit workers published and cited in several histories of the valley, including two significant volumes of interviews with Chicana cannery workers.[200]

In conducting background research for the book, I engaged in informal conversations with two dozen individuals with experience in the fruit industry from a variety of backgrounds. These conversations served to amplify historical context and clarify stories in publicly available memoirs. In some cases, I quote from these conversations with permission. I met these individuals, including canners, farmers, and seasonal workers through participation in local history events and a strong network of interpersonal connections. For instance, at a film night hosted by a local historical organization, the Fruit Cocktail Club, I met former canners Jim Zetterquist, Joe Melehan, and the Wool family, who easily agreed to talk with me about the history of the valley. One conversation led to another. The Wools introduced me to Brad Stapleton, president of Stapleton-Spence Packing Company, who remembered stealing cherries from orchards on his way to school. Brad introduced me to Mark Mariani, CEO of Mariani Packing Company, noting, "He can be trusted, unless he's talking about his golf game." Mark's brother David Mariani introduced me to Peter Coe Verbica, descendent of

Henry Coe who invented the process for dipping prunes in lye. Peter introduced me to Robin Chapman, who wrote *California Apricots, The Lost Orchards of Silicon Valley*. And I met "prune peddler" Xavier Regli because he plays racquetball with a friend and colleague of mine at San José State. For the last several years, I've remained in touch with many of these individuals and have witnessed the strong community ties that persist despite the end of the fruit industry. Many of these individuals also shared unpublished family memoirs, personal photographs, old correspondence, and ephemera. Personal artifacts bring history to life with eyewitness accounts of history and family lore that give insight into a changing valley. These personal accounts help us to frame and interpret the public record of the valley.

The personal narratives in the interviews and memoirs include a range of perspectives along gender, race, socioeconomic status, and agricultural role, including both laborers and landholders. As I conducted thematic analysis, I considered that the public availability of particular narratives illustrates marginalization of particular voices in public discourse. The public discourse of the fruit industry of the Santa Clara Valley emphasizes a Euro-centric perspective: European families who migrated to the valley and began growing fruit shaped industry discourse promoting fruit and the region. European-Americans further influenced public discourse in the establishment of newspapers, and through political and government offices. Many of the published memoirs of the valley reflect the predominance of European-American families in the establishment of the industry both in the stories they tell and by virtue of their publication enabled by the authors' educational and economic backgrounds.

I specifically sought out non-European perspectives to demonstrate the distinct senses of place articulated by various groups. For example, the experiences of Chicana cannery workers differed from those of third-generation European immigrants who held management positions in canneries. The personal narratives in the case studies are differently situated in terms of socioeconomic class, migration period, and racialized positionality, illustrating that while there are common themes across narratives, there is significance in their differences.

Through the consideration and integration of diverse discourse from the Santa Clara Valley, I attempt to "articulate the rhetorical climate of an age: how people defined the situation, what led them to seek to justify themselves or to persuade others, what storehouse of social knowledge they drew upon for their premises, what themes and styles they produced in their messages, how the processes of identification and confrontation succeeded or failed."[201] As I reviewed artifacts of public, tourist, industry, and personal discourse, I took copious notes, identifying themes and stylistic choices, and the influence of various messages. As I developed themes and categories to make sense of a broad historical narrative, I engaged in close reading of the artifacts to "deconstruct the activities of place-making."[202] To discover the rhetoric of place, I paid particular attention to "the discursive devices people use to make place, nature, and dwelling there explicit, such as place-names, [and] depictions of places including stories."[203] I evaluated communicative practices such as "the use of language and non-verbal imagery in bounding, focusing, and limiting discussion topics; the use of verbal or non-verbal strategies to include or deny participation; and the manipulation of symbols to achieve desired ends."[204] I found that as rhetorical actors attempted to define the Valley of Heart's Delight, they inscribed a historical narrative of place with implications for community and the environment.

Critical Historical Narratives

Public and personal narratives demonstrate tensions about the changing identity of the Santa Clara Valley and its significance as a place. Histories of place must be conscious of the diversity of experiences of places to reveal connections and disparities that surface the incongruities and implications of historical events and decisions. "Places, and senses of place . . . are the product of relations and interactions." No sense of place is "singular. Different social groups within any physical location may live those locations in very different ways."[205] There is no universal history; interpretation of events, explanation of decisions, and emotional attachments to place can vary. Histories of place must acknowledge that the "dominant image of any place will be a matter of contestation and will change over time."[206]

A history of place of the fruit industry in the Santa Clara Valley must track "moments of tension, digression, displacement, excess, deferral, arrest, contradictions, immanence, and desire."[207] Ideal depictions of the agricultural life in the valley need to be considered within the context of different experiences of place. Rural life is often portrayed with positive values of community. Some farmers may indeed love their land and their occupation, but for others it may be a harsh and grueling existence. Growing up on a farm may be far from romantic and the wish to escape from it may be overwhelming."[208] Thus, place-based history needs to look beyond simplified ideals that may occlude harsher realities by examining a variety of experiences.

The historical narrative of the Santa Clara Valley reveals how economic organization and social relations create "hegemonic spaces and places."[209] For example, Mexican and Asian immigrants made significant contributions to the agricultural development of the valley. They also faced distinct hardships and persecution based on race. From the 1850s on, Mexican immigrants "suffered stunning new patterns of disfranchisement and discrimination."[210] Mexican and other Latino immigrants experienced racist and often violent treatment in the Santa Clara Valley.[211] Chicana cannery workers experienced gender inequality and racial discrimination in the canning industry.[212] The late nineteenth century saw a "racial hierarchy of production" in which white Santa Clara valley growers "constructed a racialized and gendered discourse of labor" that relegated Asian migrant workers to vegetable work rather than fruit growing so as to "reconcile the family farm ideal with the prevalence of Asian farm labor."[213] Laws prohibiting the purchase or lease of farmland segregated Asian migrant workers from other groups in the agricultural community.[214] Agricultural industry practices also enabled "task segregation and discriminatory wages," and other "mechanisms of oppression."[215] Clusters of immigrant farming communities developed and "posed a challenge to the dominant class," forming agricultural cooperatives that served not only economic association but social and cultural functions.[216] For Chinese, Japanese, and Filipino immigrants, agricultural work was a means to support families, "farming was the basis of a secure thriving immigrant society"[217]

The experiences of various immigrant groups reveal diverse and distinct fruit worker experiences in Santa Clara Valley. This history integrates diverse experiences of the Santa Clara valley to emphasize that place is experienced intersectionally, and incorporates discourse of personal experiences to acknowledge that workers of color were often marginalized in the public image of the valley promoted by the fruit industry and civic leaders. Lauret Savoy reminds us that "history on this land—the events that occurred *and* the narratives told of them—can never be complete or single-voiced. Each of us participates in it. We contribute to it as players, as witnesses, as narrators, as producers and consumers, in an ongoing past-to-present."[218]

Thus, it is crucial to acknowledge that the development of the Santa Clara Valley into a premiere agricultural region was part of a great historical displacement and genocide of indigenous peoples. Estimates vary, but it is likely that between fifteen thousand and thirty thousand indigenous people known as the Ohlone lived in the San Francisco Bay area.[219] The Ohlone way of life was deeply rooted to place, emphasizing a sustainable subsistence, avoiding "conspicuous consumption," harvesting natural resources without depleting them.[220] Through "complex interactions with, and managing of, the natural environment," the Ohlone peoples produced "sustained and sustainable food surpluses."[221] The Santa Clara Valley was filled with oaks; creeks offered clean water; and the San Francisco Bay was clean, teaming with shellfish. The Ohlone lived a semi-nomadic lifestyle, sustaining themselves in harmony with the region's natural features and seasonal changes, thriving for at least six thousand years.

When Spanish settlers arrived in the Santa Clara Valley in 1769, they named the indigenous people the Costanoan. The Spanish thought little of the "poor, wretched natives [who] do not even have firewood with which to warm themselves, and they go naked like all the Indians found in this country."[222] The Spanish believed that the Missions "exerted a civilizing influence" that would assist the "aborigines of this wild country" by converting to Christianity and teaching them agricultural practices.[223] While the primary stated purpose of the missions was conversion, the missions were a tool for colonizing coastal California. This meant enslavement and forced labor marked by "harsh living and working conditions, disease, and Spanish assaults on the Ohlone religion and culture." [224] This destruction of cultural and ecological integrity had devastating impacts on the indigenous population, "as agricultural laborers, missionized Indians were largely separated from the seasonal rhythms of their own food production practices, while the growth of mission farms and rangeland for cattle initiated an environmental transformation of the Bay Area and the entire coast that destroyed much of the resource base of the indigenous economy."[225]

Spanish settlement and subsequent US colonization of California swiftly and decisively destabilized the Ohlone way of life. The growth of industry in the valley—mining, ranching, and agriculture—"initiated an environmental transformation" that destroyed the "resource base of the indigenous economy" and the "economic and environmental foundations of native life."[226] Ohlone populations suffered from the seizure of land and destruction of resources brought by colonization and state-sanctioned genocide.[227] Anglo-Americans flooded into California during the Gold Rush: "white miners, ranchers, and farmers" saw Native Americans as "threats to their prosperity and security," and believed that they were "repulsive and expendable."[228] Vigilante groups aimed at exterminating California's indigenous peoples were "legalized and publicly subsidized" by local and state governments."[229] In the first two years of the Gold Rush, 100,000 native Californians died.[230] By 1900, there were 278 Ohlone living in eleven counties surrounding the San Francisco Bay Area, with 9 Ohlone people recorded in the Santa Clara Valley.[231] Today the Ohlone Costanoan and Muwekma tribes have approximately 1,300 enrolled members and continue to work to preserve heritage and for federal recognition.[232] Despite formal recognition of tribal sovereignty the federal government continues to exercise control over indigenous people and lands. Due to lack of federal recognition, "tribal priorities may still be marginalized or subsumed within broader federal objectives."[233] The fight for recognition continues as "existing systems of power ignore and exclude native peoples and governments."[234]

Transformed Sense of Place

The intensive industries of agriculture and mining replaced the Ohlone people's sustainable subsistence in a valley now marked by a "finite and fragile natural resource base."[235] The fruit industry that developed in the Santa Clara Valley emphasized a vision of "economic viability, civic infrastructure, social interaction, and natural beauty."[236] However, the fruit industry was ultimately not sustainable due to environmental externalities and economic pressures. One hundred years later, the valley would be dramatically transformed by the development of infrastructure—houses, office parks, roadways—to support the computer industry. The swift and wholesale change of an agricultural economy to an economy devoted to technology destroyed the economic and environmental foundations of the fruit community, with significant impacts to environmental sustainability, economic scale, and community relationships.

The dissolution of the distinctive environmental and community features of the fruit-based economy in the transition from agriculture to technology has produced a *placelessness* or an "insensitivity to the significance of place."[237] The community ties built on the shared purpose of fruit work articulated in daily practices, dissipated with the decline of the fruit industry. For agricultural communities with a strong sense of place developed through cultivation of land, urbanization brings changes to that way of life, with deleterious effects on sense of place and community identity. Silicon Valley's technology companies promote placelessness enabled by technological innovation and enhanced mobility through virtual space, resulting in the loss social rootedness and continuity and a lack of attachment to community and environment.

This history demonstrates how place is experienced intersectionally: the diverse experiences of various immigrant groups articulate a dynamic, material sense of place characterized by caretaking and stewardship of the environment. The interconnectedness of power and place demonstrates how distinct groups within the valley cultivated an attachment to place rooted in community and environment. Diverse group experience challenged the dominant narrative promoted by the fruit industry and civic leaders in important ways. The development of the valley after World War II prompted rapid urbanization in the name of progress. The removal of orchards and dismantling of the agricultural economy laid the groundwork for Silicon Valley's dominant narrative of non-place. Silicon Valley's ideals of mobility and placelessness emphasize nonattachment and thus diminish the sense of environmental stewardship and community obligations that emerged across diverse relationships with place. Public and personal narratives demonstrate tensions about the changing identity of Silicon Valley and its significance for a sense of place.

My findings have implications for the study of environmental communication, sense of place research, rhetorical history, and studies of agricultural communities. This study of the Santa Clara Valley offers a cautionary tale about urbanization that accompanies industry transition for other agricultural regions in the United States such as the Corn Belt in the Midwest, wheat producers in the Great Plains, and citrus growers in Florida and Southern California. A history of place reminds us of the significance of environment and community in our agricultural regions.

PREVIEW

Chapter 1 offers the first case study, an exploration of how tourist propaganda, or booster literature, commodifies an aesthetic sense of place. I examine promotional pamphlets, postcards, and fruit can and crate labels to understand how booster literature and advertisements promoted an environmental aesthetic. I integrate this with analysis of personal discourse from memoirs. I discuss three thematic elements of the environmental aesthetic of the valley: beauty, abundance, and superior quality. These themes promote an environmental ideal that is amplified by sublime rhetoric. I conclude with a discussion of externalities that elude tourist discourse and consider how the use of the sublime occludes contrary views of the valley aesthetic.

Chapter 2 is the second case study: an examination of how rhetoric surrounding agricultural work expresses a material sense of place through articulation of embodied practices. I examine a variety of examples of corporate and industry discourse such as promotional histories and trade journals. I again integrate personal narratives from memoirs and published interviews, which allows comparison of corporate promotion and personal experience. In this chapter, I focus on orchards and canneries as two sites of the valley's integrated agricultural system and consider how distinct practices in each site are influenced by equipment and machines. I examine orcharding practices around prunes and apricots, and focus on two types of cannery equipment. I examine the embodied and material sense of place and tensions in mechanization of the fruit industry and promotion of the American agricultural ideal.

Chapter 3 is the final case study, and explores public and personal discourse surrounding the development of the Santa Clara Valley after World War II. I examine civic and political discourse including news articles about the changing industry, public reports and government documents, and memoirs and interviews. I analyze three types of discourse: pro-growth rhetoric, preservation advocacy, and coverage of the declining fruit industry. I assess how debates over land use reveal a change in land valued for its agricultural productivity to calculating land value by the amount of space for housing developments. I consider how the rhetoric of progress discounted arguments for planning and preservation, and disregarded the economic vitality of farmland. In doing so, I outline how valley development disrupted the agricultural community and environmental sense of place.

Chapter 4 concludes the book with a discussion of some implications of this research. I consider Silicon Valley as non-place and explore the impact of placelessness brought about by new technologies that offer mobility and connectivity that render physical location irrelevant. I then synthesize the sense of place and environmental community found throughout the discourse in this study. I conclude with a discussion of heritage discourse as a response to placelessness, arguing that this offers practical approaches to renewing a sense of place as well as a potent genre for rhetorical study.

ONE

_____

The World's Largest Orchard

VALLEY AS NATURAL WONDER

IN MARCH OF 1868, John Muir disembarked his steamship from New York in San Francisco. He took a ferry to Oakland and started a six-week, three-hundred-mile trip to Yosemite.[1] Muir, traveling on foot from Oakland, did not take the "orthodox" route, but "drifted leisurely mountainward, via the Valley of San José."[2] Muir passed through the Santa Clara Valley in spring, "the bloom-time of the year."[3] He noted in his diaries, "Slow indeed was my progress through these glorious gardens, the first of the California flora I had seen. Cattle and cultivation were making few scars as yet, and I wandered enchanted in long wavering curves, knowing by my pocket map that Yosemite Valley lay to the east and that I should surely find it."[4] Muir's reaction to the beauty of the Santa Clara Valley would set the tone for new European-American settlers and tourists for years to come.[5] Muir's "extensive description of the wonders" of the Santa Clara Valley are hallmarks of "exalted language, as if confirming for his readers the reality and worth of their vicarious experience."[6]

It is important to note that John Muir expressed the dominant view of Anglo-Americans regarding nonwhites. The Sierra Club has acknowledged the racism of John Muir, noting "Muir was not immune to the racism peddled by many in the early conservation movement. He made derogatory comments about Black people and Indigenous peoples that drew on deeply harmful racist stereotypes."[7] During Muir's walk across the country, he described Native American homes as "the uncouth transitionist . . . wigwams of savages." He described the homes of the very settlers who may well have drove them out as, "decked with flowers and vines, clean within and without, and stamped with the comforts of culture and refinement." He regarded Native Americans as "subhuman," calling them "dirty," "garrulous as jays," "superstitious," and "lazy."[8] While John Muir's description of the valley is historically significant, his racist statements, particularly his disregard for Native American peoples, are problematic and indicative of widespread efforts to marginalize and dominate indigenous groups.

Muir offered sensual descriptions of a verdant valley marked by temperate climate, vibrant colors, and pleasurable sounds and scents. He noted that the springtime weather was the best he had ever enjoyed. "Larks and streams sang everywhere; the sky was cloudless, and the whole valley was a lake of light."[9] The valley was alive with sounds and sights of spring. "The landscapes were fairly drenched with sunshine, all the air was quivering with the songs of the meadow-larks, and the hills were so covered with flowers that they seemed to be painted."[10] Muir found the San José sunshine "spicy and exhilarating. . . . It possessed a positive flavor—a taste that thrilled from the lungs throughout every tissue of the body; every inspiration yielded a corresponding well-defined place of pleasure, that awakened thousands of new palates everywhere."[11] For Muir, the valley air was a "flavor" to be savored. Indeed, when the fruit trees bloomed, the spring air was "sweet and heavy with the scent of the flowers."[12] Muir exalted over the beauty of the Santa Clara Valley. He was captivated by the sensual beauty of the sounds of spring.

John Muir's trip to California marked the beginning of cross-country travel to California and the Santa Clara Valley. With the completion of the transcontinental railroad in 1869, Santa Clara Valley and the rest of the West became a destination for East Coast Americans, both as a place to visit, and a place to live. Travel writers became bards of the West, writing essays published in pamphlets, magazines, and newspapers describing the wonders of California. Railroad executives chimed in about the incredible beauty and opportunity of the valley. Judge Robert S. Lovett, president of Southern Pacific proclaimed, "Nowhere have I seen such combination of the beautiful in nature and so rich in every sense."[13] Edward T. Jeffery, president of Western Pacific declared, "My conception of grandeur, beauty and commercial magnificence is realized in Santa Clara Valley."[14] Of course, Lovett and Jeffery had reason to make such statements: their railroads were the crucial link between the Santa Clara Valley and the East Coast.[15] Entrepreneurs began to promote tourism and development of the region. Chambers of commerce, boards of trade, commercial leagues, and so-called improvement clubs distributed promotional material advertising the Santa Clara Valley to tourists and speculators. Beginning in the 1870s, promoters published dozens of brochures, pamphlets, and small books promoting the

Santa Clara Valley. Pamphlets provided endless statistics about the valley's agricultural yields, miles of paved roads, and electrical networks, providing evidence for its productivity and benefits to residents. Reprinted "scholarly" articles offered climatology reports and economic assessments. This travel writing was a form of booster literature, promoting the virtues of a valley most Americans had never seen.

Travel writers told of a valley more beautiful than Europe, the richest, most magnificent valley in the world.[16] The blossoms of the Santa Clara Valley were a tourist destination. Trainloads of tourists arrived from San Francisco and Oakland, and with the advent of the automobile, visitors would "drive from all over to see and smell them." Residents remember buses and cars parked on Blossom Hill Road and other vista points, people taking photos and eating picnic lunches in the orchards.[17] Postcards provided maps and directions to the legendary Valley of Heart's Delight. For East Coast residents who might not have heard Spanish origin words pronounced, many brochures spelled them out phonetically. San José became "San Hosay" or "San Hozay."[18] Promotional literature promised a new life full of opportunity: "The achievements of your past sink into obscurity compared with the possibilities of your future."[19] In 1896, the *San José Mercury* newspaper published a hardbound book entitled *Sunshine, Fruit and Flowers,* capturing the notion of the valley's ideal society: the California version of the American Dream.[20] Promoters conveyed a sense of urgency and opportunity. "If you are coming to California, do not delay. Come immediately, and come to Santa Clara Valley."[21]

Booster literature promoted the valley as the "Garden of the World," and the "Valley of Heart's Delight." The promotion of the valley used written description and visual rhetoric to promote a valley marked by unsurpassed beauty. In this tourist discourse, landscapes were "visually attractive and enriched with sentimental associations."[22] The specific language used to describe the environment highlights the aesthetically appealing features of natural scenery. Written text features descriptions of a natural scene containing "special adjectives (wonderful, stupendous, dreadful, profound) . . . metaphors, personification, catalogs of features, broken diction, exclamations, shifts into present tense, second-person address."[23] These rhetorical strategies highlight authors' wonder at the natural world and exemplify the rhetorical convention known as the sublime. "Sublime representations can include blurring, exaggeration of detail, and compositional elements such

FIGURE 1. Promotional brochure for San José, phonetically spelling "San Hosay," 1905. *Credit:* San José Chamber of Commerce. Courtesy of History San José.

as foreground, middle ground and frame."[24] Such exaggeration may be a shift in perspective, or blurring of details so that landscapes are rendered more familiar, or alternatively, more exotic and unknown. In fact, the power of the sublime often lies in the inability to comprehend the enormity of a landscape coupled with the desire to understand it and know it. Sublime images function actively—they frame a landscape with human expectations and desires.[25] In a broader sense, "the sublime convention acts as a screen, or a projection of human preferences upon the natural scene."[26]

The sublime offers a worldview based on perceptions of beauty and taste. Representations of nature call forth an aesthetic appreciation of environmental features that have an "impact on the senses, imagination, emotion, and our sense of place with the natural world."[27] Sublime rhetoric invites and provokes a complex emotional response through "intense aesthetic engagement with nature."[28] Booster literature demonstrates the sublime aesthetic with images and language that evoke "elements of humility and humanity."[29] This is a complex environmental aesthetic that simultaneously represents human limitations and possibility.

The reputation of the "balm-giving valley called Santa Clara" grew with every published brochure.[30] Publicity efforts were wildly successful: by 1900 more than sixty thousand people called the Santa Clara Valley home.[31] Booster literature "aesthetically validated" the valley's scenery in postcards, advertisements, and crate labels that commodified the valley as a tourist attraction and agricultural opportunity.[32] The environmental aesthetic of the valley, including sublime rhetoric, is also evident in personal discourse. In memoirs, valley residents, orchardists, and farmers offer breathless recollections of the valley's beauty and exceptional description of the valley's sensual delights. These personal accounts demonstrate a significant emotional attachment to the environment and echo the sublime rhetoric of the place propaganda.

This chapter explores an aesthetic sense of place in the rhetoric of the Santa Clara Valley. I examine more than fifty pieces of promotional literature—pamphlets, postcards, ephemera, and published volumes available in the California History Center, History San José, and the Special Collections of San José State University. I analyze more than two hundred fruit can and crate labels from the collections of the same archives, as well as the personal collections of the Wool family. I also include analysis of fifteen memoirs describing the agricultural experience of living and working in the Santa Clara Valley. Review of tourist propaganda, fruit label advertising, and personal discourse reveals three themes in the environmental aesthetic of the valley: beauty, abundance, and superior quality. These themes illustrate an environmental ideal amplified by sublime rhetoric to commodify a region and its fruit. In the conclusion of this chapter, I discuss externalities that undermine this perfect aesthetic and I consider how the use of the sublime occludes contrary views of the valley.

BEAUTY

I'm sitting at lunch with David Mariani. David's grandfather, Paul Mariani Sr., arrived in Cupertino from Croatia in 1902. The Marianis, like other European immigrants, were lured by the opportunity of the Santa Clara Valley.[33] The Santa Clara Valley was remarkably different from Croatia in one respect: as Paul remembered: "There were no rocks that need to be moved and hauled away just to plant a few square feet of crops or plant a tree."[34] The soil of the Santa Clara Valley welcomed immigrants coming to make their fortune. Paul Sr. would go on to found Mariani Packing Company, which is run by David's brother, Mark, today.

When I ask David Mariani to describe the Valley of Heart's Delight, he closes his eyes. After a prolonged pause, he sighs, "It was breathtaking."[35] Like many longtime residents, David has reverent memories of the Valley of Heart's Delight. These memories are rooted in the aesthetic draw, the comfort of the valley's beauty. David expands, remembering the drive down Stevens Creek Boulevard: "Both sides of the road were planted with orchards until you reached the outskirts of the city. The orchards, in blossom during springtime, were breathtaking; the splash of vibrant colors and fragrance, for thousands of acres as far as the eye could see, was overwhelming."[36] David's description indicates the formidable task of attempting to describe the beauty of a valley full of fruit trees, incomprehensible to a resident of Silicon Valley today.

For many, it was indescribable, unable to be comprehended or explained, simply the "most beautiful place you ever saw."[37] Charlie Olson and Yvonne Jacobson's grandparents, Hannah and Carl Olson, arrived from Sweden via San Francisco in 1891 and settled in Sunnyvale, planting their first cherry orchard in 1901, with "unbounded optimism." Their Scandinavian heritage brought a "diligence and steadfastness" to working the land every day.[38] Jacobson explains in her memoir, *Passing Farms, Enduring Values*, that there was something special about living in the Valley of Heart's Delight: "The landscape was so fine it left one with a sense of quiet pleasure, an inner well-being. . . . You had a sense of vast natural beauty that had been enhanced by human hands. The orchards seemed to fit the level plain exactly. The vineyards clung in just the right proportions to the mountainsides. . . . . The vegetable fields, the berry patches, the ornamental flower shelters—all had the look of being just right."[39] Jacobson describes a sense of place in the Valley of Heart's Delight—a sense of belonging, a symbiosis between humans and nature determined by the rhythm of the seasons. Jacobson's description of the valley articulates an aesthetic sense of place as "the setting for social rootedness and landscape continuity."[40] Her language is emotional, with a breathtaking sense of awe for the vast landscape and spectrum of color. Jacobson's passage portrays the landscape as a product of hard work: it all seemed just right: a landscape perfected by humanity.

The primary consideration of the Santa Clara Valley's aesthetic is the landscape. Landscape may be broadly defined as the visible features of an area. "Landscape is a powerful term that points to both the physical places and our ways of seeing places, our ways of representing them, and our ways of interacting with them."[41] Landscapes are a primary way we understand our environment because they offer a visual perception of place. "Landscapes are not only material parts of our world but also politically and rhetorically powerful spaces. . . . Landscapes are typically conceived of aesthetically, as views and sceneries, or as natural conditions (water, wind, mountains, snow, etc.) to enjoy or contest. . . .. Thus, it is difficult for humans to separate the physical from the symbolic, or the material from the discursive."[42] Visual representations of place are aesthetically appealing because they are powerful rhetorical statements that represent human relationships with nature.

Propaganda used the words of experienced travelers to convey visions of the landscape to readers back east. Bayard Taylor, the "laureate of the Gilded Age," credited with helping spark the romance of travel, first visited the "garden spot" of the Santa Clara Valley in the 1850s.[43] Taylor asked, "How shall I describe a landscape so unlike anything else in the world; with a beauty so new and dazzling that all ordinary comparisons are worthless."[44] Taylor's use of exaggeration to communicate the enchanting beauty of the valley conveys the valley's sublime aesthetic. "Did you ever see one hundred and twenty-five square miles of vineyards and trees in snow-white blossom at one time? No of course not, for nowhere else in all the world can such a sight be seen. I who have listened to the voice of spring on five continents and in more than five score countries assure that it is worth seeing."[45] Taylor asserts his

FIGURE 2. Painting of rows of orchard trees with white blossoms used by San José Chamber of Commerce as promotion. *Credit:* L. B. Standish, Muirson Label Company. Courtesy of History San José.

own authority for comparison, offering the Santa Clara Valley's uniqueness as rationale for his superlatives.

Most propaganda literature described the valley in superlatives. A 1910 San José Chamber of Commerce brochure describes the Santa Clara Valley's environmental aesthetic: "The lure of beautiful landscapes, of inspiring panoramas, of rugged mountains and fertile valleys, of comfortable homes, of blossom and fruit-laden orchards, of wealth, ease, contentment."[46] This brochure promises the beauty of the landscapes as seen in vistas that showcased the fertile valley of fruit-laden trees promising wealth and comfort. The landscape descriptions showcase all the valley's delights with assurances of the comfortable life afforded by fruit. Booster literature commodifies the valley: landscapes reflect the dreams of opportunists seeking wealth.

Propaganda literature includes paintings and descriptions of the Santa Clara Valley that emphasize panoramic views. Very few images offer a view of the valley from up close or from within the orchards. The San José Chamber of Commerce brochure explains, "You cannot appreciate its true significance until you have climbed to a point on the slope of the mountains which form the garden wall, where the whole enchanting panorama lies before you."[47] This invitation involves readers in the enchanting scene and implicates them in the valley's splendor.[48]

The descriptions of panoramic views affirm the valley is most enticing in its entirety. These depictions of the valley landscape "exceed the usual parameters of place by continuing without apparent end; nothing contains it, while it contains everything, including discrete places, in its environing embrace."[49] Postcards and brochures emphasize a panoramic perspective with a view of the valley as a continuous orchard. From this perspective, the blossoms encompass everything else, eliding discrete places into a vision of the valley in totality. Place propaganda does not emphasize individual trees or farms or places, but promotes the valley in its entirety—better to represent the vast potential of the fruit trees. An image of an orchard in a 1930 San José Chamber of Commerce brochure is taken from above an orchard. In the center of the picture, two rows of fruit trees are discernable, while the rows radiating from the center are blurred together, extending to the edges of the picture. The caption "rows of wealth" commodifies the beauty of the landscape: interpreting its value for humans, portraying the trees' natural features as economic worth.[50] These landscapes blur the features of the valley, an example of sublime rhetoric that both exaggerates the environment and promotes self-reflexivity. In this case, to behold the miles and miles of blossoms is to see a potential future of wealth for one's self.

A 1902 article published in *Sunset* magazine, entitled "In Blossom Land: A Springtime Sketch of San José and Santa Clara County California," recommends the view of the valley from the foothills. "From these vantage points the valley stretches out as far as the eye can reach, an almost continuous vista of orchard and vineyard, formed by gently rising mountains, with the waters of the bay glistening on the north."[51] The continuous vista of the valley is a rhetorical symbol of possibility. The gently rising mountains and the glistening waters symbolize crowning achievements and unknown depths of potential. The article continues:

> It is during the blossoming season that it presents its greatest charm, whether as a panorama or seen in detail. Then the white blossoms cover it almost like a mantle of snow. It is a hopeless task to convey an impression of the beauty of this scene to one whose eyes have not beheld it. Six million fruit trees are in bloom almost simultaneously. Of these four million are prune trees and are in bloom at the same time, while with them peach, apricot, pear and cherry are mingled to give color tints to the scene, for the deep pink of the peach

blossoms adds here and there a patch of color to relieve the snowy whiteness of the general tone. Mile after mile these masses of blossoms stretch before the eye until they blend with the blue of the horizon.[52]

The article highlights the simultaneous blossoming of millions of trees, and mile after mile of orchards. The number of trees and the continuity of blossoms signify unending beauty and potential. The Santa Clara Valley's expanse is a key feature: the "largest near-continuous orchard the world had ever seen."[53] There were blossoms as far as one could see. "Mile after mile" of blossoms seemed to stretch to the horizon. In spring, the apricot, prune, cherry, and almond trees created what various observers called a "quilt" of flowers,[54] and a "sea of blossoms."[55]

The panorama of the valley is powerful because its horizon signifies unlimited potential. Landscapes "organize visual elements into a dramatic spatio-temporal structure. When we look at a country scene, we almost automatically arrange its components ... pointing to the horizon, which is our destination and future."[56] In views of the Santa Clara Valley, rows and rows of trees point toward the horizon, offering a "prospect [that] means both a broad view and a future promise."[57] A brochure published in 1887 describes this prospect in the approach of the Santa Clara Valley from the North: "The narrow roadway that skirts the salt marsh has widened to a broad and fertile valley that stretches as far as the eye can reach."[58] In this passage, the valley's fertility is infinite, the panoramic view offers an expansive future. The broad horizon of the valley offers a symbol of unlimited prospects and unbounded human potential. Landscapes help us to organize our lives, make sense of our world and plan for the future. In the visual and written depictions of the valley, the open space signifies hope and boundless potential, the broad horizon representing possibility.[59]

Landscape images and descriptions emphasize the color of landscapes. Robin Chapman recalls in her memoir, "In my memory, the warm summer days in the Santa Clara Valley have an apricot hue. The hillsides around the valley in summer are a soft shade of adobe, brightened by the apricot color of the California poppies scattered within a sea of Spanish oats. The sun in the summer afternoons is a shade of apricot too, and when the apricots ripen on the trees, they join this symphony of color."[60] The seasonal color imbued the landscape with significance, a hallmark of the rhythms of the Season. Chapman describes the valley brushed in "the off-white of the almond blossom, to the white and pink of the apricot, to the darker pink of the plum and the

SANTA CLARA COUNTY, CALIFORNIA. THE VALLEY OF HEART'S DELIGHT.

SANTA CLARA VALLEY AT BLOSSOM TIME.

FIGURE 3. Postcard of Santa Clara County at Blossom Time as a quilt of blossoms. *Creator:* Unknown. Courtesy of San Jose Public Library, California Room, Arbuckle Collection.

prune. The different colors filled the valley in their turn."[61] The harmony of color represents the seasonal orchestra, with different trees blooming in turn throughout the spring.

An article published in *Out West* travel magazine in 1909 describes the effect of the color on the landscape in the Santa Clara Valley. "Nature is here always beautiful, being as lavish of color as she is changeful of mood. In mid-winter, she paints the valley floor and the foothills a brilliant green. With the increasing freshness of spring and the springing forth of new life comes a magical change when the whole valley is transformed into a sea of billowy white, perfumed blossoms."[62] In these descriptions, color signifies life in a vibrant, fertile valley. The article expands the visual of the valley for readers. "If one's imagination can picture a scene, without the actual seeing of it, of one hundred and twenty-five square miles of prune trees in blossom and each a perfect bouquet of bloom of itself, with a fluffiness and a whiteness which can only be likened to drifting snow, he will have conceived something of the beauty of this prospect as viewed from some rise in the lower foothills. Yet it may be safely said that nowhere else in the world can such a scene be witnessed."[63] This article utilizes the sublime convention of exaggerated description to describe the snow-like fluffiness of the perfect bouquets and ethereal blooms. The scene depicts the verdant spring, and signifies the

© San José Chamber of Commerce

FIGURE 4. Postcard captioned "Blossom Time in 'The Valley of Heart's Delight.'" *Credit:* San José Chamber of Commerce. Courtesy of History San José.

prospect of the fruit economy. This passage echoes the sense of perfection that Yvonne Jacobson described as "just so." Such discourse affirms that the Santa Clara Valley was utterly distinct from anywhere else on earth.

Sublime rhetoric often uses categories of natural features to elicit an emotional response.[64] Descriptions of the various seasonal colors aim to delight and awe. The *Out West* article continues, describing the changing colors of the season.

> Passing on to summer, we find the color scheme has changed from the purity of the driven snows of the prune blossoms to a composite of the dark green foliage of the fruit trees, lightened plentifully with the amber red of the apricot, the purple and red of the cherry, the yellow of the peach and the blue bloom of the prune and the grape. The autumn follows with fields and hills verging into the golden, russet and brown, while in the wild growth of the woods, clambering vines have changed their foliage into brilliant hues of red and yellow.[65]

This description ascribes virtue to color: the purity of the white blossoms, the plentifulness of the red blossoms. The rainbow of color in the valley's fruit blossoms suggest the fruit harvest as the pot of gold, assuring the fortunes of all who seek it. The article conveys the expansion and movement of the valley with depictions of "clambering" vines and vigorous growth. This rhetoric emphasizes the valley's ecological health as an economic asset, framing the fecundity of the soil and productivity of the trees as a means to prosperity.

The brilliance captured in these descriptions refers not just to nature's beauty but to the force of the seasonal changes. A 1904 San José Chamber of Commerce brochure promotes the valley's year-round color show: "Lavish of color is nature here. In midwinter, she paints the floor and foothills of the valley a vivid green. In spring, she waves a wand, and, lo! billows of white, perfumed blossoms, beginning with the foothills, roll down upon and submerge the lower levels. Nowhere else in the whole world are there one hundred and twenty-five solid square miles of trees in blossom at once, and every prune tree a mound of scented snow."[66] This description imbues nature with agency: The green floor and foothills are vivid and alive. Nature affects gentle seasonal changes with the waving of a wand, causing billows of blossoms to roll down and cover the valley. The suggestion of the magic of the seasons portrays the valley as a natural wonder, deflecting from the intense cultivation that established those blossoms. Tourist propaganda proclaims the valley to be a miraculous place. The seasonal colors and vast expanse of the valley symbolize the fertility and promise of nature. The descriptions of the valley's natural features were designed to elicit an emotional response to the valley's prospects.

ABUNDANCE

Propaganda lured people with an aesthetic of abundance that promised beauty and bounty: an appreciation of both the beauty of the valley and its potential cultivation. In this aesthetic, the beauty of the valley is a symbol of its wealth. The blossoms that inspire awe become fruit that promise wealth. Take this proclamation by the Santa Clara County Fruit Exchange in 1905:

> Nowhere in the wide world can you find orchards better tended, in healthier conditions than ours. . . . Level as a floor, the land stretches along for miles and miles. The trees in never ending rows, reveal vistas of surprising beauty. Each tree is a huge bouquet, cream-colored and fragrant. Under arches of cream-colored blossoms marking themselves against the azure of the sky, with the busy hum of bees all around us, forgetting sorrow in the beauty and

enchantment of the moment. That is a spring day in the orchards of Santa Clara County.[67]

The hallmarks of the abundance aesthetic are evident: the landscape features, panoramic views, the infinite horizons. The rows are tended, and the orchards are healthy. The vistas reveal the possibilities and abundance of the season. The passage continues:

> The petals begin to drop, a snowy shower descends to the earth. The fruit has set and is growing lustily; slyly it peeps out from under the leaves, receiving the kisses of the sun. Its color at first a vivid green, changes to a bright red, soon to deepen to the royal purple of the ripe fruit. Undisturbed by the hand of man, it is allowed to finish the process of its ripening, to finally drop from the tree in the fullness of its perfection. A carpet of richest purple soon covers the ground around the trees; harvest time is at hand. Gay laughter of merry boys and girls fill the land. They have come with their pails and baskets to gather the prunes from under the trees."[68]

The passage emphasizes the colors as a sign of ripening fruit. The lusty fruit and kissing prunes inspire delight in humans who come to harvest the fruit. The aesthetic sense of place emphasizes an emotional attachment to the valley's stunning beauty and temperate climate and the wealth and comfort afforded by its abundance. Propaganda commodified the valley as an agricultural ideal: a beautiful and productive valley that promised to sustain one's self and one's family. The Valley of Heart's Delight signified an aesthetic sense of place, a delight of the senses and a comfortable life: a connection to the environment based on beauty and productivity.

Propaganda promoted the beauty and temperance of the valley—nature's beauty signified a healthy environment and an abundant harvest. For many Easterners, the temperate climate of the Santa Clara Valley was a draw. Propaganda promoted the favorable conditions of the Valley's topography that prevented extreme weather. The *San José Mercury* wrote in the volume *Sunshine, Fruit, and Flowers* in 1896: "The cool breeze from the ocean lowers the temperature in summer and prevents the ardent rays of the sun from burning the leaves and trunks of trees. The same breeze in winter seems warm, and tends to remove from the atmosphere any crispness caused by winds from snow-covered peaks."[69] This description evokes an idyllic retreat that combines the ideas of visual beauty and gentle winds. The topography offers protection so that the elements of the weather are kind. The *San José Mercury* continues, "Snow may cover the summits in winter, and in the valleys a semi-tropical warmth prevails, while flowers bloom everywhere in the open air. . . . The air, too, may be almost stationary in the valley, and moved by gentle zephyrs in the foothills, while a brisk breeze sweeps over the summits."[70] The gentle winds and blooming flowers in this description were a stark contrast to Northeast winters. Brochures described the Santa Clara Valley as gentle and supportive of human endeavors. The temperate climate promised ease, contentment, and comfort.

Tourist propaganda declared that productivity was made possible by the valley's temperate climate and emphasized the gentle change of the seasons. The San José Chamber of Commerce published a brochure in 1930 noting: "One season slips unnoticed into another."[71] The *San José Mercury* portrays the Santa Clara Valley as perpetually sunny: "A year of broad sunshine and long-continued fruitage, where elements are gentle and climate kind." Indeed "summer lingers so long in the lap of winter that set calculations cannot be relied upon."[72] In these brochures, nature is gentle, kind, and lingering. These descriptors help form an emotional attachment as part of an aesthetic sense of place. A 1915 brochure promises, "Winter falls gently. . . . Winter is never a period of storm and frost, or blizzards and fear. It is the seed time that heralds the voluptuous growth of spring, the season that is rich with the prophecy of hopeful husbandry. The change of seasons brings no fear of heat, no dread of cold."[73] This passage describes spring as voluptuous and rich: the temperate climate offers comfort and protection from fears of a long winter that might threaten successful cultivation of resources.

The *San José Mercury* describes the seasonal changes as playful. The first clouds of fall "go floating lazily over the valley, and their shadows play hide and seek on hill and dale, but it doesn't rain. They are little bits of baby rain clouds, but wouldn't hurt anybody. Dark they are for a time, but the sun soon puts upon their frocks the prettiest white edging imaginable, and at sunset the silvery color turns to gold."[74] The description personifies the clouds as lazy, with playful shadows, wearing pretty dresses, suggesting the gentle seasonal change and hospitable climate. The *Mercury* continues:

> In February and March spring hides its face behind an occasional cloud and masquerades as winter. It approaches so quietly that one scarcely knows when it came. It has been lurking about all winter, and now, in April, abandons its mask and smiles continually. Wild flowers tint the hillsides, birds fill the air with melody, and the gentle breezes go laughing o'er the wheat. The sun shines more frequently, vegetation is more luxurious, and cherries are blushing a deeper red. Sometimes during the latter part of this month it

seems like summer has stepped over into spring. . . . Winter dropped asleep amid the flowers.[75]

This passage articulates the heart's delights of the valley. The seasons are like playful children: Spring hides and smiles while winter falls asleep, the breezes laugh, and cherries blush. Nature is personified as kind and friendly. *The San José Mercury* concludes that of the Santa Clara Valley, "it may be always said that the elements are gentle and climate kind."[76] The personification of nature exemplifies the perspective of the sublime and the emotional attachment of environmental aesthetics. Propaganda links the emotions invoked by the views of the valley to the valley's promise. Sublime rhetoric, "in praise of natural scenery, the very background and source of human endeavor."[77] Propaganda emphasizes nature's kindness to suggest the valley's generosity and the promise of wealth, and thus commodifies the valley's beauty as a setting for agricultural pursuits.

Booster literature commercializes the valley's temperate climate to convey a pleasurable life made possible by astounding productivity. A 1909 article connects the emotional attachment to the Santa Clara Valley's beauty to the wealth of its crops: "Rich as this valley is in sunshine, fruit and flowers, its richest crop is found in the broad kindness of the royal hearts of its royal people."[78] As J. J. Owen, founder of the newspaper now known as the *San José Mercury News*, wrote in 1873, "Justly considered the garden valley of the Pacific Coast . . . a vale of surpassing beauty and fertility . . . a region of remarkable fertility, susceptible of the highest degree of cultivation."[79] The valley's productivity was due to its remarkable soil—ten feet of top soil created by rains "washing loam from the mountains into the valley, where it has gathered layer upon layer."[80] The valley's temperate climate and rich soil were ideal growing conditions that with human cultivation had enormous potential. In their 1893 promotional volume, *Picturesque San José and Environments*, H. S. Foote and C. A. Woolfolk describe how, through cultivation and hard work in the valley, humanity has "reversed the processes of Nature and constrained the courses of the seasons."[81] Propaganda promoted a sense of place that drew upon the valley's beauty as a setting for human achievement.

Just as booster literature used exaggeration to describe the valley's beauty as so incredible as to be unbelievable, propaganda also described the valley's productivity as so immense as to be incalculable. Similar to sublime descriptions of the Santa Clara Valley's beauty, propaganda used the sublime convention of exaggeration to describe productivity. An 1887 brochure boasts, "The yield of our orchards is so out of proportion to anything to which the Eastern people are accustomed, that they are inclined to be incredulous when they hear stories of our golden harvest."[82] Tourist propaganda commodified the valley's beauty with visual and written depictions of physical features that facilitated incredible productivity. "The broad floor of the valley and the rolling foothills beyond are wonderfully productive and horticultural, viticultural and agricultural pursuits have reached a state of unusual perfection."[83] Multiple publications refer to the valley's perfection. "The valley and foothill land is tillable, capable of producing to a high state of perfection such a multiplicity of products . . . [it is] wonderfully fertile and productive."[84] The possibility and promise of the landscape is verified by descriptions of opportunities promised by valley fertility. An 1887 brochure promises "A small amount of money, combined with a small amount of labor, invested in our orchards and vineyards, will secure a comfortable living for themselves, and a competence for their children."[85] Propaganda articles argue that while nature's magic is responsible for the harvest, humans have constrained the seasons, and thus the valley's natural productivity is amplified by human endeavor.

Importantly, in an effort to sell the valley to potential orchardists, pamphlets promise that "up to this time the immense resources of Santa Clara County have only been foreshadowed—not developed. We only stand on the margin of the great sea of possibilities."[86] The valley's beauty and fertility were symbols of incredible potential wealth. An 1887 brochure describes the valley as "a vale of plenty."[87] In 1890, another promotional publication promises untold wealth in "the brightest, fairest and most desirable portion of the world, the present Mecca of the hopes of thousands and the future homes of millions."[88] The desirability of the "bright" and "fair" valley is part of its aesthetic—the lure of the blossoms is in part due to the riches they promised.

SUPERIOR QUALITY

Propaganda literature sold the valley's beauty and abundance. The San José Chamber of Commerce boasted, "Santa Clara County is literally the most fruitful valley in the world. One-half of the prunes produced in the United States are grown here. No other county in the United States raises so many cherries; none other so many apricots. Of greater importance, Santa Clara Valley raises the very best of each of these fruits."[89] The superior quality of the fruit was the symbol of the valley's abundant aesthetic. While boosters sold the valley, fruit growers had to sell the fruit. As fruit production increased and businesses increased, growers and canners had to design ways to promote their fruit in a competitive market. The Valley of Heart's Delight became part of many company's branding. "Advertising began with labels. . . . Image often made the difference between profit and loss. . . . Brands helped wholesalers to distinguish the shipment of one grower from that of another."[90] At first, the fruit had to be sold to buyers, those who brokered fruit between orchardists and consumers. Growers advertised on crate labels, which established a brand's aesthetic with artistic renderings of fruit and valley.

The focus of labels changed from brokers to consumers in 1916, when a grocer in Memphis, Tennessee, revolutionized the way Americans bought food. Clarence Saunders moved his merchandise from behind the counter; he placed food products and other household goods onto shelves in store aisles so that customers could select what they wanted.[91] The self-service trend caught on, so grocers wanted "products with a strong consumer brand appeal, attractive labeling, and aggressive in-store merchandising backup— products that would sell themselves."[92] Now advertising turned to consumers. Agricultural journals had emphasized the importance of advertising on can and crate labels for years. *Orchard and Farm* explained the need for pleasing the consumer, noting that American products were packed in ordinary boxes, whereas French producers shipped fruit in "fancy boxes, decorated, and often with glass in sets in the covers, showy and attractive."[93] This 1910 article suggests such packaging would convey the superior quality of the valley fruit.

On April 21, 1917, CalPak placed an ad for Del Monte peaches in the *Saturday Evening Post*. This marked the first time a fruit company marketed directly to consumers in a national audience. That same year, California Prune and Apricot Growers started marketing under the Sunsweet brand, starting a nationwide campaign for prunes with the slogan "eat 'em like candy."[94] The goal of these ads was to overcome the widespread perception that canned fruit was only for a "rainy day."[95] Growers had to appeal to new consumers. "The old marketing offered fruit to a hungry public; the new marketing encouraged consumption for its own sake and employed publicity, name recognition, uniformity of product—merchandising."[96] Marketing cooperatives began to promote canned fruit as "pleasurable consumption."[97] Fruit ads appealed to the aesthetics of fruit: both the taste and the valley itself.

Canners recognized labels as a "vehicle for advertising. Professional lithographers designed these miniature billboards to create a pleasant impression in the auction room or on the floor of the produce market."[98] Many labels featured the fruit itself.[99] Smaller canneries like F. G. Wool did not have the budget for national marketing, so labels were advertisements in themselves: conveying tastes and pleasures of the Valley of Heart's Delight. F. G. Wool sold their fruit under the White Oak label in honor of the trees on the family property. Many labels used landscape as a way to sell the fruit.

George Muirson came to San José from Indiana in the 1880s. After working at newspapers, he started a printing firm in the 1890s and founded the Muirson Label Company in 1916. He created most of the labels for the Valley of Heart's Delight. The Muirson Label Company operated from 1916 to 1970, the only label company in the valley. When Muirson died at age fifty-eight of influenza in the epidemic of 1918, the *San José Evening News* mourned the loss of one of the valley's "best known, best loved and most useful citizens."[100] Ralph Rambo started working at Muirson in the foundry the year it opened. After a year, George Muirson heard he had "faint traces of art ability" and promoted him.[101] Rambo "established himself as the one-man Art Department." The Art Department grew, and Rambo remained Muirson's principal artist and art director for nearly fifty years.[102] Hand-drawn and lettered, labels were carefully designed to represent the valley's fruit in a pleasing way. These labels conveyed the aesthetic of abundance to market the fruit to grocers and later consumers.

A review of more than two hundred fruit labels from dozens of fruit companies in the Santa Clara Valley revealed prominent themes of the aesthetics of abundance. The label ads used visual images to "express consistent, memorable and marketable place identities. As such, place branding strategies play a significant role in the composition of landscape imagery, including 'natural' environments"[103] Nearly all labels reviewed include an image of the particular fruit that was in the can or crate. Many labels also depicted scenes from the Santa Clara Valley. In this way, the labels articulated the simple causal relationship promoted in the propaganda literature: the beautiful valley grew the best fruit. I offer examples of labels that demonstrate these themes.

Fruit labels from different fruit growers depicted familiar landscapes of the valley on their labels: rows of fruit trees with white and pink blossoms flanked by hills. For example, a crate label for Embarcadero Fancy Santa Clara County Pears depicts two pears on a branch in the foreground, and

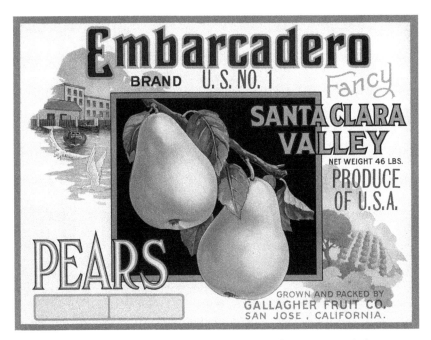

FIGURE 5. Embarcadero brand fancy pears label. *Credit:* Muirson Label Company. Courtesy of History San José.

a background view of orchards and foothills. A Paradise Valley Brand Apricots label features a pair of bright apricots hanging from a branch in the foreground, and a view of the valley in the background with rows and rows of orderly green fruit trees, a river running through the valley and mountains framing the scene. A label for Sunnyside Brand Yellow Cling Peaches is similarly structured: one side of the label features an image of two bright yellow peaches in a glass bowl. The other side of the label depicts the valley: rows of green fruit trees near a river, with redwoods and a mountain in the backdrop. A Garden City Jam Kitchens label features a valley of houses nestled among trees framed by the sun shining over the mountains in the backdrop. A Heart's Delight Apricots label does not feature the fruit at all. The label is drawn to appear that the label has been ripped away from the can to reveal what's inside: the view of the valley—rows of fruit trees with white and pink blossoms. In this example, the label promotes the superior quality of the fruit with an image of the legendary valley.

Of course, most labels feature the fruit itself. For example, a label for a one-pound can of Valley View Prunes is a tryptic: images of prunes on a

FIGURE 6. Paradise Valley brand apricot label, packed by Bisceglia Brothers Canning Company. *Credit:* Muirson Label Company. Courtesy of History San José.

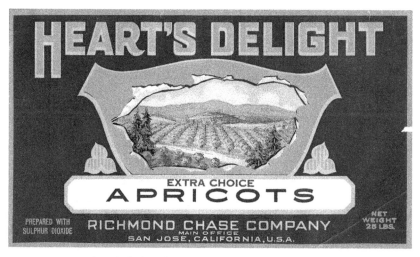

FIGURE 7. Heart's Delight brand apricot label, packed by Richmond Chase Company. *Credit:* Richmond Chase Company. Courtesy of History San José.

dish, fresh plums on a branch, and a view of the valley: white blossomed-trees in rows, flanked by rolling hills and a distant snow-covered mountain. The name "Valley View" links the visual aspect of the valley aesthetic with the taste aesthetic of the fruit and celebrates the landscape. The can labels demonstrate the hyperbole of the sublime: the glistening fruit and the incredible beauty of the orchards. A label for Ajax Brand Fancy Santa Clara Prunes proclaims, "Greetings from the Valley of Heart's Delight," echoing a postcard a tourist might send. In this case, the fruit is a souvenir of the valley. The can depicts an orchard scene with rows of trees that disappear into the horizon, with a white house and red roof and a barn. In another panel, prunes hang from a branch. A label for Cortese Brothers Bing Cherries features bright, shiny red cherries in the foreground of a valley with expansive orchards, rolling hills, and mountains. These cans sell fruit using images of the valley that echo the paintings and descriptions of tourist propaganda. The valley is a selling point. The view of the valley on the cans offers a way to promote the famous Valley of Heart's Delight, selling the fruit on the basis of the valley's reputation. The images of the valley, trees, rivers, house, and mountains promote the American ideal of an agricultural landscape. These labels sell an agricultural ideal where environmental conditions and hard work realize the promise of a life of comfort and wealth. The labels use rhetorical strategies of the sublime to sell the hope of the promised land of the Santa Clara Valley, exaggerating the superior quality of the fruit with images of perfect fruit and scenic valley, cultivating an attachment rooted in the flavor and aesthetic appeals of the fruit, and asserting human potential in the valley's promise of opportunity.

CONCLUSION

The promotional discourse of the valley, pamphlets, ads, and labels, sold an agricultural ideal, commodifying the region as a promised land with beauty and abundance. Early promotional literature often acknowledged that the reputation of the valley must seem too good to be true, and used different arguments to show that this was not just a fantasy. Many would provide statistics about the valley's agricultural yields, miles of paved roads, and electrical networks, providing evidence for its productivity and benefits to residents. Others used description with superlative language describing the valley's scenery, climate, and ideal life. All of these strategies attempted to demonstrate that the Santa Clara Valley was the promised land. This propaganda reflects the Eurocentric view of a natural beauty civilized in its cultivation by agricultural entrepreneurs. The use of sublime rhetoric to promote the most beautiful productive valley in the world used exaggeration to blur the details of the orchards. It also had the effect of hiding the deleterious effects of the agricultural industry on the environment. I offer two examples here.

First, the images and descriptions of the valley in promotional literature emphasize the pristine natural environment: clean air and a gentle breeze. The world-famous panoramic pictures of the valley left unseen one of the most obvious pollutants from the orchards: smoke from the smudge pots widely used in the Santa Clara Valley. Farmers placed pots between trees on early spring nights when freezing was likely for more than an hour.[104] "Each pot was about two feet long and a foot wide. It stood on legs. A stack like a stovepipe projected from the top."[105] These "small kettles of burning oil" produced a blanket of warm black smoke that protected trees from frost damage.[106] The smudge pots were effective at protecting crops, but they created intense particulate matter. It wasn't unusual for orcharding families to wake up to "find everything outside covered with a thick layer of black soot from the ranchers' smudge pots. . . . Any housewife who had left her wash on the line the night before would wake to find it covered in soot."[107] As one farmer noted, "In the morning one had to do a good job of nose cleaning."[108] Smudge pots were recognized for their unpleasantness, but were part of the process for growing the valley's famous fruit.[109] While smudge pots might only be used a couple times a year, until smudging was banned in the 1950s, it was an accepted part of farming in the valley—clean air sacrificed for fruit products.[110] This early example of agricultural pollution reminds us that air pollution remains a significant environmental justice concern.[111] In landscape pictures and descriptions, the air is clear, the sky is blue, with hardly a cloud. The valley vistas emphasize landscapes that are unmarred, the clean air a sign of the health of the valley, and an essential feature of the valley's beauty used to market the region's fruit.

Second, valley propaganda promoted clean water. In their 1893 promotional volume, H. S. Foote and C. A. Woolfolk exult that the "the water supply of San José is drawn from the crystal streams and limpid fountains of the Santa Cruz mountains, and is bright, sparkling and pure. . . . Water from the bowels of the earth can be obtained in unlimited quantities and at little expense."[112] In 1930, the San José Chamber of Commerce promised the valley's water to be "pure, plentiful and wholesome . . . no typhoid in its sparkle."[113] This would turn out to be too good to be true. All of the valley's crops depended on water, so growers pumped water from deep in the ground to irrigate. The valley's shrinking water table threatened the overall water supply.[114] In the late 1920s, "critical water conditions continued to rally the orchardists around the conservation cause."[115] In fall 1929, the Santa Clara County voters approved the Water Conservation Act, which allowed for the creation of water districts to manage water supplies and act to protect and conserve as necessary.[116]

Agricultural wells, built in the late nineteenth century started to create a problem within a few decades.[117] Between 1915 and 1933, groundwater pumped from the valley increased from 25,000 to 134,000 acre-feet annually.[118] The valley was slowly sinking. Water was depleted faster than it could be replenished.[119] The water level in one downtown San José well fell eighty feet below the land surface by 1933.[120] The Santa Clara Valley water table was "discernibly dropping, the land was subsiding as a consequence, and traces of saltwater from the San Francisco Bay were beginning to show up in the valley's aquifer."[121] Increased nonagricultural use of water during the 1940s, and population increases and development in the 1950s, would intensify demand for valley water. A 1959 report found that "local water supply sources, both surface and ground water, are barely adequate for present irrigation, domestic, and industrial needs" in Santa Clara County.[122] In 1964, that downtown San José well fell to 235 feet below land surface.[123] Potential water shortages are not promoted in booster literature as this would belie the public image of a pristine and inexhaustible water supply. This omission highlights a final aspect of the aesthetic of abundance: a promise of infinite resources. The promotional literature promotes an aesthetic that does not account for the environmental impact of agriculture or any externalities that might place limits on production or affect the beauty of the valley. In reality, water scarcity is a significant environmental justice concern both in the United States and globally, with low-income areas and communities of color facing disproportionate barriers to accessible clean drinking water.[124] The promise of the aesthetic of abundance is that it is eternal: a naturally fertile valley with unlimited potential when enhanced by human enterprise.

The environmental aesthetic promoted in tourist literature commodifies landscapes as the ultimate symbol of the valley's beauty and possibility. Views of the valley feature the valley as a whole—a continuous orchard whose blossoms stretch endlessly into the horizon. The landscapes are powerful symbols of human achievement and potential. This aesthetic emphasizes an emotional attachment to the fertility and productivity of the valley. The gentle and kind elements of the valley support the human endeavor that has cultivated the fruit trees and harnessed the elements of nature for wealth. This valley aesthetic promotes an agricultural ideal that emphasizes infinite abundance.

Propaganda promoted a sense of place that relied on the continuity of an environmental aesthetic and a profound emotional attachment to the land. This aesthetic and emotional attachment is confirmed in the personal narrative discourse. Personal accounts acknowledge the environmental impacts of agriculture in ways that do not detract from the cachet of the Santa

Clara Valley. Memoirs contribute to the historical narrative of the valley that echo Jacobson's claims that it was "just right." This narrative describes an agricultural ideal: humans and nature in harmony; a valley made more productive by human cultivation. The aesthetics of abundance exemplifies nostalgia for the agricultural ideal. At times, this ideal can be problematic, as exemplified in John Muir's view of wilderness. Richard White notes that "Muir's image of pristine wilderness unshaped by humans only existed if native people weren't part of it. Even though they had been there for thousands of years, Muir wrote that they 'seemed to have no right place in the landscape.' American Indians needed to be removed in order to reinvent those places as untouched."[125] Muir demonstrates an idealized notion of the past: ideal nature devoid of Native Americans and waiting for European-American cultivation and preservation. The emphasis on the perfection of the landscape reveals the significance of an environmental aesthetic in a collective sense of place, and also the desire to remember the best of the history, thus producing an idealized memory of the past. Conventions of sublimity such as blurring of details and exaggeration offer slights of hand that allow propaganda and personal recollections to dismiss detractors and assert the Valley of Heart's Delight as an ideal. The aesthetic abundance of the Santa Clara Valley, commodified in public promotional discourse of the valley and affirmed in personal discourse of memoirs and recollections, demonstrates an unwavering sense of place based on the beauty of the valley and the promise of its harvest.

TWO

———

Prune Pickers and 'Cot Cutters

VALLEY AS FRUIT FACTORY

LYMAN BROWNELL WAITED FOR the Overland Daily Express at the San José train depot. The train was scheduled to leave Sacramento at 1:20 p.m., but delays at any of the stops, Stockton, Merced, and so on, could make it late.[1] In 1874, the excitement of meeting a train with transcontinental passengers was still new, even though Brownell and his family had themselves come to San José three years earlier from Vermont.[2] The transcontinental railroad made it possible to cross the country in less than eighty-five hours. Just ten years earlier, the journey would have taken weeks by sea or months by land.

The train pulled into the station and Frederick and Jane Wool disembarked with their three children. While the ride from Sacramento had taken just a few hours, they had been traveling for weeks, including a stop in Chicago to visit family. Jane, just twenty-six, had developed "lung difficulty," and so the family moved from Vermont to California for a better climate.[3] The promotional brochures promised: "There is not a better, more salubrious, tonic and health-giving climate on the Pacific Coast than in Santa Clara Valley."[4] As the train had descended the Western slope of the Sierras and passed through the Sacramento Valley, Fred Wool thought the green hills dotted with yellow poppies was "the most beautiful sight" he had ever seen.[5] Jane vowed never to return to the snow, ice, and cold of Vermont.[6] As the Wools disembarked, the packing sheds and fruit warehouses lining the north side of the station were the first sight to greet them. The temperate April afternoon was a far cry from the dregs of winter left behind in Vermont.

The Wools bought twelve and a half acres of "bare land" in the Quinn orchards, three miles east of downtown San José. The family moved there in September 1877 and began farming. Fred would rise in the morning to go to work building wagons. After a day's work in town, he would come home and plant fruit trees in the evening, while Jane held the lantern.[7] Jane worked in the orchard during the day while Fred was at work.[8] In the burgeoning agricultural region, land cultivation was the basis for the household economy. As the valley developed, many workers in large canneries also operated their own small orchards.[9]

Orchards were rapidly expanding at the time, and growers had more fruit than they could sell fresh. Families like the Wools had to preserve the fruit so as not to lose money on their crop. Early packinghouses were open-air metal sheds where families sorted, peeled, and cut the fruit by hand. From family operations grew packing plants that canned and dried fruit for distribution around the world. From the backyard shed, F. G. Wool Packing Company grew, building a "steam plant, requiring seven hundred gallons [of water] per minute to operate the machinery [with] a capacity of four thousand pounds per day."[10] Today, the Wools are modest about the start of the family cannery, but the construction attracted the notice of a national survey of California: "On his fine twenty-acre fruit ranch, at the foot of Quinn avenue, two and half miles south of San José, Mr. Wool is erecting an extensive cannery, and will be prepared to handle fruit, vegetables, etc. during the present season, 1904."[11]

With its concentration of orchards and packing houses, the Santa Clara Valley was a fruit factory. The production of fruit consumed valley residents: farming, harvesting, and processing required everyday practices of cultivation. These practices fostered an agricultural community rooted in "the physical geography and topography of the locality . . . embellished by the cultivation of the land and by the social and cultural associations that follow from this."[12] Agricultural work fostered a sense of place distinguished by an attachment to land nurtured by daily labor, and identification with the practices of the work. One fruit worker remembers "the clang of a prune bucket being dragged along the base of an orchard tree and the feel of dirt clods crumbling under our knees."[13] The work of the valley created an intense connection with the land, and a sense of place developed in daily fruit work. "The nature of everydayness is perhaps best understood through our encounters with tools, pieces of equipment."[14] For agricultural workers, the various methods and tools used to grow, harvest, and process fruit define their relationship with the land. This chapter examines how agricultural work creates a sense of place by examining the embodied, material rhetoric in corporate discourse, industry publications, and personal memoirs.

Corporate discourse, such as ads and published histories, describes the process of fruit production. "Corporate rhetoric is itself material, and it is located in places and spaces that produce structures of feeling or (affects) about the environment."[15] Films, labels, and brochures are all advertisements, material effects that promote affection toward the environment. Corporate discourse is a "material force that is made manifest in the architecture of places, spaces, and entire communities."[16] I examine five published corporate histories from Del Monte, Sunkist, NatureRipe, Sunmaid, and Sunsweet, and three promotional films produced by CalPak and the San José Chamber of Commerce in the mid-twentieth century. I also analyze a range of industry publications available in the archives of History San José, the California History Center, and as shared by the Wool family and Jim Zetterquist. I review issues from six different trade journals published from 1885–1985: *Western Canner and Packer, Canning Age, Blue Anchor, Orchard and Farm, American Fruit Grower,* and *California Agriculturalist.* I examine eighteen publications of five exchanges and organizations published from 1895 to 1985: Santa Clara County Fruit Exchange, California Cured Fruit Association Fruit Growers' Convention, California Canners and Growers, and the *Sunsweet Standard.* Because industry rhetoric only presents a partial narrative of the agricultural labor economy, I also include personal discourse with analysis of fifteen memoirs and numerous published interviews with people describing the agricultural experience of living and working in the Santa Clara Valley.

This chapter focuses on two sites of the integrated factory of the valley: orchards and canneries. These work locations feature distinct practices influenced by equipment and machines. The discussion of orchards centers around two kinds of fruit and the practices of harvesting and processing them: prunes and apricots. The discussion of canneries considers rhetoric surrounding two types of equipment used to process fruit products: the continuous can sterilizer and the conveyor belt. Examining how an embodied and material sense of place is rhetorically framed in corporate and industry discourse alongside the personal descriptions of lived experience in memoirs allows us to explore tensions in the promotion of the American agricultural ideal.

ORCHARDS

Corporate rhetoric promoted a farming ideal. Booster films of the mid-twentieth century glossed over the challenges of a weak economy and corporate competition facing farmers. Produced by the San José Chamber of Commerce, the 1948 film *Valley of Heart's Delight* promotes the Santa Clara Valley's agricultural heritage. The film narrator explains that, "Ideal climate makes year-round orchard work a possibility. Every spring, miles of orchard land are cultivated. During mild winter months, growers carry on extensive pruning operations to ensure better crops and easier more accessible picking."[17] The film, like earlier booster literature, declares farming life a pleasure, as growers, workers and consumers share the sensual delights of the valley. *Valley of Heart's Delight* emphasizes the joy of the pickers, asking, "And who wouldn't enjoy nibbling while he worked? Especially these juicy mouthwatering cherries. "'Cherries are ripe' is the keynote sounding/starting off the long fruit harvesting season."[18] This film portrays the harvest as easy work, as a leisurely pursuit, where pickers have time to taste the fruit, disregarding a picker's economic incentive to ensure that every piece of fruit goes into the bucket.

The 1948 film *Valley of Heart's Delight* touts the Santa Clara Valley's agricultural roots. *Valley of Heart's Delight* emphasizes the beautifully productive landscape. The film portrays farming life as pleasant and idyllic. Scenes of farm life are accompanied by light quartet music. The narrator describes "waving fields of grain" that provide winter feed for dairy animals and livestock.[19] The accompanying footage of wheat blowing in the wind pans out to farmers walking in a field followed by a tail-wagging dog. The narrator explains, "Harvesting under ideal weather conditions makes outdoor work a pleasure. With an average daily temperature mean of 58 degrees workers enjoy golden sun-drenched days tempered by cooling ocean breezes."[20] The film's images and words portray harvesting as recreation. Even newspapers portrayed the work as delightful. *The Pacific Rural Press* portrayed migrant workers as vacationers, "going from crop to crop, seeing Beautiful California, breathing its air, eating its food."[21] This echoes the agricultural ideal promoted in corporate films and the booster literature. Propaganda works rhetorically to promote an idyllic orchard setting, beyond the aesthetic of abundance seen in the beauty of the valley, to incorporate an agricultural ideal of happy workers.

Prune picking season arrived in August. Prunes are a specific type of plum that have high enough sugar content that they can be dried without fermenting. A common local aphorism declares, "All prunes are plums, but not all plums are prunes."[22] The *petit d'Agen* prune, brought to California by Louis and Pierre Pellier, is an ideal prune for growers because the fruit falls off the tree when it is ready. So, prunes are picked from the ground rather

FIGURE 8. Workers picking prunes, 1946. Photographer Unknown. Courtesy of History San José.

than from the tree. Prunes were a symbol of the Santa Clara Valley's status as the nation's premier fruit producer. In late summer, ripe prunes filled the valley with a strong perfume. For many, the scent of prunes ready to pick would recall "past seasons of drudgery, with thoughts of the hard and miserable way in which one had to work for a mere pittance."[23] The rhetoric of fruit work in the personal discourse of those who worked the Season reveals a sense of place directly linked to agricultural practices.

The fruit industry required a seasonal labor force. At the height of each season, the growers and packers employed 86 percent of manufacturing workers in Santa Clara County.[24] During the four months of the fruit season each year, the valley population grew by tens of thousands as migrant families traveled to the Santa Clara Valley to pick and pack fruit. In the 1930s, Mexicans, Filipinos, and American refugees from the Dustbowl did "the lion's share of hard, migratory farm labor."[25] Rudy Calles traveled with his family from Pasadena to pick fruit in the Valley as a teenager. Calles's memoir, *Champion Prune Pickers,* tells the adventures of his family's travels each year to the Santa Clara Valley from Pasadena. He remembers the drives well, and they were not always smooth. The family always carried spare tires "in anticipation of the usual flats."[26] For his first trip in 1925, his parents told him they were going on vacation. He remembers his surprise to find he would be doing work that was "a combination of pure misery, dirt, painful backs, aching knees, sunburned hands and neck."[27]

During the Season, Calles's family, like other migrant fruit pickers, lived where they worked, camping in and around the orchards, in "tents, make-shift shelters made from prune drying trays, or just under some large ever-green tree."[28] The summer residents would cook with wood. These open fires also served to light the area. Some growers provided outhouses and water, but often there were no restroom facilities in the fields, and many workers relied on whatever they brought with them.[29] In the summer, the orchards were filled with music, laughter, and shared meals. The "hustle and bustle of a prune ranch during picking season" included physical labor and sense of community.[30] The embodied practice of fruit work cultivated a sense of place including not just the work itself, but also the collective lived experience in the orchards during the harvest.

Personal accounts of orchard work give meaning to embodied practices and insight into the fruit-worker life. A memoir collection, *Voices from the Orchards*, includes statements from two dozen residents of the Santa Clara Valley who worked in the 1940s, 1950s, and 1960s, speaking to the experience of Chinese, Croatian, English, Italian, Japanese, Mexican, Spanish, and Swedish immigrant families. Anthony Zerbo, who graduated from San José High School in 1951, remembers his first day picking prunes: "I was really enthusiastic about picking prunes. I thought it'd be an easy way to make some money. After the first couple of hours, I found out it wasn't easy. I was on my knees picking up these prunes and the buckets didn't fill up that fast. I tried to make a picking machine out of myself and I wasn't very successful."[31] This was not easy work; efficiency did not come quickly to newer pickers. In his memoir, *Gulchin' Out*, Vince S. Garrod, whose father, R. V. Garrod, headed the California Prune and Apricot Growers (which became Sunsweet), notes that prune pickers were identifiable by "a pair of jeans or overalls with pads sewn onto the knees with holes worn into the pads, shoes with the toes worn out from dragging on the ground."[32] Agricultural workers' clothes are markers of work—evidence of the physical labor of picking prunes.[33] Garrod explains that besides the dust and heat, the picker "had to put up with a sore back, tender knees, sticky and sore hands, and buzzing flies that constantly flew around your face and head."[34] Picking prunes was a difficult physical labor. Agricultural work is "deeply enmeshed in both physical labor and dirt."[35] These memoirs demonstrate that material conditions shaping farm work are rhetorical: workers develop a collective identity as they describe and remember fruit work.

Andy Mariani, cousin of Mark and David Mariani, who still grows fruit on his orchard in Morgan Hill, explains: "You have to kneel. You get all of this crud—smashed prunes and dirt and mud on your knees. You pick so fast that—what are these called? Cuticles. The cuticles start to peel back, then the acid from the prunes gets in there. It's painful, and you're putting band-aids on. It was tough."[36] The fruit and dirt stuck to workers' knees, and the fruit acid seeped into their fingers. The work of harvesting plums makes an imprint on workers' physical bodies. Anthony Zerbo continues, "By the end of the day I was very tired. I had been on my knees for eight hours and my hands were all dirty and my hair was kind of dusty. . . . The next morning when I woke up, I didn't feel very good; my back was hurting me. My knees were bruised and I was sunburned. They told me to bring a hat but I didn't do it."[37] Zerbo's rueful story about the elusive delights of picking prunes reveals the discrepancy between the easy orcharding life promoted by boosters and the reality of working in the valley. The practice of picking prunes fosters an embodied sense of place through a distinct relationship with the land attuned to the feeling of working in the dirt and the corporeal effects of a day's work. Fruit labor fostered physical attachment to land marked by bodily aches and pains. Fruit labor also brought enjoyment of community gathering. Juan Manuel Herrera remembers, "My favorite part of the day was the lunch break. My mom always had such good food. It felt great sitting around with everyone. We would always look forward to the burritos that were coming, hot and tasty, bean, chorizo, rice, and sodas."[38] The daily embodied practices of both work and community gathering created physical and emotional identification with place.

On smaller family farms and before modernization, prunes were picked, dipped, and dried by hand. Emma Stolte Garrod, Vince Garrod's mother, notes, "It seems impossible now, but after grading all this fruit by man and woman power, Father patiently dipped it all through the boiling lye water, then through clean water to wash off the lye, pailful by pailful."[39] Vince Garrod describes the work required to use the prune dipper, the mechanism that lowered prunes into the water and then dumped the prunes onto a tray: "Two men could do this operation, but it was much faster to have three men. Once the water was hot, the unit would take about one box a minute or just around two tons per hour. After [they were] spread out, the trays were then hauled out to the field to be spread out for the sun to dry."[40]

FIGURE 9. Workers with trays of drying prunes, c. 1900. *Credit:* Andrew P. Hill. Courtesy of History San José.

Descriptions of prune work—patiently dipping by the pailful, hauling trays—emphasize the embodied practices that rhetorically construct a sense of place. Frank Preglascio, who grew up on a ranch in Los Gatos, remembers the manual labor involved in dipping the prunes before families afforded mechanical dippers.

> We had an old-fashioned dipper. We had a big steel kettle. We had to work it by rope. We had a brick oven. We'd keep a fire underneath to keep it hot. My father'd dump a whole can of lye in the water. The lye helps crack and wrinkle the skin. The skin is broken up a little. And, then we had a wire basket and a pulley. We'd drop it in there for a couple of dips. Then, we'd pull them up and dump them on the tray. Everybody that had money, had a dipper that worked mechanically. We did it the hard way.[41]

Workers were close to the fruit, handling it and processing it by the bucketful. Rudy Calles, the teenager from Pasadena, describes the work of collecting the prunes from the dipper:

FIGURE 10. Workers sorting prunes, c. 1930. Photographer unknown. Courtesy of San José Public Library, California Room, Arbuckle Collection.

When the handle was pulled back, the washed prunes would roll onto the wooden trays. One man would stand at each end to push and pull the tray smoothing out the wet prunes. The trays were then loaded onto a flatbed truck and driven out to the drying field. Two men carried the loaded trays all the way to the end of the field and spread them out so the fruit would dry under the warm California sun. A tray of wet prunes weighed about one hundred pounds. Lifting those trays, sometimes overhead, could get to you.[42]

The prune dipper defined the daily practice. Workers would pull the handle to release the prunes and personally smooth out the prunes into one layer. The prunes were handled one by one, pound by pound. This practice is rhetorical: these passages describe embodied practices such as rope pulling and fire tending that highlight material conditions of fruit work—the feel of the rope, the heat from the fire. Workers felt the weight of the fruit as they lifted buckets, moved trays, and processed fruit through the valley. Calles describes the push and pull of the tray to smooth the prunes—this is a metaphor for the push and pull of efforts all season, to harvest and process the fruit in the context of the valley's changing externalities.

Prunes were the most recognizable product of the valley, but the valley produced tons of other fruit, including apricots. Both prunes and apricots required "the constant reiteration of practices that are simultaneously individual and social. Places in this sense are intensely embodied and dramatic [with an] emphasis on bodily subjectivity and constant process."[43] Workers' bodies were integrated into the production process—fruit picking and processing required great levels of physicality; workers experienced the Season with their bodies. Samantha Senda-Cook defines such practices as "mundane, embodied, and repetitive actions; they are the daily arguments and compromises that compellingly convince us of who we are and how we ought to act." These practices demonstrate our participation in a collective identity.[44]

Tim Stanley, in his memoir, *Last of the Prune Pickers,* remembers picking apricots from the tree:

> A 'cot picker is up and down a rickety 3-legged ladder all day and cannot avoid looking into the sun more than what is comfortable. Extending the arms out to pick fruit will build the muscles but makes them quite sore first. Frequently the picker must reach into the tree and push the small branches aside to get to some of the fruit. The reward when withdrawing the arm is often not just the fruit but a slap in the face from one of the small branches. The larger branches are scaly and rough, and tear at the skin. And splinters from the wooden ladders are unavoidable.[45]

While prune pickers' knees had an intense familiarity with the ground, apricot pickers had an intimate relationship with the tree. Memoirs describe the physical effects of picking fruit, and reveal a close-up view of the orchards. Tourist discourse highlighted the soft, pillowy blossoms, but fruit trees had more prickly physical attributes up close. Memoirs emphasize the intimacy of embodied practices of fruit labor, rhetorically constructing a visceral sense of place.

Just like prunes, apricots were processed in the orchard until the modern cannery changed long-held practices. After harvest, apricots were cut in half and pits removed before being spread on trays, a process known colloquially as "cuttin' 'cots." The apricot cutting shed, an open air structure near the orchard, was a busy place. Local families would join migrant workers, and each shed would house dozens of women and children cutting the cots. It was hot

FIGURE 11. Workers in an apricot shed, c. 1910. Photographer unknown. Courtesy of California History Center.

and messy; flies buzzed around, attracted by the sticky apricots. 'Cot cutters used special paring knives. Gerrye Kee Wong, a third-generation Californian, remembers that her friend showed her the system. "I had never cooked before or held a knife. I cut myself a lot of times. After the first day, I had all these Band-Aids on. It never dawned on me not to go back. That money was very attractive. It was the first time I ever earned money. Growing up in the times of the depression we didn't have an allowance or money."[46] Wong emphasizes the physicality of the work and also its inevitability—it was what everyone did in the summer, and for teenagers, it was good money.

Dorena Berryessa Penner, whose ancestor Nicolas Berryessa arrived with Juan Bautista de Anza in 1777 and founded the city of San José, remembers "other people could do it very fast. . . . I was a little slow and sloppy. . . . I cut my hands very slightly. I was careful. I was more concerned with not cutting my hands than about how much money I made. I just wanted to have some spending money."[47] Leslie Rose Takamoto, a third generation Santa Clara Valley resident born at Hart Mountain Internment Camp in Wyoming, remembers the cutting shed: "we were outside. You cut your fingers ten times a day."[48] The work involved dexterity, not only to cut the fruit correctly, but also to avoid injury. Memoirs and other personal discourse frame work as a skill, learned through experience. Skilled cutters could "slice the apricot evenly around and push out the pit, all in one circular movement."[49] Dorena Berryessa Penner remembers that experienced workers distinguished themselves with their skill: "I remember looking at their hands. They would use a little rounded knife to cut the 'cots with. They would do it so quickly and theirs would be even. . . . Their hands were cut and stained from the fruit. You could see all the marks where they had cut themselves. It was a kind of orangey color, kind of rusty and dirty."[50] The physical labor of agricultural work involves risk of injury.[51] These passages reveal this was expected—that even experienced apricot cutters had scars from days of learning. The stains and marks on their hands were symbols of embodied practice, evidence of many seasons in the shed and of the impact of fruit work on the body.

Families worked together processing fifty-pound boxes of apricots. Cutters placed fruit halves on eight-foot trays, supported by wooden sawhorses. Felix W. Ribbs, who moved to San José with his family in 1922 at two years old, remembered cutting apricots as a child: "When you got emptied, you'd just holler 'Cots!' Then, they'd bring you some more. And you just kept on cutting. You'd put them out on the tray, face up, as close together as you can so you'd have a full tray."[52] When a tray was full, cutters would yell "tray!" and workers would take it away. Once the stack of full trays grew too tall to work on, a family would move to another area of the shed.[53] Women wore tags pinned to their shoulders that supervisors would mark to indicate every tray the family cut.[54] Memoirs of fruit work in the valley reveal a collective identity. Work was communal, families were part of a production line, moving and processing the fruit physically. The cutting shed was bustling as workers carried trays of whole fruit to be cut and cut fruit to be dried.

Cutting apricots was a social event. Tim Stanley reflects in his memoir, "It was an opportunity to be with friends and earn some money for school clothes at the same time. The work stations were close together and, unlike picking, the work was light, so it was easy to talk to your neighbors or even to yell at someone across the shed."[55] Vince S. Garrod remembers that the shed was full of children and "required a shed boss to keep some semblance of discipline. At times, the shed boss had no more discipline than those who worked under him."[56] At the end of the day, apricot fights would start. Margaret Martins Rendler, who grew up on a family apricot ranch in the Evergreen area of San José, remembers, "We'd use the squishy ones and hit each other."[57] Prunes were also too tempting. Carol Beddo, whose parents

FIGURE 12. Fruit workers at canning tables sorting fruit at Richmond-Chase Cannery, c. 1925. *Credit:* Denton's Industrial Photographers. Courtesy of History San José.

migrated to the Santa Clara Valley from Oklahoma during the Dust Bowl, explains, "Prunes were meant to be thrown."[58] Fruit fights would break out after a long day of work; more often as the Season wound down. The collaborative work (and play) in the cutting shed built community, cultivating social ties in the daily work.

Some workers did stop to taste the fruit. Gerrye Kee Wong recalls, "The apricots were wonderful. After a while, you got to know a really good one. One that was a nice deep orange. After I'd cut it, I'd eat it because that was a precious one. No, I never got sick of them. I love apricots still."[59] Leslie Rose Takamoto disagrees wryly: "Course, nothing tastes good after you got 200 loads of it."[60] Takamoto's comment reveals the distinction in the sensual sense of place promoted in brochures and labels. Rarely featured in labels and propaganda, fruit workers have a different sense of place than the aesthetic appreciation of the valley's beauty promoted in booster literature. Fruit workers' memoirs offer corporeal rhetoric of embodied practice: their bodies were an integral part of the fruit production process. Fruit workers vividly remember the practices of physically processing the fruit, whether kneeling on the ground to pick up prunes, carrying buckets of apricots up and down a ladder, dipping prunes into an open pail of lye, or cutting apricots while attempting to avoid nicks on their fingers. Memoirs demonstrate that a sense of place can be a powerful attachment to place without a positive affinity for place. Rather, sense of place is part of an attachment to, a visceral connection to place. Personal memories of the Season disclose that fruit workers cultivated a sense of place through hard experiences and a collective sense of contribution. In this way, sense of place is nuanced: a physical place, a mindset, and a culture. As the valley modernized, labor became mechanized, changing the embodied practices of the fruit industry in significant ways.

CANNERIES

In 1916, five major canning groups merged to form one company: CalPak. This enormous company now included all eighteen canning companies in the California Fruit Canners Association, which was already the "world leader" in fruit canning and drying.[61] CalPak began operations the next year, building a fifteen-thousand-square-foot warehouse on the site of the old San José Fruit Packing plant.[62] CalPak "controlled every aspect of food processing from ground to market."[63] To ensure consistency in product, CalPak relied on long-term contracts with growers, who became essentially part of the company.[64] This consolidation meant CalPak controlled millions of acres of fruit production.[65] CalPak would become the world's largest packer of foodstuff with sixty-four food processing plants in ten states, and more than twenty thousand acres of agriculture in California alone.[66] CalPak would become Del Monte, and another conglomerate, The California Prune and Apricot Growers, would become Sunsweet Corporation. These two corporations would produce a majority of fruit coming out of the Santa Clara Valley, and thus control fruit processing. In 1947, the canned fruit and vegetable industry was the largest manufacturing employer in California. Santa Clara Valley workers produced about 90 percent of California's fruits and vegetables pack, which accounted for 25 percent of the national fruit and vegetable production.[67]

The division of labor in the canneries was divided along gender lines. Men were supervisors, heavy lifters, and machine repairers: jobs that required physical strength or managerial authority. From the very beginning of the industry in the 1860s, women "performed the seasonal tasks of washing, cutting, canning, and packing California produce."[68] By the 1930s, Santa Clara Valley's thirty-eight canneries were the largest employers of women in California.[69] This work "reflected the domestic work that women did in their own kitchens."[70] The seasonal nature of food processing "reinforced the notion of women's participation in the labor force as temporary or supplemental."[71] Gendered assignments in the canneries reflected assumptions that as heads of households, "men needed full-time year-round work to support their families" while women were only working to earn extra money.[72]

Orchards and canneries became integrated. "The modern farm is often vertically integrated with a cannery that is in turn is integrated with a merchandising outlet." Thus, the fruit process from orchard to consumer could be controlled by one firm.[73] Through mergers, cooperatives, and associations, the fruit industry had a powerful influence on "people, spaces, and resources. The economic and political power of the fruit canning industry and its production networks shaped cities, agricultural land, and workers' lives."[74] Orchards became more industrialized as manual work in the prune yard and the cutting shed became mechanized. Canneries developed like conventional factories and were central in the "industrialization of agricultural spaces, which had previously included fields and outbuildings."[75] Modern canneries were vast warehouses—buildings the size of four football fields with machines running constantly.[76] Fruit was packed ripe, so the size of the harvest determined the length of the workday. During the Season, workers clocked in eighteen hours a day or ninety-six hours each week.[77]

As machines did more and more of the work of canning, human labor changed: fruit workers used to bear the weight of the prunes in the dipper, or eyeball the amount of syrup that would go into a batch of fruit. Mechanization meant that workers were pushing a button or monitoring a meter, removing the need for much of the physical contact with the fruit and knowledge of the product. With the new machines, embodied practices changed—mechanization removed much of the human element of fruit processing.

Working conditions in canneries influenced the embodied practices of fruit workers. Modern canneries moved workers out of the cutting sheds and away from outdoor prune dippers into huge buildings. More complex technologies allowed for mechanization of different aspects of fruit production.[78] Fruit processing plants streamlined production "by means of belts, flumes, and gravity feed conveyor systems. Mechanical choppers, peelers and pitters took the place of the more time-consuming manual operations."[79] As the tools changed, fruit work changed, transforming workers' relationships with the product and the environment. Two technological developments, the Sterilmatic continuous canning sterilizer and the conveyor belt, each revolutionized the canning process. Personal memoirs and corporate

FIGURE 13. Fruit worker operating a conveyor belt with boxes of prunes. Photographer unknown. Courtesy of History San José.

discourse rhetorically demonstrate how machines changed embodied practices and sense of place in the Valley of Heart's Delight.

The prune dipper was critical in the human effort of prune processing. Personal accounts offer visceral memories of working prune dippers in the orchards. The weight of prune-filled pails and sound of the pail against the tree reveal the intimacy of these embodied practices. William C. Anderson, Willow Glen orchardist, patented a "hinged basket system" for a state-of-the-art prune dipper.[80] He formed the Anderson Prune Dipper Company and expanded to other fruit processing equipment, including graders used for sorting fruit, dipping tanks, and various storing solutions. Anderson merged with another agricultural company to settle a patent dispute, becoming Anderson Barngrover, accelerating the mechanization of fruit processing. The first cannery equipment sold was a syruper that could fill twelve cans at once. The operator controlled the syrup with a foot pedal and "eyeballed" the fill line.[81] At the turn of the century, Anderson machines processed 90 percent of California fruit.[82] In 1901, Anderson Barngrover hired a twenty-one-year-old engineer, Albert R. Thompson, to help with equipment design. Thompson began working on a sterilizing machine to solve a critical issue arising with the mass production of canned goods. Canning required sterilization accomplished by "cooking" cans in a water bath at high temperatures. As valley orchards grew, more fruit required processing, and canners were faced with the problem of how to ensure consistent processing with a high volume of cans.

The common technique of sterilization was in a closed pressurized tank. Workers loaded small batches of cans in baskets and stacked the baskets in the cooker. Once the cans were cooked, they had to be cooled and baskets full of cans retrieved from the tank.[83] Cans often exploded or were otherwise damaged.[84] The process was laborious, requiring up to fifteen workers; time consuming, because it took a long time to heat the cans' contents thoroughly; and imperfect, because batches had to be started and stopped. Humans ran the machines, introducing inconsistencies and inefficiencies. The solution was "continuous sterilization" to eliminate steps and possibility for human error. Thompson designed the first continuous cooker. It could "receive filled, sealed cans from mechanized lines and process them without manual handling." The cooker's "precisely synchronized steam-tight pocket valve plopped cans accurately into the reel channels in perfect timing, and . . . retrieved them with equal dexterity." The Sterilmatic, as it came to be called, cooked cans quickly at high temperatures, and then quickly cooled them to prevent damage. Importantly for canners, it allowed "perfect uniformity, each can was handled exactly like all the others. And it was fast—up to 400 cans per minute."[85] The Sterilmatic introduced precision and enabled mass production. The descriptions of the Sterilmatic rhetorically frame the disembodiment of cannery work. The reference to its "dexterity," a term typically used to describe efforts by human hands, describes the machine's efficiency by assuming the agency of the workers it replaced. The descriptions of the machines emphasize precision and perfection, rhetorically eliding individual workers from the process and signifying that modern fruit work was disembodied and mechanized.

The Sterilmatic was the world's first continuous-stream automation of the cooking and cooling system for canned food. It was the "most significant piece of canning equipment to come from Santa Clara County."[86] By sterilizing, cooking, and cooling cans in one continuous process, the Sterilmatic eliminated several steps of manual labor, reducing the number of people required to can one batch from fifteen to one.[87] The sterilizer helped to create conditions for complete mechanization of the canning process.[88] Machines also changed the material conditions of the working environment. The heat from steam and running motors of industrial machinery like the Sterilmatic defined the cannery setting. It was hot. Working in a cannery was like standing in a "sauna" all day.[89] There was no climate control. Harvest and processing time for apricots and prunes was August to October, the hottest months of the year in the Santa Clara Valley. Depending on the weather, the interior of a cannery could reach temperatures over 100 degrees.[90] The steam expressed from the Sterilmatic would linger in the air. Condensation would collect on the ceiling. Fruit workers' accounts emphasized the oppressive nature of working indoors with the machines. Jennifer Wool, of the F. G. Wool cannery family, explains: "It would rain on you. You are standing there, and it would drip down your back. Oh, I hated that! It would be right here in front of your face or it would go down your neck."[91] The material conditions of the canneries affected the physical experiences of fruit work: the machines that replaced workers had commanding presence; cannery workers were surrounded by enormous industrial machinery. As the work setting changed from the apricot shed to industrial canneries, machines changed the work itself.

The conveyor belt was introduced in 1920 to move fruit through the cannery more efficiently.[92] The industry magazine *Canning Age* showcased the "complete system of inter-departmental conveyors," installed in the George E. Hyde Canning Company in Campbell that year.[93] Industry discourse highlighted the rhetorical shift from the agency of workers to machines. While the conveyor belt reduced the number of personnel needed to move the fruit manually through the factory, workers were still needed to monitor and sort the fruit as it moved along the conveyor belt. With the exception of hand sorting, the jobs on belt were "essentially machine tending, with workers overseeing the smooth movement of the product along the conveyor belt or operating cutting or pitting machines."[94] Workers watched the machines, helping fruit move along the belt as the machine did the processing. "The workstation approach itself embodied the principles of scientific management. Men and women learned simple tasks they repeated perfectly hundreds of times a day during the packing season."[95] Workers became accessories to the machine, repeating tasks throughout the day at a pace determined by the belt. Material conditions of the factory changed the embodied practices of fruit work: where workers' bodies once determined the pace and quality of work, machines now controlled the fruit production process including the very movement of workers' bodies.

The conveyor belt streamlined transportation within the plant. Fruit was brought in from the railroad car, weighed, and placed on a conveyor belt that moved it to the sorting table. This eliminated jobs in canneries: labeling cans and packing them into cases was done by machine, and workers were no longer needed to move fruit around the factory on carts.[96] Women inspected and sorted fruit, placing it in boxes, which were then delivered by conveyor to cutting tables. After other women cut the fruit, conveyors delivered fruit to the peeler and then to a final sorting station.[97] The conveyor belt set the pace of cannery work—beginning in the section of the cannery where fruit was prepared, through sorting, washing, canning, quality control, warehouse, and shipping.[98] Analysis of personal discourse regarding the cannery experience demonstrates the shift in embodied practices for employees from diverse backgrounds and workplace positions.

Workers no longer moved through the orchards or the sheds. Machines moved fruit through the factory. This pace was unnaturally fast, visually and physically disruptive to workers' natural movements. Jennifer Wool describes the stress of standing at the belt: "Here come all the peaches. And they're coming out. And then they're on this belt. And they move along. And you have to either look for bad ones or flip them over. Well, pretty soon, the belt seems like it's standing still and you're moving. Because you're staring down and all these peaches are moving and you're never really looking up because you don't want to miss anything, right? And pretty soon you feel like your body is moving. I couldn't handle it."[99]

The mere mention of the conveyor belt today provokes visceral reactions from former cannery workers. "Hypnotic! It's horrible!" Joe Melehan exclaims. Joe cohosts the Fruit Cocktail Club with Jim Zetterquist. Joe's grandfather, Joe Perrucci, founded Mayfair Packing in the 1930s. Melehan says he couldn't fall asleep at night because he could still see images of fruit moving along the conveyor belt.[100]

"Nothing was worse," Jim Zetterquist agrees. Sorting on the belt was a "tedious, monotonous, and sickening job. You had to sit there. You couldn't lift your head. You had to sit there and just sort."[101] Workers couldn't lift their gaze because they became dizzy staring at fruit rolling by. New employees would have to become accustomed to the motion: one veteran cannery worker explains: "A new girl, she doesn't know that, so she looks up and down all the time and pow! She falls right over dizzy."[102] Women working on the lines sorting described their jobs as tedious and boring. In an interview with Patricia Zavella, Lupe Collosi stated: 'I don't like the monotony

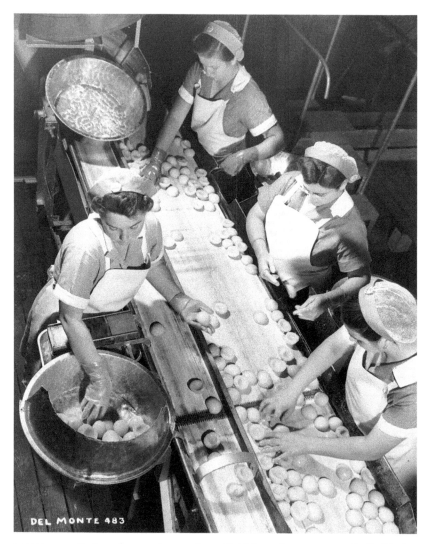

FIGURE 14. Fruit workers sorting peaches at Del Monte Cannery, 1945. *Credit:* Moulin Studios. Courtesy of History San José.

of the belt. I hate standing all day. It's noisy; it gives me a headache. The line makes me dizzy, and sometimes I get sick."[103] The machines had corporeal effects such as nausea, vertigo, and dizziness that were distinct from physical exertion of the manual labor of fruit processing.

Workers described how machines changed the embodied practices of the work itself. The conveyor belt mechanized the movement of the factory such that workers no longer moved the fruit through the cannery, but stayed in one place as the fruit moved past them. Sorting was assembly line work. "Workers used both hands to sort the produce into various grades—choice, standard, or nectar. They performed the same tasks all day, had no control over workspace and little control over techniques, and were confined to their stations on the line. They stood in one place, concentrating on doing the job quickly."[104] Patricia Zavella interviewed Chicana women who noted "how demanding the work was and how it strained their bodies." Lisa Hernández said, "You're just standing there moving your hands, and it hurts your lower back."[105] Cannery machines restricted workers' movements so as to maximize efficiency.

Personal discourse reveals how machines restrained the workers' movement and thus disrupted the sense of place engendered in agricultural work. Sorting jobs were characterized by "confinement in one place, endlessly repeating a single task [that] provided little intrinsic reward."[106] Margaret Martins Rendler remembers, "It was just an awful job. You had to stand right there. When you were cutting 'cots at home you would cut one section and kind of move around a little bit, but there, you just had to stand right there."[107] The work was different from the fruit orchard. In the cannery, workers' activities were dictated by machines—the conveyor belt's movement was so fast and unnatural that it disrupted sleep patterns. Rendler remembers, "That was the worst job I ever had. I went home after an eight-hour day and I would be so exhausted. When I would go to bed, I would be moving my hands around like I was still working . . . I remember my fingers were cut and my wrists hurt."[108] The rhetoric of fruit workers reveals a disruption to sense of place cultivated in the orchards and sheds—in the cannery, workers describe a disembodied experience as tasks require unnatural movements in a confined space.

Cannery work was "grueling."[109] Government reports noted poor working conditions: poor ventilation, wet floors, and hazardous machinery.[110] While some plants were "airy and sanitary," many in the 1930s were "bona fide sweatshops."[111] Women "stood for hours working with acidic fruit," washing fruit, cutting it and placing it in the can.[112] Such "exacting" work caused "severe damage to their hands; not from traumatic injuries but from the small nicks and cuts from cutting fruit by hand."[113] Rendler remembers working with the mechanical 'cot cutter: "they would have somebody standing on one end of the line and pouring boxes of fruit into this machine. The machine would cut them. The cots would come down a conveyor belt. You would have to wear gloves or you'd have your hands be torn up. Even with the gloves, they'd get cuts in them. The apricot pits were pretty sharp. They would be coming down the belt and we'd have to pull the pits out and flatten them out face up."[114] Workers had to move fast to manipulate the fruit at the pace set by the belt, while trying to avoid injury. Women had their hands in water most of the day, so the cuts frequently became infected.[115] Moreover, peach fuzz irritated women's hands and arms; workers shared cold cream with newcomers to relieve irritation and inflammation.[116] Jim Zetterquist remembers, "Peach fuzz is itchier than poison oak."[117] These personal accounts of the mechanization of fruit work illustrate how the embodied practices of fruit work were intensified by cannery machines.

In addition to changing the physical nature of fruit work, material conditions of the cannery also changed the social nature of fruit work. Fruit processing was no longer a social activity. Although kinships and tight bonds developed, largely along ethnic and gender lines, the socializing of the cutting shed wasn't possible in the cannery. Workstations were spaced far enough apart that it was difficult to talk due to the background noise of the factory.[118] Canneries were loud: characterized by what Jennifer Wool describes as a "certain roar."[119] The conveyor belt was "deafening." Workers had to yell to be heard over the sound of tin cans rattling on metal rollers.[120] Jim Zetterquist describes a can manufacturing plant as the loudest plant he'd ever been in: "I was a jackhammer operator for a while. It was louder than that. It was deafening. The empty cans were the loudest. Clanking. Thousands and thousands of cans, up to thirty conveyor lines, with the fastest lines running up to eight hundred cans a minute. Can you imagine the noise?"[121] The canneries disrupted the sense of place fostered by the work in the orchards and the sheds. The work happened inside, and the cannery machines created a wall of sound that was disconcerting and completely disconnected workers from the outside world, severing their attachment to the land.

The conveyor belt also affected the traditionally cooperative nature of fruit work. In the cutting shed, women would help each other fill boxes.[122] In the cannery, this turned competitive. Women were paid very little, and on a piece-rate scale, which means they were paid by the pieces of fruit they processed.[123] To ensure access to fruit pieces, women workers needed to "secure a favorable position on the line, which was always a spot near the chutes or gates where the produce first entered the department."[124] In an interview with Vicky Ruiz, Carmen Bernal Escobar recalled:

> There were two long tables with sinks that you find in old-fashioned houses and fruit would come down out of the chutes and we would wash them and

put them out on a belt. I had the first place, so I could work for as long as I wanted. Women in the middle hoarded fruit because the work wouldn't last forever and the women at the end really suffered. Sometimes they would stand there for hours before any fruit would come down for them to wash. They just got the leftovers. Those at the end of the line hardly made nothing.[125]

Women working along the conveyer line were discouraged from working cooperatively due to the piece-rate scale and the pace of the work set by the machine. As Escobar notes, a worker's position on the conveyor belt line determined access to fruit, so women at the end of the line would often process substantially less fruit than other workers, and sometimes none.[126] Technology changed workers' relationships with each other. The machines introduced competition rather than collective action, further disrupting the collective sense of place cultivated in the orchards by weakening relationships between workers.

The change in a sense of place is seen rhetorically: the nostalgia with which fruit workers remember the work in the cutting shed dissipates when they recall working in the cannery. Cannery machinery increased the pace of the work, which became increasingly repetitive. Women noted "the dehumanizing aspects of line work, especially the fast pace and speedups." In an interview with Patricia Zavella, Josie Flores said, "I'm just like a robot, a cog in the machine. It's so inhuman to me."[127] Fruit work became disembodied as machines processed fruit and set the pace of the work. The dizzying pace of the conveyor belt and the mechanization of the canneries signified the changing nature of the valley and the onslaught of progress. Across the diverse perspectives offered in the memoirs and interviews of fruit workers in the valley, from managers to family members of family-owned canneries to seasonal workers, common themes emerge. The personal discourse of the valley suggests material conditions of fruit work profoundly influence a sense of place characterized by strong relationships to community and attachment to land.

EXTERNALITIES

Mechanization arrived at valley farms in the mid-1930s.[128] California's "farm economy" was characterized by an "intimate relationship between agriculture and industry."[129] The life of the farmworker gained publicity in the American media with the publication of *Factories in the Field*, Carey McWilliams' exposé of "farm industrialists."[130] Dorothea Lange's photography further publicized the plight of laborers across California. The partnership between farmers and packers produced "a pattern of low wages, oppressive working conditions, and unspeakably bad living conditions."[131] As many costs in growing and processing fruit are fixed and unpredictable, labor was often the first cost-cutting measure.[132] Packers and canners, whose profit depended on the quality and quantity of produce, were eager for mechanization and approached farm problems from "strictly economic or technological perspectives."[133] Investing in one machine with a repair budget provided more certainty than fluctuating labor pools and risks of striking workers.

The 1930s saw intense and prolonged labor unrest. It was hard to promote the pleasures of canned fruit when Americans didn't have money for basics. Canners and packers faced significant profit losses and, wanting to ensure low wages during seasonal operations of picking and packing, resisted workers' attempts to organize.[134] In the 1930s, the partnership between farmers and packers produced "a pattern of low wages, oppressive working conditions, and unspeakably bad living conditions."[135] Agricultural work in orchards and canneries was often "grueling labor that fell disproportionately to immigrants, people of color, and women."[136] In response to dangerous and unsanitary working conditions and low wages, the 1930s "ushered in a wave of labor unrest unparalleled in the history of California agriculture."[137] During the 1933 season, more than 47,500 farmworkers participated in thirty-seven major strikes across the state.[138] Waves of strikes "erupted throughout the summer and fall as each crop ripened for harvest."[139] Strikes continued through the decade, culminating in 1938, with the "Apricot Wars" of the Santa Clara Valley as cannery workers went on strike, joined by fruit pickers. Incidents of arson, violence, and property destruction made the news. The *San José Mercury Herald* reported "widespread violence" throughout the county, as apricot growers attempted to prevent other growers from selling to canneries for less than the agreed price.[140] Growers threw fruit from loaded trucks and burned boxes en route from ranches.[141] Workers "succeeded in demonstrating to employers their labor could not be taken for granted."[142] As the California Farm Bureau noted in April 1934, organizing was a "vital factor in the agricultural life of the Santa Clara Valley."[143]

The mechanization of agriculture had important implications for California farm labor. Increased mechanization highlighted the precarious position of small family farms amid broader corporate entities. Family farms with limited acreage were at a competitive disadvantage, lacking capital to invest in machinery and having no marketing support, while larger farms were able to purchase machinery and could hire more labor.[144] Farm mechanization "helped to doom the small family-farm system."[145] Large-scale farming established itself rapidly in California, incorporating industrial values into traditional agricultural practices.[146] With the mechanization of agriculture, the material conditions of place changed for fruit workers. "In any given place we encounter a combination of materiality, meaning, and practice. . . . Places have all the material things that pass through them—commodities, vehicles, waste, and people."[147] Mechanization of agriculture in the valley affected the way that fruit moved from the tree to the consumer, how people moved in the orchards and the canneries, and how by-products of agricultural production moved across the fields and through the factories. The shift in agricultural sense of place in the valley is seen rhetorically in the personal and public discourse regarding agricultural work.

The mechanization of agriculture allowed more intense cultivation, which exacerbated already looming environmental issues. In the 1930s, Santa Clara County had one hundred thousand acres of orchards and an additional twenty thousand acres planted in vegetables.[148] The scope of orchards in the Santa Clara Valley planted with mostly the same species of trees, "made a wonderful environment for all sorts of pests and diseases to develop in quantities never seen before in orchard areas."[149] Trees full of prunes, apricots, cherries, walnuts, and peaches lured more than forty different pests.[150] Pesticides became indispensable for ensuring quality crops. The term used in memoirs and industrial publications alike is *spray*. Dominic Cirone, born in San José in 1912, remembers: "Spraying, oh yes. We had to spray the apricots. We had to wear hats and boots. Those wagons carried the spray. The tractor pulled it. . . . After you sprayed, you had to wash yourself."[151] Charlie Olson remembers "coming in from spraying the orchards covered in blue residue [and] bathing in kerosene to wash it off."[152]

The effects of pesticides on farmworkers are well documented today.[153] Historically, pesticides were applied without caution. On a "hot sunny morning," Rudy Calles, the teenager from Pasadena, reported for work along with fifty other laborers at a field next to Moffett airbase.[154] He recalls one morning when an airplane flew ten feet above the field, spraying powdered insecticide.

> We watched the plane as it flew right over us. The powder had a temporary blinding effect. Also, it stuck to the skin, leaving an uncomfortable itch. . . .
> The next day the same airplane sprayed the plants and us, first flying the length then the width of the pea field. Some of us developed a coughing spell, all the while the field Boss yelling, "Can't you guys take a little dust, hell

don't let that bother you mojitos!" . . . I earned $9.00 for six days of stooped labor in 90-degree temperature[s] and lungs full of powdered insecticide.[155]

Calles's story animates the direct effect of industrialization on workers' bodies: the spray blinded workers and stuck to their skin, and invaded their lungs. The personal discourse of fruit workers shows the materiality, meaning, and practice that shape their sense of place.

Pesticides were used widely to ensure healthy crop yields in the Santa Clara Valley's monoculture, despite the undetermined cost to workers' health. Additionally, older pesticides that contained lead or arsenic are "tricky pollutants. They break down slowly, persisting in soil for decades or longer."[156] More than fifty former agricultural sites in Santa Clara County have required clean-up due to pesticides. Vince Garrod explains, "No one realized they were enveloping the county in a chemical blanket that would last long after the orchards disappeared."[157] Pesticides were a necessary externality whose impact was disregarded by growers concerned with the most productive harvest. Today, research demonstrates that pesticides have acute and long-term impacts on human health and ecological integrity. [158] While the impact of pesticide use on environmental and human health was not questioned at the time, another by-product of the cannery industry gained public attention.

After World War II, public concern grew about the environmental impact of cannery waste. Canneries were "dumping rotting peelings, fruit and liquids into the south bay. The wastes continued to rot, killing all of the fish in the south bay and generating clouds of hydrogen sulfide gas."[159] The State Board of Public Health banned dumping of raw sewage following a 1946 report that concluded, "The disposal of raw or inadequately treated sewage and industrial wastes in the waters of the Lower SF Bay has destroyed its aesthetic character."[160] The California State Fish and Game Commission required canners to install screens to collect solids from cannery wastewater.[161]

The canning industry and the valley's growing population also created capacity issues for the sewage treatment plants. The primary sewage treatment plant, completed in 1956, was designed to accommodate thirty-six million gallons of daily flow. In 1961, the actual daily flow through the San José sewage treatment system was sixty million gallons daily.[162] By 1959, wastewater from fruit processing imposed a disproportionate load on treatment in the valley compared to other sources of wastewater. The annual output of fruit alone in Santa Clara County exceeded all other counties in the country. A 1959 sewage report found that, "Canneries within the service area of the San José sewage treatment plant produce about 12 per cent of the national peach pack, 20 per cent of the pear pack, and 45 per cent of the fruit cocktail pack."[163] The concentration of fruit processing plants in the valley put remarkable pressures on the sewer. The seasonal nature of the canning industry created more issues. The overloads occurred during peak canning times. The problem was exacerbated by the timing of the canning season, which occurred during the summer and early fall, when the water table was at its lowest.[164] The issue of cannery waste would call into question the fruit industry's sustainability in the Santa Clara Valley.

The San José City Council voted in March 1976 to double the sewage fees charged to canneries.[165] In 1975 and 1976, cannery sewage taxes increased 250 percent.[166] In 1977, canneries in San José were paying about 20 percent of the city's total sewer costs.[167] In 1982, sewage rates increased again, this time by 50 percent.[168] Canneries discharging more than twenty-five thousand gallons of sewage a day saw their sewage fees rise 135 percent. The sewage rates were the last straw. In 1982, a *San José Mercury News* article headlined "Sealing the Fate of a Dying Industry" explained the end of an era: "The heyday of the San José canning business is over, and everyone in the industry knows it. The city's canneries—the victims of high fuel and sewage costs, a growing national taste for fresh food and the flight of agriculture to the central valley—are disappearing quickly."[169] Externalities such as pesticide and sewage were products of the increasing mechanization of agriculture and further changed the material conditions of work. These external pressures and costs would ultimately prove the fruit industry unsustainable.

CONCLUSION

The industrialization of the valley brought new practices and a change in the intimate relationship with the land seen in smaller canneries. In family operations, "identity intersects with place both in the sense of home as the domain of a 'private' domestic life and a rootedness within a locality."[170] Workers keenly felt a sense of place in their aching muscles, cut fingers, and lingering pesticide residue. For farm families and canning communities, the everyday practices in the canneries and orchards created a sense of place rooted in material conditions of their embodied lived experience.

With the industrialization of the fruit industry, the land was increasingly viewed solely as an economic resource, disrupting the sense of place attached to it. "This materialist perspective sometimes overshadows the sense that land can also be seen as a component in people's social or cultural make-up. . . . The land and the surrounding environment are an integral part of their being."[171] Increasing corporatization of agriculture and development of land is "constituted by production, an industrial attitude, rather than the possibility that land can be inflected with symbolic meaning depending on one's relation to it."[172] Industrial agriculture thus shifts "solidarity from one's local community to economic interests," largely through a change in material conditions that disrupts the environmental and community connections engendered by more traditional agricultural work.[173] A shift in the rhetorical expression of the collective sense of place from the orchards and sheds to the canneries reveals a changing attachment to environment and community.

Mechanization changed the nature of agricultural work in three ways: First, embodied practices of fruit processing became disembodied work. The mammoth canneries were a stark contrast to family fields and farmhouses, where prunes were graded, dipped, and dried by hand. In the canneries, machines set the pace of the work and controlled the movement of fruit through the cannery. In the cutting shed, people moved trays of apricots from stack to stack; in the cannery, fruit moved to different stations via conveyor belt. In the cutting shed, counts were done by pinning a number to a person's apron; in the cannery, this was done by automatic sensor. In the cutting shed, fruit cutters brought fruit directly from the orchard, human bodies moved the fruit, bearing the weight of the buckets and trays of fruit: this provided an overall sense of the work. In the cannery, the conveyor belt removed the physical movement of fruit and people through the factory. The stream of fruit was endless; it came from a cart, or a chute in the wall, but there was no direct connection to orchard. The sense of place is disembodied in the modern cannery because human workers monitor machines, rather than working with the fruit by hand. Place relies on embodied practices; to be "disembodied is not only to be deprived of place, *unplaced*; it is to be denied the basic stance on which every experience and its memory depend."[174] Industry and personal discourse reveal a disruption to sense of place as agricultural production in the valley shifted from worker to machine.

Second, the mechanization of work in the cannery and the orchard separated workers from the environment. Debbie S. Dougherty notes that farming is by nature "dirty work," framed by material conditions and social constructions.[175] Mechanical intervention separates farmers from physical labor: "Equipment places an increasingly large metal and rubber layer between the farmer and the dirt they are working with . . . [and] dirt is not as deeply imbedded in the work that they do."[176] This is not to say that the fruit workers harvesting with tractors or sorting on conveyor belts do not get dirty or work hard; rather, the machines separate fruit workers from the natural environment in specific ways, weakening the intimate sense of place derived from working with the land. The canneries moved production inside, away from the orchards. The infamous rains of 1918 are one example of the importance of measures to protect the fruit harvest from the harshness of the weather. Personal accounts reveal that work in the apricot sheds was intimately tied to the environment—workers remember swatting flies, dodging bees, and being aware of the weather. When work moved to the cannery, the workers left the natural environment. The canneries were large factories that, except for their proximity to the orchards, could be anywhere. Canneries were not emplaced locations; rather, they weakened workers' ties to the natural environment.

Finally, mechanization changed the communal nature of agricultural work. The cooperative, social aspect of the work depicted in the orchards and cutting sheds was lost in the larger canneries. Cannery workers did develop kinships, largely along gender and ethnic lines, but these carried out mostly over lunch breaks and commuting to work.[177] Personal recollections emphasize the noise of the cannery and how the stationary workstations discouraged conversation and camaraderie. Furthermore, the piece-rate payment system encouraged a competitive environment among workers that isolated each worker in a solitary pursuit of wages. Thus, the cannery distanced workers from the fruit, the environment, and each other. This chapter reveals through personal and industry discourse how the industrialized cannery changed the sense of place in the valley from a focus on environment and community to a focus on efficiency and economy.

THREE

———

From Farmland to Metropolis

VALLEY AS SYMBOL OF PROGRESS

THE AUGUST AFTERNOON IN 1943 was a pleasant 74 degrees, a surprise to the one hundred New Yorkers leaving behind another oppressive East Coast summer. As the special train pulled into San José's Southern Pacific Railroad Depot, the passengers were welcomed with a key to the city.[1] They were IBM workers who would operate the company's first card plant on the West Coast at the corner of 16th and St. John Streets in downtown San José.[2] IBM moved to the Pacific Coast because of its potential as an "industrial district" after the war.[3] IBM's arrival in San José marked the beginning of a new era.

Excitement about new technologies abounded. In response to the Great Depression, San José business leaders wanted their city to be more than a cannery town. Half the city's workers were employed in canneries, so a common refrain was that San José "feasted in the summer and starved in the winter."[4] The Chamber of Commerce and Merchants Association formed the Progress Committee, a political organization composed of business owners, landholders, and others who would benefit from growth. The Progress Committee represented "extensive disillusionment with agriculture throughout the valley and the building momentum of high tech in the north county."[5] It campaigned to build "a new metropolis, in the place of sleepy San José."[6]

In 1944, Progress Committee candidates won election to the San José City Council. They immediately ousted the frugal city manager, Clarence Goodwin, and began to implement ideas for industrial growth.[7] That year, San José's Chamber of Commerce spent nearly sixty thousand dollars to attract industry.[8] The Chamber placed ads in *Business Week* and *Fortune*, and prepared a forty-page promotional booklet that advertised opportunities in the Santa Clara Valley.[9] This campaign echoed propaganda promoting the promise of the fruit industry a hundred years earlier that urged opportunists and entrepreneurs to come to the Santa Clara Valley without delay.[10] The Chamber of Commerce campaign worked, creating an "industrial rush" to the valley.[11] As the economy diversified after the war, a number of factors attracted industry to the valley: government support for electronics research, readily available large sites for plants and factories, and incentives offered by eager cities and developers.[12] Westinghouse Electric bought the Hendy Iron Works in Sunnyvale in 1947. Ford relocated to Milpitas in 1953, Lockheed located its Missile and Space Division in Sunnyvale in 1956, General Motors moved a plant to Fremont in 1956, and IBM opened a bigger factory in San José in 1958.[13] The San José Chamber of Commerce campaign lured two thousand industries in five years.[14] The economy shifted toward year-round jobs bolstered by three major firms: Ford and Westinghouse Electric each employed three thousand people, and FMC Corporation employed more than two thousand workers.

The change in the Santa Clara Valley played out in planning offices and empty fields, in hotel lobbies and orchards. Seemingly innocuous political battles over housing, city limits, and sewage brought about profound change to the Valley of Heart's Delight. As the Santa Clara Valley gained attention amid national changes after World War II, debates about the purpose and best use of land emerged in public discourse. Public rhetoric about the future of the valley reveals "overt and covert social practices that embed in place-making behaviors notions of ideology, power, control, conflict, dominance, and distribution of social and physical resources."[15] Public debates about the future of the fruit industry featured disputes over territorial boundaries and reflected tensions surrounding development and preservation. Public and personal discourse shows community tensions over competing economic and environmental interests and attempts to control the future of the valley.

This chapter examines how debates over land use reveals a disrupted sense of place in the Santa Clara Valley agricultural community. I examine civic and political rhetoric, industry discourse, and personal memoirs and published interviews. Local public discourse on the development of the Santa Clara Valley after World War II offers a breathless celebration of the progress of industry and development while personal discourse, planning reports, and national discourse present a more skeptical view of the changing valley. I examine hundreds of news articles from local newspapers, primarily the *San José Mercury News*, from 1940–2000. I examine twelve public reports and government documents concerning annexation laws and farm bills in the California Legislature, and the effects of San José's development on urban sprawl, including three national reports from Ralph Nader, the *Stanford Law Journal*, and Leonard Downie Jr., journalist and future editor of the *Washington Post*. I also include analysis from fifteen memoirs describing the agricultural experience of living and working in the Santa Clara Valley. The divergent perspectives of public and personal discourse reveal three impulses in public and personal discourse: growth and speculation, preservation and resistance, and declining industry.

GROWTH AND SPECULATION

One hundred years to the day after San José was incorporated as a city, a "dynamo of a man" walked into the red brick building of San José's city hall.[16] A. P. "Dutch" Hamann was the City Manager of San José, appointed by a split City Council vote. Arriving in San José to manage the city, the forty-year-old had no training or experience in government work, but "was a skilled politician and a public relations expert."[17] In the five years since the end of World War II, two thousand new industries had arrived, and the San José City Council wanted a manager to build a city to accommodate the rapidly expanded population. Hamann fit the bill: "completely unflappable—an open, friendly, super-salesman politician."[18] He came into the manager position with a fervent growth agenda and "strong ideas about what was good for a city and what was not."[19] Hamann's arrival signaled a change in the valley and launched a campaign about what it meant to be a modern city. For Hamann and his allies, that meant growth and development.

The Progress Committee's propaganda and industrial incentives attracted hundreds of thousands of new residents: the region saw astounding population growth for the next twenty years. The Santa Clara Valley population tripled from 1948 to 1950.[20] In ten months between April 1950 and January 1951 twenty thousand people moved to the valley.[21] In 1961, three hundred thousand arrived in San José within eighteen months: a rate of sixteen thousand per month.[22] Between 1945 and 1965, California's population grew by 77 percent, while Santa Clara Valley's population increased by 188 percent. As people streamed into the valley, a "vigorous real estate market emerged."[23] In the first quarter of 1951, thirteen subdivisions broke ground, which would add seven thousand single-family homes to the valley.[24] More than ten thousand new homes were built in 1958.[25] San José was not the only city with a

FIGURE 15. San José city manager Dutch Hamann, center. *Credit:* Del Carlo Studio. Courtesy of History San José.

building boom. Sunnyvale's 1955 Annual Report celebrated the number of companies moving into "the city with the built-in future." The report noted that Sunnyvale's growth was so fast that "statistics become obsolete hourly."[26] Industry and civic discourse celebrated rapid population growth as an opportunity for economic expansion. Just as booster literature a century earlier promoted opportunities of the fruit industry, city boosterism promoted opportunities of development and growth of population and industry.[27]

In San José, Dutch Hamann dived into his role. In his first few months in office, he successfully lobbied for a bond issue to pay for repaving San Carlos Street, a major artery from downtown to the west side of San José. Instead of repaving the street, however, Hamann unapologetically used the bond funds to pay for a new sewer for the IBM plant in South San José. He explained, "it was a far better use of the money."[28] Hamann often "ignored the niceties" in favor of making progress on his agenda.[29] He accomplished his agenda with a "mix of rustic charm, saber-rattling toward opposing communities, and shrewd juggling of bond issues."[30] Hamann disrupted existing ways of politics and asserted his direct political influence; for example, he routinely met with the city council privately before public meetings.[31] His power and ability to push through his proposals were helped by an "unofficial kitchen cabinet that wrote the public agenda and pushed the passage of bond issues needed to finance capital improvements and make even more growth possible."[32] The group had success raising money for several bond issues with contributions from home builders, business leaders, utilities, real estate industry, and construction companies.[33] Hamann and associates met for lunch at the Hyatt House in San José, jokingly referring to themselves as the "Buck of the Month" club, a riff on the "Book of the Month" clubs that were popular at the time.[34] The group exchanged financially beneficial information about zoning and development between government officials and bankers and developers.[35] All had a vested interest in paving the way for the city's growth. The city's collective shrug about the Buck of the Month Club reflected the prevailing attitude that such dealings were legitimate and necessary to ease the path of development. Growth rhetoric prevailed, privileging progress over place, disrupting the fruit community by endangering the orchards that were central to its livelihood and sense of place.

Government reports and news articles portrayed growth as inevitable. In his annual reports for the city, Hamann repeatedly emphasized San José's "appointment with destiny."[36] He testified before a state board using the line that defined his tenure: "They say San José is going to become another Los Angeles. Believe me, I'm going to do everything in my power to make that come true."[37] He told a *San Francisco Chronicle* reporter, "It's hard for a San Franciscan to believe, but we will be the biggest city in Northern California—little old San José!"[38] Hamann rhetorically defined San José's destiny as a modern city, and framed his vision with an unyielding belief in the desirability of economic development and population growth. As a result of Hamann's efforts, San José's growth and development "was absolutely unbridled."[39] In 19 years as city manager, Hamann oversaw growth of San José that "can only be described as staggering."[40] San José's population grew from 92,000 to 460,000.[41] The city annexed 1,377 parcels of unincorporated land to grow from 17 to 137 square miles in twenty years. For comparison, after Hamann's term, San José grew 40 miles in fifty years to reach its present area of 180 square miles.[42]

Urban expansion reflected the city's reactive approach to growth: annexing land to accommodate the separate demands of each company that could be convinced to move to San José. The city limits expanded based on individual land acquisitions rather than broadly planned expansion. Hamann followed a strategy that became known as "strip annexation." He was empowered by state law that allowed cities to annex territory with fewer than five people per acre without voter approval.[43] San José would annex territory around revenue-generating development projects to secure the tax revenue. Outlying land was cheap and thus most attractive to developers. In some cases, San José would merely annex the street that led from the existing city limit to a far-flung piece of land, and then pressure adjacent landowners until they capitulated and the city could acquire the land itself.[44] Known as "cherry stem" annexations, these created "serious obstacles to efficient public service provision."[45]

Hamann was persuasive, he used his personal touch to convince property owners to sell. Dave Cortese recounts the story of Hamann meeting with his grandfather, Vincent Cortese Sr. In the Cortese kitchen on McKee Road, Hamann explained that the city could only do contiguous annexations, and so, Dave Cortese explains, "my grandfather and my father went door to door all the way down McKee Road, at Dutch Hamann's behest, and got every other property owner to agree to annexation."[46] Hamann's assistants "fanned out across the valley, stopping farm by farm, cajoling and pestering orchardists to allow property to be annexed."[47] His staff became known as Dutch's Panzer Division, named after the main offensive line of the German army in World War II, for "relentlessly plowing through farms like tanks, letting nothing impede their progress."[48] Public and personal discourse framed Hamann as too powerful to fight. Farmers who resisted saw the land around them annexed, with the assumption that they would inevitably have to yield and become part of San José.[49] National reports retrospectively observed that the city "crept along highways and leap-frogged pockets of empty land, creating an octopus of a city that thrusts its tentacles into a 340 square mile sphere of influence."[50] The city map looked like an "irregular spider web." The city borders "zigzagged 200 miles to enclose just 20 square miles of incorporated city area."[51] These reports rhetorically framed the city as the agent of change, growing erratically of its own accord, devouring empty land, becoming more powerful and destructive. Strategies for development hinged on territorial expansion and thus the view of place as bounded and controlled. Annexation created boundaries for political and economic reasons regardless of environmental features or agricultural plots.

Hamann's success largely depended on the support of the newspapers. Joe Ridder, editor of the *San José Mercury News,* quickly became an ally for Dutch Hamann. He believed "fervently in the gospel of growth" and campaigned for Hamann's policies in his editorials.[52] Like Hamann, Ridder was open about his ambition to make the *Mercury News* "a vital and constructive force in the development of San José and its territory."[53] Under Ridder, the *Mercury News* "aggressively promoted expansion and business development."[54] The editorial support of the paper, coupled with eager developers and starry-eyed city council members, contributed to unchecked growth. When Ridder was asked about his zealous support of San José's growth when it destroyed the orchards, he candidly replied, "trees don't read newspapers."[55] Ridder's phrase "development of territory" demonstrates the view that place is space that needs to be defined and controlled. His quip that trees do not read newspapers explicitly removes nature from consideration in development. This is particularly poignant in a region where growers still tended orchards, and to whom trees meant a great deal.

Newspaper publishers were giddy about population growth. In April 1955, the San José Newspaper Guild held its annual dinner. The program featured an illustration of an astronaut standing on the moon next to a sign reading "San José City Limits."[56] The caption explained the "push to spread the boundaries of the Garden City over the earth may someday even reach beyond the stratosphere."[57] The loudest laughs of the night came from this joke:

Can you tell me where the San José city limits are?

No, but if you wait right here, they'll be along any minute.[58]

These comments demonstrate the wide held belief that the growth machine was unstoppable.

The city added acres weekly. In the first week of October 1967, San José added more than 500 acres and 7,200 people.[59] The *Mercury News* headlines reveled in the frenzied annexation:

"San José a Little Larger, Expands by 249 Acres."

"City Nudges 110 Square Miles in Size."

"San José to Add 4,000 More Acres, Another Blow to Morgan Hill."

"The Law and County Crazy Quilt."

"San José Grew by 7,200 Persons, 500 Acres in First Week of October, 1967."

"San José Well on Its Way to Metropolitan Status."[60]

These headlines position the city as the active agent: expanding, adding acres, growing, and nudging boundaries. This adds to the sense of inevitability, that growth is out of human control. One headline acknowledges the unplanned nature of San José's growth as a "crazy quilt." This references a quilting technique that uses patchwork without repeating patterns or discernable motifs, emphasizing the seams and stitching. The crazy quilt is an apt metaphor for the expansion of San José, where carefully tilled agricultural plots were sold piece by piece as random patches of land that were less important than the boundaries themselves.

Public rhetoric emphasizes dizzying growth. In 1965, the Santa Clara County Planning Department reported, "whether by stork, train, plane or automobile, one new resident arrives in Santa Clara County every ten minutes."[61] Every two weeks a new subdivision broke ground.[62] The map of San José changed so often that instead of redoing the main map, local map-makers issued monthly packets of stickers to place over existing boundaries and add new streets and geographical areas.[63] These images and descriptions portray change as constant, framing place as unstable. Hamann's tactics worried officials in surrounding cities. Several cities incorporated so as not to be annexed by San José: Cupertino in October 1955, Los Altos Hills in January 1956, Saratoga in October 1956, and Woodside in November 1956. A national report declared Santa Clara County's sixteen cities a "confused jigsaw puzzle with no discernible boundaries and little sense of community."[64] National public discourse reflecting on Hamann's legacy highlighted the key role of annexation in fragmenting communities. The city was a puzzle whose pieces did not make a whole.

In 1961, San José was named an "All America City" by the National Municipal League for "winning a race to keep up with its own successes."[65] Dutch Hamann got credit. He accepted the award on April 25, 1961, in front of 1,800 supporters who applauded wildly when he walked on stage.

Hamann was the driving force behind San José's unbridled expansion and still today receives much of the credit (and blame) for the effects of the city's growth. But his policies had support from the San José City Council, as well as from voters, who passed his sweeping bond measures and backed Hamann in nine votes of confidence.[66] Upon his retirement, the *Mercury News* published a special section devoted to his accomplishments, declaring San José "the house that Dutch built!"[67] Upon his death, the newspaper credited Hamann for guiding San José from "farmland to metropolis."[68] The accolades affirmed Hamann's vision for an American city. The rationale that San José won a race to keep up with its own successes demonstrates the self-fulfilling nature of growth rhetoric—growth is good for growth's sake. The phrase "from farmland to metropolis" celebrates the move to the modern city and also demonstrates that there was no compromise—farmland had no place in the modern city. In most public rhetoric at the time, no tears were shed for the orchards or fruit growers.

In a 1963 *New Yorker* article investigating the aggressive development of the Santa Clara Valley, an unnamed San José resident offered support of the growth mindset: "We're going to keep right on building our city, expanding, pushing ahead, tearing down, putting up regardless. Nothing can stop us!" The article noted, "On the surface, he appeared confident, a booster at peace with his world, but there was a note of terror in his voice."[69] This passage reflects the assumption of inevitability in development rhetoric, building the city required expansion and demolition, "regardless" of the consequences. A 1973 San José Chamber of Commerce brochure depicts a view of downtown's buildings and freeways with the caption "It's Happening" on the front and the elaboration "What's happening today in downtown San José is no longer a dream! More than $322 million in new and committed developments have transformed the core area of San José—creating a fresh human environment."[70] This frames the development of San José as desirable and inevitable.

Orchardists faced unyielding pressure. San José's developer-friendly approach started intense land speculation. The valley's expansive acres were an opportunity for industry and builders. Speculators bought farmland in undeveloped areas, and resold it at inflated prices to developers, who in turn doubled or tripled the land price as profit on the land.[71] Farmland worth $500 an acre could sell for $5,000 or more to speculators, who would then sell it for $10,000 per acre to developers who could sell to homebuyers at $15,000 to $20,000 per acre.[72] Karl Belser remembered, "It was not unusual for land to double in price while changing hands in a single day."[73] Financial burdens

FIGURE 16. Cover of a brochure titled "It's Happening / Downtown San José. *Credit:* San José Chamber of Commerce. Courtesy of History San José.

prompted some farmers to sell the land a bit at a time. This served to increase pressure to sell the rest later. The resulting "severing of properties" doomed many farms.[74] Remaining parcels that were too small to farm profitably were passed down through several generations.[75] Strip annexation meant farmers were increasingly surrounded by housing, "creating pressure on all sides for the few remaining farmers to sell out to development, even if they didn't want to."[76] Development dismantled the Santa Clara Valley's continuous orchard into disjointed plots of land with no overarching vision of the landscape. The remaining fruit growers became outsiders, holdouts from the past. Personal and public discourse show how the rhetoric of land speculation promoted the inevitability of annexation, portraying the sale of the land as the only option for farmers. Speculation about the future ignored the legacy of the past.

Farmers' property taxes increased sharply. As farmers sold, tax assessors "wasted no time in establishing new urban land values on adjacent lands based on the elevated prices paid to those who sold out. Thus, the entire rural community was confronted with a financial crisis."[77] Remaining farmland was reassessed based on potential real estate value based on the selling

THIS IS SAN JOSE

FIGURE 17. Cover of a brochure titled "This Is San Jose." *Credit:* San José Chamber of Commerce. Courtesy of History San José.

price of nearby land.[78] Farmers were often the larger landowners in an area, and although they were not contributing to the increased service load, they paid disproportionately for "new sewage, street lights and schools" for new suburban populations.[79] Increased taxes caused farmers to panic. "Even those farmers who did not want to sell were driven out."[80] Changes in industry created changes in land use and land value. As land speculation, tax increases, and development pressures mounted, struggling farmers sold their land. This was "their last and most lucrative harvest, the land itself—there seemed little reason for a landowner to worry much about, or invest much time and money in, the *agricultural* future."[81]

Promotional literature defined the new San José. The San José Chamber of Commerce published a brochure proclaiming "This is San José" above an image of buildings and freeways.[82] Public rhetoric largely ignored the farmers' perspectives. Public officials and developers were "exuberant in the intense activity of boundless development and expansion" and so "the anguish of a few at the miracles of the chain saw and bulldozer went largely unheeded."[83] Physical displacement of the trees disrupted the fruit community and sense of place. The vision of the Santa Clara Valley's future did not include fruit. Public rhetoric signaled a shift in a view of the valley as ecologically productive to an economic vision divorced from the valley's ecological health. Public discourse about land development emphasized property values in opposition to agricultural value.[84] Richard Novy, president and CEO of Dried Fruit Association of California explained that Silicon Valley "pushed out all the prunes into condos."[85] The symbol of the valley changed from the fruit of labor to buildings to house the labor force. The land itself was no longer valued for distinct environmental or agricultural qualities that were celebrated and cultivated in the Valley of Heart's Delight.

PRESERVATION AND RESISTANCE

Karl Belser was director of the Santa Clara County Planning Department, and one of Hamann's chief opponents. Belser had "a deep, almost spiritual commitment to the continuation of agriculture in Santa Clara Valley."[86] He and his staff conducted nearly thirty planning studies and surveys regarding the county's "sphere of influence."[87] The rhetoric of the planning department under Belser offered a counterpoint to Hamann's pro-growth rhetoric. He proposed a greenbelt to "preserve agricultural land" and at the same time "lend definition to the urban areas."[88] To persuade landowners and government officials, Belser made dozens of presentations to civic organizations and farmers groups, city council meetings and town halls.[89] Belser's public rhetoric of caution and deliberation responded to Hamann's rhetoric of inevitability.

San José resoundingly resisted the county's plan. City officials and local developers criticized Belser's blueprint as a "first step toward delimiting annexable areas and thereby controlling urban expansion."[90] City rhetoric disavowed limits to control growth. San José's City Council consistently refused to outline policies to guide city planning. The city grudgingly developed a master plan after California passed a state law requiring it, but it was primarily "vaguely worded platitudes" and maps with little detail.[91] This response highlights the pro-development contention that growth should not be controlled and, more specifically, that oversight is an inappropriate limit on development potential. Public discourse about the appropriate boundaries and control of growth in San José reveals changing views of the best use of land, and thus a disrupted sense of place.

The profound lack of oversight made Belser's role as county planner exceedingly difficult: Santa Clara County hosts seventy-two local governments including fifteen municipalities and nearly sixty special districts.[92] New streets and developments were built without warning, with no communication between cities and the county.[93] Developers took advantage of rampant lack of coordination to shop around, comparing building codes and service requirements of various cities so they could invest the least amount of planning and money for the most profit. One report describes the result: "slipshod construction, wasted land and a general lack of community amenities."[94] This phrase encapsulates the preservationist view of land changes: where land is not utilized fully, but wasted, sitting empty, and that resources and infrastructure for the community were largely neglected. Preservationist rhetoric emphasized the importance of land for community, echoing the emphasis on human stewardship of the environment in booster literature and personal discourse.

In fact, this uncontrolled, unsupervised development was not an accident. City, county, state, and federal officials had broad legal powers to control development and preserve farm land. California laws protected agricultural land and open space from development; new housing needed backing of state or federally backed banks.[95] Development proposals had mandated review by city planners and independent water and sewer agencies. "Many of these sentries proved to be less than trustworthy."[96] The country and all levels of government were eager to build highways and housing in the postwar boom, and so ignored or denied attempts to control development. Karl Belser saw this lack of oversight as deliberate misplanning. He declared, "San José is not an *unplanned* city; it is a *misplanned* one."[97] One study found that new developments contradicted the master plan more than half the time.[98] Belser's rhetoric emphasized the importance of planning and the need for control, and he attributed the unbridled development of San José to willful

FIGURE 18. Aerial photograph of Highway 280/Guadalupe freeways in downtown San José. *Credit and Courtesy:* History San José.

neglect and an impetus to undermine attempts to plan development and manage growth.

Thus, growth and development proceeded unabated. Urbanization was swift. Between 1945 and 1950, twenty-three thousand acres of Santa Clara Valley farmland was developed annually.[99] Farmers concerned with land protections began to sound the alarm with county officials and began to formally resist uncontrolled development. By the early 1950s, as the valley reeled from the first wave of the industrial rush, farmers formed a taskforce and appealed to the county to protect agricultural land.[100] In September 1953, Santa Clara County adopted the first county land-use law with exclusive agricultural zones.[101] Farmers sponsored several bills in the state legislature that proposed exclusive agricultural zones that would protect farmland from city expansion, and outlaw the type of annexation tactics used by San José.[102] Farmers were successful. In 1955, the California legislature passed the "Agricultural Exclusion Act," which established that county land zoned for exclusive agricultural use required owner consent to annex.[103] Known as the "Greenbelt Law," it also ended the provision that cities could annex large portions of land without annexing the abutting property.[104] In the most egregious example of this practice, San José had annexed a strip of land along Monterey road that was seven miles long and only four hundred feet wide.[105] The efforts of the Santa Clara Valley farmers to protect farmland instigated a "battle to enact state agricultural land conservation legislation."[106] From 1955 to 1970, 115 measures were introduced in the California State Legislature that "dealt, in whole or in part, with the preservation of agricultural or other open-space land."[107] The preservationist rhetoric in these measures emphasized the value of land for agriculture or as undeveloped open space, advocating for an environmental sense of place.

On November 27, 1956, a subcommittee of the state legislature met in San José to review the effects of the county's greenbelt zoning law. The subcommittee determined that "the greenbelt legislation has been a workable tool in the county's program to protect farmers against premature and unwarranted urban expansion and should be reenacted on a permanent and statewide basis at this session."[108] Such rhetoric advocated for planning and tempering expansion, but while county officials approved of the protections, city representatives condemned it.[109] Speaking at the hearing, Karl Belser countered that the law had not affected the growth of cities: "Over 8,000 lots were subdivided and 35,000 people came into the county." Between September 7, 1955 and November 26, 1956, San José, Sunnyvale, and Mountain View alone made 108 annexations adding 5,337 acres to these cities.[110] The laws did not prevent the growth of cities, and yet city officials fought restrictions of any kind.

Karl Belser remembers the rhetorical pressure when a developer's request for a zoning change was brought to the county planning office for review: "Every day, someone would come in and say, 'Karl, you have to approve this because it's good for the county.'"[111] The phrase "good for the county" meant for the benefit of the combined interests of those who would profit from growth: landowners, construction companies, real estate developers, and bankers.[112] The planning commission itself included a realtor, two building contractors, and the president of the Merchants Association.[113] Business leaders gave sizeable contributions to campaigns for bond measures that funded infrastructure for new development.[114] These leaders were anxious to support Hamann's growth policies, and "reap the profits of housing the flood of new-comers."[115] With political and economic will steadfast in support of headlong growth, Karl Belser was unable to prevent the urbanization of the Valley of Heart's Delight.[116]

In 1965, California passed the Williamson Act to provide property tax relief for farmers. Farmers could declare their land as exclusively agricultural and thus be taxed only at the value of the land as farmland. The Olsons took advantage of the Williamson Act in 1968, which R. C. Olson cited as "the biggest reason we are still farming."[117] However, agricultural zoning laws were too late to stop the momentum of the growth of the Santa Clara Valley. Farmers continued to fight annexations at the city level. In her memoir, Yvonne Jacobson remembers that her father R. C. Olson "developed ulcers as he [staffed] the telephone with other worried farmers and helped to devise schemes to counterattack the cities' drive to annex."[118] Personal discourse reveals the disruption to sense of place. Deborah Olson remembers, "It was a really hard fight. Everybody was very angry about the city taking away parcels of land."[119] As urbanization increased, cities needed more land to develop infrastructure to support the growing population. In the early 1960s, Sunnyvale launched a plan to widen El Camino Real and Mathilda Avenue.[120] The Olson orchard was in the path of construction and the city pressured Olson to sell. R. C. Olson was reluctant: "We have the most fertile land in the world right here. What more could I wish for? We are doing what we want to do, so why should I want change?"[121]

Personal discourse of orchardists like the Olsons reflects a sense of place ignored in public rhetoric. Olson was portrayed in the press as a "mulish Swede" who wanted to be left alone.[122] His refusal to sell his land was seen as "impeding progress."[123] The newspapers portrayed farmers who resisted as out of touch with inevitable growth. When Olson finally agreed to sell three acres so the city of Sunnyvale could widen the road, the local paper, the *Sunnyvale Standard*, rejoiced: "At long last, Mathilda extension deadlock appears to be broke."[124] The headlines echo the rhetoric of inevitability in San José's rhetoric. Deborah Olson remembers her grandfather "was never the same. . . . When that happened, he was just bitter at the city."[125] She remembers how her family fought and fought to keep growing fruit as the city changed around them. "I just remember my grandfather fighting City Hall, and I remember my dad fighting City Hall, and then I had to fight City Hall and everything. So, it's been a fight. . . . Any land owner, especially farmers who want to remain on their land, they're always fighting the city or the Goliaths."[126] Personal discourse portrays the resistance to growth as a battle to protect the land and preserve a way of life. For the Olsons and other family farmers, the relentless pressure was a "disenfranchisement, a separation, of the majority of people from the land."[127] As development expanded, there was no land left for crops. One farmer told a newspaper reporter, "we're defying the law of gravity here—we're hanging on by the skin of our teeth"[128] The news coverage and personal reflections portrayed farmers who attempted to resist development as standing in the way of progress. Too late, newspapers began covering the impacts of urbanization. The *San Francisco Examiner* pleaded in 1981, "Let's conserve the vanishing farmland."[129] The use of "vanishing" suggests the farmland was simply disappearing, rather than falling to the effects of growth. The emphasis on inevitability in public rhetoric deflected any need to consider the implications of growth on the environment and community.

Karl Belser retired "early" in 1967 after years of "frustration and disappointment and disillusionment."[130] That summer, Belser published an article entitled "The Planning Fiasco in California," explaining that he retired because he was "consistently countermanded in his recommendations by elected officials" and was tired of ramming his head "against the stone wall of political expediency day after day."[131] Belser lamented in a speech at the University of California at Berkeley in the summer of 1970, "Why is it, that in a county that had 850 thousand acres of which less than 10 percent were good, solid, agricultural acres, why is it that we had to take that 10 percent, that grassland and ruin it?"[132] Karl Belser did "more than any single individual" to slow down San José's growth.[133] Belser's rhetoric emphasizes the agricultural worth of the land, presenting an alternate view of growth in which land is considered valuable for what it can grow in the soil—a view rooted in primacy of place. In this way, public rhetoric around San José's progress is a debate over land use. Preservationists argued the land was valuable for its support of a way of life whereas proponents of growth and development portrayed the land's value as space to build to support population growth.

In almost immediate hindsight to Dutch Hamann's tenure, three major reports published in 1970 and 1971 by Ralph Nader, the *Stanford Law Journal*, and a reporter for the *Washington Post*, decried the "sluburbanization" of the Santa Clara Valley.[134] These reports gained national attention, but sparked "surprisingly little notice, comment or controversy in the valley."[135] However, San José's unbridled development became the subject of national derision. *Newsweek* noted: "Growth came so fast to San José and with such disastrous results that the city's experience serves as a dire warning of what

FIGURE 19. Aerial photograph of freeways and houses in Cupertino, California. *Credit and Courtesy:* History San José.

can happen if residents fail to watch what is happening in their community."[136] *Business Week* reported: "Urbanists cite it as the archetypal slurb, a sprawling confusion of look-alike houses, shopping centers and filling stations, crisscrossed by freeways that whiz shoppers and workers away from a once bustling downtown district."[137] Karl Belser described it as: "what so recently had been a beautiful productive garden was suddenly transformed into an urban anthill."[138] These articles note the disruption to sense of place and attribute the changes to powerful development forces and call for community input to prevent such change. The national coverage decried the changes as sprawl, and labeled the places as lacking distinct character and existing only for consumption and transportation. These descriptions of the valley suggest a change in the community as well— the valley, previously characterized by trees and farms, was now defined by buildings and roadways. As the fruit industry reeled from the changes and headed toward its eventual cessation of operation, the rhetoric of loss became more prevalent in reports and news articles as planners and fruit growers expressed dismay at the destruction of agricultural land and with it, loss of community. This disrupted sense of place is a precursor to the feelings of disconnection and non-place engendered by Silicon Valley.

DECLINING INDUSTRY

Meanwhile, orchards were aging. Many trees in the Valley of Heart's Delight were planted in the 1880s and 1890s. Some groves of trees were nearly one hundred years old. In the 1950s, many orchardists were deciding whether to start another cycle of sixty to seventy years of trees.[139] Aging trees would need to be removed, and new ones planted. Newly planted trees typically take seven years to yield a profit. The expensive process of replanting an orchard meant farmers had to survive on savings or go into debt while waiting for the new trees to produce a gainful harvest.[140] "The choice was to sell out and take a large gain on the price of the land, or to hang on and replant in the hope that a viable climate for continued agriculture would be maintained."[141]

Disease limited productivity of existing orchards. In the 1960s, 40 percent of crops were "destroyed by disease, and farmland began to be cleared for homes and businesses."[142] The summer of 1965 was a particularly bleak one for apricot growers across the valley. Brown rot severely damaged the apricot crop.[143] Pears were next, attacked by a fatal fungus.[144] The *Mercury News* declared, "Time runs out on once-thriving pear industry."[145] Another headline read, "How the pears got bulldozed."[146] Farmer Harold Beckman complained, "There's too damned many subdivisions and not enough pears."[147] The discourse of these news articles signaled the inevitability of growth, suggesting that the pear industry had run its course naturally.

In the 1980s, Charlie Olson's cherry orchard began dying. Local news coverage of the Olson's predicament reveals a discourse of change. Between 1983 and 1986, 25 percent of the orchard succumbed to a root disease. In 1986, heavy, late rains hit "just as Olson's trees were in full blossom. The storms tore off most of the blossoms, leaving trees filled with new green leaves but few cherries," ruining all but 25 percent of the remaining crop.[148] By 1988, the root fungus was killing one hundred of Olson's cherry trees a year.[149] Then, the 1990 cherry season suffered because of relentless rain. Charlie Olson had "never seen damage as serious" after a weekend with nearly two inches of rain. The cherry trees "were in the midst of a crucial growing period. The big rain in a short time caused the cherries to grow so fast they burst out of their skins." Once the skins break, the fruit molds within a few days. In previous years, the orchard shipped fifty tons a year, but in 1990, the Olsons shipped no cherries at all.[150] The news articles of the Olsons' declining crop focused on natural causes, such as the fungus and ill-timed rains, emphasizing natural disasters while excluding discussion of external pressures faced by farmers.

By 1991, something had to change. The orchard's yield was unprofitable.[151] After a few years of consideration, in 1994 the Olsons sold ten acres to a developer to build sixty homes. It was a "very emotional . . . unfortunate economic decision," Deborah explained.[152] "I'd like to do this for the rest of my life, and my father would, too," she said, "but it's just not paying the bills."[153] Olson continued to farm the remaining eleven acres, and the fruit stand maintained a brisk business with loyal customers. The 1996 cherry crop was near zero, less than 5 percent of the previous year, largely due to the winter's warm weather. "The Santa Clara County Cherry Crop Is the Pits," the *Mercury News* headline read.[154] Interviewed for the article, Charlie Olson described the cherry crop as the "worst in his memory." Deborah pointed out, "There might be all of five cherries on a single tree. Our trees look half dead."[155] The news articles faulted the weather as the reason for the declining crop yields and described the orchard's singular economic situation as the reason the Olsons had to sell more land. This rhetoric ignores the broader context of industrial growth and development that precipitated the destruction of the orchards.

In 1997, after several years of extremely poor yields, the Olsons made the decision to look into development options and requested the Sunnyvale City Council to allow residential and commercial development on their agriculturally zoned land.[156] The Olsons leased sixteen acres of land on the corner of El Camino Real and Mathilda Avenue, to a developer for the construction of luxury apartments and nearly sixty thousand square feet of retail.[157] Deborah Olson told the *Mercury News*, "We held on as long as we could, but we just can't do it anymore."[158] Charlie Olson explained the financial determination to the *San Francisco Chronicle*: "It's an economic decision. Some neighbors have complained about runoff when we water. Some of the trees are dying. And the availability of farm workers has dwindled because of the cost of housing. We're no longer a farm community."[159] Olson cites the external pressures on farmers: "It's very simple. Very simple. Farmers were desperate and, bluntly, they weren't making any money. They weren't making a living."[160]

His sister, Yvonne Jacobson, expounds: a "farmer's decision to sell precious land has been forced by harsh economic realities, increased costs of labor, fuel, water, fertilizer, sprays, equipment, and taxes, costs that have not been matched by increased profits."[161] Olson and Jacobson cast the plight of the orchard as a fight against changing externalities. These externalities, enhanced by the growth of the city around the remaining orchardists led to inevitable decisions. Karl Belser explains that when farmers saw their neighbors leaving the economic stress of farming behind, they became "less and less firm in their desire to fight for survival."[162] Personal discourse reveals the externalities and pressures elided in news reports. Fruit families describe growth as disruptive—the pressures to sell influencing their attachment to the land, and a changing valley disrupting their community and identification with place.

On Labor Day of 1999, a bulldozer tore out sixteen acres of the Olson's one hundred-year-old cherry trees. "It was quite a sad day," Deborah Olson recalls. Lightening "ripped through the sky" as the cherry trees fell on what happened to be the one-hundredth anniversary of her great grandfather's birth.[163] The Olsons' orchard removal was a high-profile event, but throughout the valley, as Mac Hamilton put it, "they were just gobbling up the orchards."[164] The march of development was relentless. Bruce and Jennifer Wool remember family conversations about the changes in the valley: "'Oh they're putting in another [subdivision]; you can drive down the road and they're putting in more housing,' stuff like that."[165] Bruce recalls, "You'd see the tractors and trees piled up." Jennifer chimes in, "And you'd see all the big sewer pipes going in."[166] People in the fruit business found a new use for tractors and trucks. Bruce Wool explains that people with tractors developed businesses taking out orchards—pulling out trees instead of tilling soil.[167] These recollections reveal the physical changes of the land—trees are pulled up to make way for sewer pipes laid down—as the landscape was altered to suit the expansion of housing and business.

For David Mariani, one day symbolizes the changing valley. He remembers driving down Stevens Creek Boulevard on a family shopping trip.

> We saw a big orchard being bulldozed. The trees were being ripped from the ground and heaped into a huge pile. . . . A week later a fire was set, and all the uprooted trees, with leaves still green, were burned, leaving a great empty space where, a few weeks before, there had been acres on acres of flourishing trees. What followed was even more puzzling. Earth-moving equipment, cement trucks, and workers came flooding in and started building. We couldn't imagine why anyone would build, especially on such scale, in

the middle of an orchard in the middle of nowhere. We were witnessing the building, in 1955, of our first regional retail shopping center.[168]

Mariani describes specific changes that were confounding to residents of the orcharding town. He describes the changes in land use—"empty space . . . in the middle of nowhere," rural areas that were then filled with buildings of "such scale" to support future population growth. Development altered the scale of the valley's material conditions. For long-time residents, the changes to the valley were disruptions to their sense of place.

For years, the sharp sounds of "cracking limbs and splitting trunks [echoed] throughout the countryside . . . bulldozers ripping each tree from the earth and tossing it aside."[169] Piles of trees became "tangled pyres" with embers lighting the barren land for several nights.[170] It was easy to fell the greatest orchards in the world. They "topple easily" under "the power of a diesel engine . . . the trees tumbling without a fight."[171] These personal accounts portray trees as victims to the powerful march of urbanization. In 1963, the *New Yorker* described the onslaught: "The subdevelopments have got the upper hand. . . . There's no stopping them. Turn your back for an instant and there are new roads, new houses, new people. . . . Orchards are the primary victims of the expansion. Trees in and around San José are the first things to go. They cannot fight back."[172] This article depicts a battle between trees and buildings, where concrete development overwhelms natural features. This echoes the discourse of inevitability in Hamann's promotion of growth. Indeed, the rate of development suggested such inevitability. In the late 1950s, an acre was bulldozed every ninety minutes.[173] Tim Stanley notes in his memoir that "nearly the entire Valley was covered. . . . The 'Garden of the World' was laid to rest under a blanket of asphalt and concrete."[174] The term blanket here continues the metaphors of the expanse of the valley, described in tourist literature as a sea of blossoms and a carpet of fruit. Rather than a symbol of life and productivity drawn from the soil, however, the concrete blanket formed an impermeable barrier between the community and the land.

First the orchards went, then the factories.[175] For some time, even as orchards were disappearing, canneries continued the pack. In 1977, the *Mercury News* described the canning industry as thriving: "Little is left of the wall-to-wall orchards that once carpeted the Santa Clara Valley so beautifully, but the canning industry they spawned still thrives. The sweet aroma of peaches and fruit cocktail; the pungent smell of stewed tomatoes—fragrances

An Aerial View of Progressive, San Jose, Calif.   S-J 3

San Jose Chamber of Commerce   71417

FIGURE 20. Postcard captioned "An Aerial View of Progressive San José, California." *Credit:* Tichnor Brothers. Courtesy of History San José.

reminiscent of San José's past still waft across the valley at the height of yet another multimillion dollar canning season."[176] One detail in the story sticks out: "Trucks from the central valley travel the state's highways loaded with fruits and vegetables destined for Santa Clara County canneries."[177] This scene is a stark change: trucks bringing fruit *to* the Santa Clara Valley. Tim Creswell reminds us that, "Places need to be understood through the paths that lead in and out."[178] Public accounts of fruit moving through the valley reveal a changing sense of place as the valley went from producing fruit to processing it.

Jennifer Wool shakes her head as she explains how "little things kept building up. We had to go over to the valley to get the fruit instead of the fruit being in the valley because farmers had sold off their orchards. . . . It would take a good two hours for those trucks to bring over the peaches and the pears."[179] For orchardists who moved to the Central Valley, shipping fruit to the Santa Clara Valley for processing was expensive, and the quality of the unprocessed fruit suffered from being shipped long distances. The cost of the trucking route to San José would become too much for many canneries.[180] The disruption of the fruit industry was ongoing— economic pressures created further change in agricultural economy and community.

At the same time America's tastes were changing. In 1986, the *Mercury News* reported, "There's just not the demand for canned fruit anymore. . . . People want fresh fruit. So, fruit canneries have become nearly extinct."[181] The market for canned fruits and vegetables declined as awareness of the health impacts of sugar and salt increased.[182] The shift in American diets paralleled the increased availability of fresh fruit from around the world.[183] As Tori Hamilton explains: "At a certain point, you could get fresh fruit anywhere. It started coming out of South America. Once you could do that, who wants canned fruit when they can get fresh fruit?"[184] The public and personal discourse points to externalities that created a situation where change was inevitable. So, the canneries and other fruit packing plants began closing. In 1960, the Santa Clara Valley was the world's top fruit-producing region: 215 fruit-processing plants included eighty-five canneries, twenty-three dried fruit plants, twenty-five frozen food plants, and eighty-five fresh packers. In 1985, only seven canneries remained.[185] Between 1980 and 1984, Santa Clara County recorded 13,236 jobs lost with 118 plant closures.[186] By the summer of 1986, only two major canneries, employing fewer than 1,200 people, operated full time in San José.[187] One longtime resident remembered the news read like "a graveyard of canneries and packing houses."[188] The *Mercury News* headline called the decline of the industry an "extinction," and indeed, news of the declining industry read like an obituary. Public rhetoric highlighted the significance of the demise of the industry on the community. More than 30,000 California cannery workers ended up losing their jobs between 1980 and 1986.[189] Many of the displaced cannery workers were longtime employees, local men and women who had spent their adult lives working for the same cannery. As plants closed, laid-off workers swarmed remaining canneries looking for employment. Each morning, more than 150 cannery workers would gather outside the union office on Race Street, a bleak coda for a place that was "once the heart of a thriving San José canning industry"[190]

In 1999, Del Monte closed its last plant in the valley. Employee Mary Lou Reyes sobbed as she explained, "We are not only losing a job, we are losing our friends." Joey Fahey, local union president explained: "It's not just breaking up a work crew, it's breaking up a family. They openly care about each other."[191] Patricia Nevarez, safety coordinator at Del Monte who worked at the plant since 1972 lamented, "more than half my life, all my youth, went into this plant."[192]

When Del Monte closed its cannery in 1999, the *Mercury News* headline read: "The Valley of Heart's Delight came to a symbolic end."[193] At

11:46 a.m., "the last can of Del Monte fruit—pineapple tidbits—rolled off the last conveyor belt at the last major fruit cannery in San José. . . . Then came a downright eerie moment. After 154 straight days of three shifts a day, seven days a week, an around-the-clock clamor stopped."[194] This was the final obituary for the canning industry. An industry defined by growth, progress, and production just stopped.

CONCLUSION

As part of its promotional campaign for industry, the San José Chamber of Commerce produced a short film, *Valley of Heart's Delight*. In addition to promoting agricultural work as a "breeze," as discussed in the previous chapter, the film depicts the ideal suburban life: "Orchards interspersed among residences" throughout the Valley offered the "convenience of a city home in country surroundings."[195] Mid-century promotional films portrayed the valley as retaining its agricultural heritage amid the exciting throes of progress. "Mild climate, ideal living conditions, agriculture and industry geared to a high level of productivity all mean better incomes and more abundant living."[196] This propaganda promised development opportunities and high quality of life enabled by the proximity to farming land and open space. A 1952 San José Chamber of Commerce postcard entitled "An Aerial View of Progressive San José," featured an in illustration of the city buttressed by thick orchards and green hills: portraying balanced development in the progressive city.[197] Even as housing and office buildings replaced orchards, chambers of commerce and developers continued to promote the idyllic image of the valley, and would-be residents literally bought it. Headlines proclaimed, "It's blossom time again in Santa Clara Valley!"[198] News articles breathlessly reported on the thousands of visitors touring the valley.[199] "Even while orchard after orchard was plowed under for housing tracts, the Chamber of Commerce maintained its national advertising campaign, boasting the valley's best features."[200] Buyers typically signed housing contracts sight unseen, based on the valley's reputation. Working-class families flocked to the area, especially susceptible to the American dream sold by valley promoters.[201] "Many home buyers undoubtedly bought their houses under the presumption that the open space surrounding their neighborhood would be maintained."[202]

The orchards were the central appeal of the Santa Clara Valley: the very trees being torn out to make room for newcomers. Newspaper coverage reveals the tension. Readers opened the *San José Mercury* to see promotions for orchard tours and the annual Blossom Festival juxtaposed with advertisements for new housing and articles reporting on astounding population growth and the housing boom. On March 7, 1953, the *Mercury* featured two headlines that revealed this tension: one read, "Fruit Trees Displaced by Homes."[203] Another celebrated the contradiction: "Booming, Blooming— That's Santa Clara County Now!"[204] These news headlines rhetorically presented the changes as harmonious, downplaying the incompatibility of the orchards with wholesale development.

Five years later, the *Mercury* still proclaimed the orchards could stay: "The trees, blossoms, and crops are still here, but so are more homes, more and better roads, more water conservation, sewerage, and drainage projects."[205] This rhetoric promotes the rural ideal with the urban promise that development would preserve beauty and promise modern amenities. Orchards were replaced with suburban plazas and housing tracts with "sentimentally rural names such as Pruneridge Shopping Center, the San Tomas Orchards housing development, or the Blossom Hill Manor subdivision."[206] These names offer superficial homage to the agricultural infrastructure that these buildings replaced. News coverage and promotional discourse suggested that the valley could have it both ways— the trees would survive alongside the housing subdivisions and that development could happen without destroying the orchards. This type of public rhetoric obfuscated the volume of farmland sold and developed, and the inevitability that buildings would replace the orchards. This type of coverage, and the fragmented nature of San José's annexation may have had the effect of hiding the reality of the wholesale change to residents.

When longtime residents recall the changing valley, they noticed changes here and there, with the changes slowly becoming more constant. Mark Mariani reflects on the pace of change:

> It was so slow. There wasn't a moment, I wish I could bring some dramatics there, but no, it was just so slow. . . . When you see signs, it was the strip malls that unfortunately we start see going in and then slowly but surely, they take Stevens Creek Boulevard's beautiful orchards, [first] a strip mall, small little packing house, an orchard, another strip mall and then you could see, between the '60s and '70s, and '80s, that now [an]other orchard was sold out, another strip mall, so it was like a chain link that went all the way down from Monta Vista, down into San José.[207]

These recollections of slow change differ from the statistics that show the Valley's rapid growth. Mark Mariani explains: "We saw that there was a trend of something that we didn't understand, as farming families, and had no idea, other than we began to see speculators coming in and buying land from our neighbors."[208]

The tensions of blooming and booming confounded attempts to document and stop change. This could explain public malaise about the decline in farmland. As Michael S. Malone notes, "In the excitement of the postwar boom, as we bought our tract houses and cheered each new freeway, who had time to worry about the rapidly disappearing Valley of Heart's Delight? It was only after the last orchard in the neighborhood was uprooted that we began to wonder if we might want to preserve something to show our children what life was once like."[209]

Thus, slowly but definitively, the community relationship with the environment changed. For rural communities, "land remains central to the sense of place . . . with the fluidity of connections appropriately mirroring the dynamism of place."[210] Cindy Spurlock reminds us that public discourse promoting the valley relies on "rhetorics of development and growth that ignore the vital role that farming plays in community health and economic independence."[211] Dutch Hamann and other development proponents ignored preservation rhetoric from the County Planning Department and the California State Assembly. The development of the valley was pursued without attention to preservation and with disregard for the existing community's sense of place. Resistance to growth was unsustainable, and piece by piece, agricultural land disappeared, and with it, the fruit industry. Spurlock continues: "The ways in which we use and re/value land, be it for subdivisions, sustainable agriculture, recreation, or conservation, are of profound importance, but not simply because land is a limited natural resource."[212] As the value of land transitioned from agricultural cultivation to "development" of city infrastructure, the fruit community was uprooted. The expansion of the city and the development of housing and office parks was at the direct expense of the orchards that were at the heart of the community of the Santa Clara Valley. As Senator James D. Phelan opined, "I fear the day when Santa Clara Valley shall have been discovered. Like any other tide, the human tide is devastating and sweeps things away."[213]

FOUR

Conclusion

IT IS POURING RAIN as I drive south on US Highway 101. The suburbs of San José give way to wide-open fields, fruit stands, and a tractor supply store. Before the highway, Monterey Road was the only route between San José and the farms in South Santa Clara County.[1] Storefronts had wooden sidewalks and hitching posts. "Imagine so many head of cattle being herded down a dusty, dirt Monterey Road that it takes hours for them all to pass by."[2] Turning off Highway 101, I pass strip malls and gas stations, which give way to a long country road lined by farmhouses. Going too far, I turn around in a brightly colored subdivision. These stucco homes are part of what Andy Mariani describes as the "inexorable march through the countryside."[3]

Andy Mariani still grows fruit in his eponymous orchard in Morgan Hill, twenty miles south of San José, doing brisk business in "chin-dripping, exquisite" heirloom stone fruit.[4] That is the market these days, and the Santa Monica farmers' market in Los Angeles provides steady customers. Andy's tree-ripened fruits "have a cult-like following."[5] *Gourmet* called him a "horticultural wizard," noting his signature Baby Crawford peach has an "unmatched intensity of flavor."[6] When an NPR reporter tasted an heirloom peach called Gold Dust, she wrote, "This peach is so juicy, I'm an immediate mess. And wow, is it delicious: sweet, but with a bright acidity that sets my taste buds alight."[7]

My tires crunch on the gravel as I pull into the driveway of Andy's Orchard. Buds on the fruit trees hint at fruit to come in a few weeks. The screen door of the old barn creaks as I walk into the orchard's farm stand. Andy Mariani walks from behind some fruit boxes to greet me, his blue eyes smiling under his trademark baseball cap as he firmly shakes my hand. We sit down amid boxes of dried fruit. Even though it is the off season, the screen door creaks with a steady stream of visitors. Andy greets them all: "No, we're actually not really open, but come on in." Andy's phone rings intermittently throughout our conversation: "This is Andy. . . . No thank you . . . I don't want a free cruise. . . . This is Andy. . . . We won't have fresh fruit until the season, but we are open on weekends with dried fruit. . . . This is Andy. . . ."

The downpour on the barn's tin roof nearly drowns out the conversation as Andy Mariani explains what it is like to be one of the last orchardists left in the Santa Clara Valley. Andy quotes Wallace Stegner, describing the Valley of Heart's delight as a "brief Eden, an unbelievable place with a Jeffersonian ideal."[8] He explains the decline of fruit production in the Santa Clara Valley: Fruit from the valley "went from a commodity that was sold all over the world in bulk, twenty-five-pound cases, to cutesy little things like this. You're selling nostalgia."[9] He frowns when I ask him what happened to the Valley of Heart's Delight: "People were kind of half asleep when it happened. That was, the changes were so subtle, you didn't realize it."[10]

In the south Santa Clara Valley today, Andy Mariani encounters the same challenges orchardists faced in the post–World War II development of Silicon Valley. "As farmland becomes suburb, the lifestyle of the new suburbanite comes into conflict with the farmer's established practices."[11] Orchard operations produce dust and noise, which can annoy nearby residents. Farmers experience trespassing and vandalism.[12] Andy tells me, "Toxic waste from Silicon Valley was dumped right in our orchard."[13] Andy explains the impacts of farming on the urban fringe today. "We're right here by a school. We can't spray during the weekdays because school's in. On the weekends, the joggers, the bicyclists, everybody's out. So, when do you spray? Spray at night?" Moving around in his chair to adjust his back, Andy tells the story of an encounter with his neighbor after new regulations for spraying went into effect:

> One of our first sprays was in January. We sprayed at night over here. [He gestures to the orchard across the road.] And a lady, she called Morgan Hill police, she called the Sheriff's office. She said, "I don't know what they're doing over there, but they're disturbing my sleep. Lights are shining in my bedroom. The noise is unbelievable." And she raised hell with them. And then she calls me, and I told her in the nicest way I could, it's not that we want to spray at night we're just complying with the regulations. And then she said "Well I got a job that pays such and such," like six figures. "And I've got to have my sleep." Okay.[14]

Andy shrugs. Most people who bought houses in the area didn't understand the realities that come with an agricultural setting. Like the boosters of the Santa Clara Valley in the mid-twentieth century, today's developers promote a bucolic orchard setting. Andy explains, "They were selling it and it said, 'Surrounded by open space and an agricultural preserve.' That was the way they presented the house. And they didn't say anything about spray, noise."[15]

Andy tells another story about driving his tractor one morning: "I was going real slow, and the guy zips around with I don't know what it was, a BMW I think, he zips around and he flips me off because I am interrupting his fast-paced urban lifestyle. And yet, he's probably the one that would like us to stay here."[16] Andy adds that he thinks he saw that BMW driver at the orchard for a weekend fruit tasting. Charlie Olson explains simply: There are just too many people, too suddenly and too close."[17] Deborah Olson agrees: "People are upset because the bees are buzzing around, and [we are] irrigating, and burning brush. And you can't burn brush anymore. So, people want this bucolic setting, yet they complain a great deal" about the reality of farming.[18]

Andy Mariani fields questions all the time about how long he'll stay. The love of premium quality fruit and the farming life motivates him to continue. Andy notes, "Every time I talk to Charlie and Deborah [Olson], we say we're in it for the beauty of it."[19] Local newspapers and food magazines write feature articles about him almost every season. Each article paints him as the last orchardist in town. Andy explains what keeps him going: "Well, I get up in the morning, and I think, God, I'm gonna taste this great peach that's just starting to ripen, and this and that. I'm gonna be able to plant this and I'm gonna buy a new tractor and I'm gonna do this or I'm gonna do that. And it just keeps me going all the time."[20]

SILICON VALLEY AS NON-PLACE

I drive north on Highway 101 from Andy's Orchard to Silicon Valley, the open space in the south valley gives way to housing and shopping centers anchored by big box stores. Driving through San José, the residential sprawl gives way to office parks and corporate campuses. US Highway 101 is "the tech industry's Madison Avenue."[21] Digital billboards hawk cloud communication platforms and data security, and showcase stunning #nofilter photos taken on an iPhone. Office buildings boast familiar logos: Oracle, Evernote, Intel, PayPal. Google Maps' directions to Silicon Valley end with, "Merge onto CA-237." As the freeway span crosses the railroad tracks, my phone chirps, "you have arrived." I'm surrounded by houses and office parks. This is Silicon Valley.

The iconic Silicon Valley remains elusive. "What does Silicon Valley look like? Where could one send tourists—or even locals for that matter—hoping to 'see' it?"[22] A *New York Times* travel feature on Silicon Valley explains: "Unless you're the next Mark Zuckerberg, the high-tech campuses that dot the valley are off-limits. But there are ways to sneak a look."[23] Tourists report their disappointment on the travel website, Trip Advisor. One visitor reports the campuses are "just office building so not much to see except you take photos with the signs."[24] Another visitor concurs, "There is not anything to really do. There's a sign outside Facebook that you can take photos with and then at Google there's a shop and you can walk around the campus. We got told to not use the Google bikes as they are for employees only, which was a bit of a shame as we were only trying them out! Not worth going out of your way for."[25] The signs are "unremarkable, but symbolic" of a region built on virtual environments.[26]

There's a reason we cannot find Silicon Valley. "Silicon Valley isn't so much a place as it is an idea. More than with any specific landmark or point of geography, Silicon Valley is identified with the spirit of innovation."[27] Public discourse about Silicon Valley celebrates technological revolution and newly minted millionaires. The eponymous HBO series glorifies the trials and tribulations of startup culture. The world of ideas in Silicon Valley replaced the place-based community of the Valley of Heart's Delight.

Silicon Valley exudes what Edward Relph calls "placelessness," which he defines as "the casual eradication of distinctive places and the making of standardized landscapes that results from an insensitivity to the significance of place."[28] He cites mass production and an increasingly mobile world.[29] Mark Augé takes up the term *non-place* to mean "spaces formed in relation to certain ends (transport, transit, commerce, leisure)."[30] Non-places are characterized by the insensitivity that Relph ascribes to placelessness. Non-places are "marked by a lack of attachment, by constant circulation, communication, and consumption that act against developing social bonds and bonds between people and the world. These non-places are marked by a plethora of texts, screens, and signs that facilitate mediated relationships between people and places rather than direct ones."[31] Non-place is characterized by non-attachment and non-identification. Placelessness and non-place characterize the Santa Clara Valley today in three ways.

First, as Santa Clara Valley developed, office parks and houses overtook the orchards. The Valley of Heart's Delight is "now one giant parking lot. Silicon Valley proper is soul crushing suburban sprawl [with] fabulous weather."[32] In non-place, the distinct characteristics of place are lost to homogeneity: "Place is being lost to an increasingly homogeneous and alienating sameness.... Strip malls and chain stores replace the elemental variety that once characterized the landscape. Everywhere is increasingly alike as we all spend more of our time in non-places such as airport lounges, shopping malls and on the Internet, living lives increasingly without any sense of place whatsoever."[33] Silicon Valley has no distinct character: "Along its Prius-choked roads, it looks like Anywhere, USA: single-family-home suburbs south of San Francisco, bordered by chain stores, auto dealerships and corporate parks—lots of beige, boxy corporate parks."[34] Norman Mailer described Silicon Valley as "one of the ugliest places I've ever visited. It's abominable."[35] Silicon Valley could be anywhere—anodyne shopping malls, agnostic subdivisions, freeways, office parks, and parking lots—these are the hallmarks of non-place. Non-place is characterized by non-identification: offering familiarity without distinction. Shopping malls, chain restaurants can be reproduced anywhere and thus lack an identification with a particular place. Edward Relph describes placelessness as "the casual eradication of distinctive places and the making of standardized landscapes that results from an insensitivity to the significance of place."[36] Silicon Valley's housing tracts and freeways facilitate a placelessness that uprooted what made the Santa Clara Valley unique: the top soil that nourished the orchards, which in turn nurtured community.

Second, Silicon Valley emphasizes connectivity instead of rootedness. Silicon Valley is the place where placelessness is made possible. Computing technology allows virtual living, connectivity without attachment. Fiber-optic cables connect our ideas, but untether us from geographic place. "The world is marked by a speeding up of communications and information flows that leads to a bombardment of images of spaces and times other than the one a person may be immediately located in. [This causes] a shrinking of the planet due to time–space compression."[37] The never-ending flow of information, and the intense connectivity of social media networks unmoor us from place. "Electronic media have . . . weakened the relationship between social situations and physical places."[38] Our screens substitute for information and companionship: we look at our phones as we walk by our neighbors and check the weather online rather than going outside. We delight in being any-where and everywhere: we hail rides with strangers, answer our doorbells remotely, and have packages delivered anywhere. Virtual living means that we don't think about the way we move through the world.[39]

Today, the valley thrives on connectivity, which facilitates nonattachment through a profound efficiency. Our connections are not bound to place, to the valley itself; rather, life in Silicon Valley is characterized by an intense mobility. Connectivity enables non-place, an existence without regard to physical conditions or location marked by nonattachment, which offers ease of movement without obligation. Nonattachment can be desirable: the ease of online shopping, the convenience of food delivery, the predict-ability offered by online reviews are just a few examples. The freedom of movement heralded by rideshare companies and remote working platforms enables virtual living based on the assumption that "space is uniform and objects and activities can be manipulated and freely located within it."[40] The technological advances of Silicon Valley have "reduced the need for face-to-face contact, freed communities from their geographical constraints and hence reduced the significance of place-based communities."[41]

Third, the cachet of Silicon Valley is innovation—the pursuit of the lat-est electronic gadget or smartphone application. The emphasis on cutting edge stresses the "urgency of the present moment."[42] Non-place accentuates "solitude and similitude. There is no room for history unless it has been transformed into an element of spectacle, usually in allusive texts."[43] The focus on the present, on the newest innovation disconnects us from history: "One of the reasons many Americans may no longer seem to 'know their place' is that they no longer *have* a place in the traditional sense of a set of behaviors matched to physical locations and the audiences found in them."[44] Non-place weakens ties to physical place. An ad from Intel Corporation quotes founder Robert Noyce, urging, "don't be encumbered by past his-tory, go out and do something wonderful."[45] This epitomizes Silicon Valley's disregard for the past and emphasis on innovation and the future. Social media's focus on constant updates and the planned obsolescence of both hard- and software cause laser-like focus on the future, without regard to the physical environment. The result is what Danny Harris, former director of the Knight Foundation in San José, explains as "place-agnostic:" the absence of the "texture of our rich cultural and historical heritage."[46]

Placelessness is a global phenomenon and the problem of non-place is fa-miliar to agricultural communities around the country facing diversification of industry and loss of family farms. While not limited to Silicon Valley, placelessness is a result of Silicon Valley's innovation: heightened mobility and virtual connectivity causes a detachment from place. New media technologies are designed to be "disruptive of place, and the sense of place, itself represents a serious challenge to cultural heritage as such, since that which is culturally significant is not mere 'information' but is itself tied to particular places and things, and to the practices and narratives that cohere around them."[47] Whereas place is a location full of meaning that cultivates profound attachment for people and the environment, the proliferation of screens has dissipated that attachment. The profound nonattachment offered by Silicon Valley is marked by the "undermining of place for both individuals and cultures, and the casual replacement of the diverse and significant places of the world with anonymous spaces and exchangeable environments."[48] San José State University anthropology professor Jan English-Lueck explains that Silicon Valley's "ethos of cultural flexibility may encourage creativity, but [Silicon Valley residents] also expressed concern about the difficulty in making meaningful connections, or in sustaining a 'deep' sense of belonging."[49] Silicon Valley culture supplanted the palpable sense of community in the Valley of Heart's Delight. As server farms replaced fruit farms, the primacy of the idea superseded the importance of place.[50]

The tech industry transformed the Santa Clara Valley from a community rooted to the land through agricultural work to the radical placelessness and "intense mobility" of Silicon Valley. Broad changes to the landscape—buildings replacing trees—eradicated the material conditions and environmental aesthetic that were the basis of a profound sense of place. The fruit industry in the Santa Clara Valley engendered a collective sense of place based on shared experiences of daily fruit work and seasonal change; it allowed meaningful participation in environment and community. This place attachment was erased by the radical placelessness and intense mobility of Silicon Valley. The technological amplification of "processes of mobility and communication in the modern world [means] that place is becoming insignificant in a world of placelessness and non-place."[51]

SENSE OF PLACE AND ENVIRONMENTAL COMMUNITY

Place is the condition of all things, a way of knowing and believing. A sense of place engenders an "attitude of enduring affinity with known localities and the ways of life they sponsor."[52] In the Santa Clara Valley, the sense of place was not just in the orchards, but in the way of life they supported. Fruit was a way of knowing the earth and affirming the importance of one's own participation in that community. This research demonstrates a multi-faceted agricultural sense of place with direct influence on attitudes and behaviors toward the environment that may be instructive in future studies of environmental change.

A place aesthetic fosters an appreciation of beauty and an emotional attachment to place. This aesthetic connection cultivates a view of places as "beautiful and worth preserving."[53] As orchards disappeared, little usable open green space replaced them. Vast orchards that used to quilt the valley are now a blanket of concrete. Fruit trees were "replaced by endless stretches of tract homes, jumbles of commercial signs, and the noises and odors of freeway traffic."[54] Early news reports about the changed valley offered dire descriptions: "Automobiles push and shove through crowded concrete. . . . Here and there, small isolated groves of the last surviving fruit trees fight strangulation by the surrounding subdivisions, factories and freeways. Acres of roofed box houses huddle tightly together, back to back and side to side, without open spaces, parks or even sidewalks."[55] As one of the early reports condemning the changed Santa Clara Valley mused, "The most scenic public land left in the valley may be the carefully tended and regularly watered tropical flowering greenery along the shoulders of the several crisscrossing freeways."[56]

The impact of the urbanization of open space is "difficult to quantify," but the orchards "provided a very real benefit to the city's residents. One only has to imagine seeing them in bloom, smelling the freshness of the air, and hearing the peaceful sounds of the county to know the benefit was real."[57] The orchards allowed valley residents "to enjoy peace and quiet, to commune with nature, and to appreciate the beauty of the natural environment."[58] Open space invokes an appreciation for the natural environment, which promotes preservation of wilderness, and conservation of natural resources.[59] This is more than an aesthetic change. The Valley of Heart's Delight cultivated a sense of place, a connection between the land and the community. Life in the valley was defined by participation in the natural environment that was an important part of one's identity and one's community.

The loss of the orchards changed the aesthetic and the material conditions that were the basis of place attachment. James Cantrill reminds us that, "The landscapes we habitually experience and our perceptions of who we are in those environments shape our worldly engagements, thereby influencing what we think about when presented with environmental communications."[60] The change in the valley environment and the infrastructure of the fruit industry altered historically situated material conditions. "Humans understand and process various claims and arguments regarding the human relationship to and responsibilities for managing the natural world."[61] In agricultural communities such as the Santa Clara Valley, "rural economic foundations and community cohesion are intricately linked to these natural systems."[62] A rural sense of place offers vital connections to the environment. Communities with attachments to the environment more often have an ethical sense of responsibility to that place and are thus more likely to act to preserve local natural resources.

The development of Silicon Valley disrupted a sense of place cultivated in the Valley of Heart's Delight, weakening attachment to and identification with place that diminished the sense of environmental stewardship and community obligations. The implications of a weakened sense of responsibility to environment and community can be seen in documented environmental justice concerns with electronics and computer manufacturing practices.[63] In early Silicon Valley, technology companies disposed of hazardous materials from the production of computing electronics in dumps disproportionately located in low-income areas and communities of color.[64] Electronic industry workers are predominantly "women, immigrants, and people of color. Compounding the pollution in their neighborhoods, these workers hold jobs that are more toxic than those found in any other basic industry."[65] Stephen Pitti cautions that "rushes to celebrate the Silicon Valley obliterated memories of mercury mines and fruit orchards, and they too often ignored the present circumstances of nonwhites."[66]

The development of Silicon Valley changed the material conditions of the valley and altered community connections that characterized the region's agricultural economy. Tori Hamilton describes the changes from her perspective. "Just think there is just so many people and it is such a beautiful place to live that you are going to lose everything. You are going to lose everything that you have and it's going to be a paved city. That's all it's going to be. It's going to end. . . . Because we don't in this country understand the concept of keeping people's space, of people having space. . . . You are going to lose all the history. You are going to lose everything."[67] Charlie Olson concurs: "Saving some trees will be good for the children. . . . These young kids could grow up never knowing what a good apricot tastes like."[68] Hamilton and Olson describe a relationship to the land cultivated through social interactions and community activities focused on fruit work that create a connectedness, a feeling of belonging. Keith Basso describes such a place-based identity: "Fueled by sentiments of inclusion, belonging, and connectedness to the past, sense of place roots individuals in the social and cultural soils from which they have sprung together, holding them there in the grip of a shared identity, a localized version of selfhood."[69]

Long-time valley residents speak of the beauty of a place sustained by community. Mark Mariani remembers the Valley of Heart's Delight as "very community minded. Church was probably only five miles away from our farm or ranch, but after church it always took about two and a half hours to get home, because we would stop at the different farm houses and say hello and have a cup of coffee and so forth."[70] This recollection indicates a palpable sense of place and community, based on pace of life influenced by community relationships and the natural rhythms of the harvest. Ralph Rambo, the label illustrator, has similar memories of trips to San José: "how leisurely were our trips to and from old San José sixty years ago as Dad and I drove down the rural Stevens Creek Road with our horse-and-buggy. This road, the 'grass roots of my childhood' had a beauty not only of the land but in the happy associations with the people we met along the way. We knew every neighbor, every orchard, every tree and windmill on the route."[71] This affirms Tim Creswell's claim that a sense of place is more about "routes than roots."[72] Here we see both—the leisurely ride to and from home marked by conversation and connection.

Considering the "diverse and diffuse" immigrant experiences in the Santa Clara Valley allows us to "appreciate their geographical identities through the lens of regional inspection, across settlement scales, and through time."[73] The variety of experiences affirms that a sense of place is not always congruous, and allows us to "imagine how we are intimately tied to broader conceptions of human and planetary life . . . which demonstrate our common and difficult histories of encounter."[74]

Mark Mariani remembers how immigrant families arrived with no money, and the community had to work together to survive: "You helped each other plant your trees and you helped someone build their first two-room house. When you do those basic things, you build friendships and trust for life."[75] Andy Mariani echoes the importance of community that continued across ethnic lines: "We had a community here of Portuguese and Italians and Croatians and all that, and we helped each other. If somebody had a big crop of apricots and he needed some extra ladders, and the neighbor had some extra ladders, go ahead. Borrow them. Bring them back. And that was our community."[76]

While cannery machines changed embodied practices of fruit work, the companies were anchors for the community. Jennifer Wool explains, "The cannery really meant a community. . . . The cannery was the soul of the family. It really kept us together."[77] Brad Stapleton of Stapleton-Spence Packing company, founded in 1951 in San José, remembers: "It was a different time and a different place. We all had jobs in the canneries when we were kids. There was a real sense of family because we all tended to work in these enterprises together. It was beautiful."[78] Jim Zetterquist remembers, when "our company went bankrupt, I had the hardest time. I was thirty years old. . . . I'd known this cannery all my life. . . . When it came time that it was going to be bulldozed, I couldn't fathom. To me, it was like tearing down the Roman Coliseum. It had been there all my life and it seemed so ancient to me and so permanent. . . . I had a hard time with it. . . . We lost such an important part of our community."[79]

The Valley of Heart's Delight cultivated a collective sense of place based on interpersonal relationships, a sense of community, and a connection to the land nurtured through work with fruit. Yvonne Jacobson explains: "That the life was hard cannot be denied; that it engendered a special relationship between people and the soil, between families and the natural world, was equally true. Add to this the honesty in human relations, the concern for those around you, and you had a place where there were few if any anonymous people."[80] The Santa Clara Valley fostered a place-based identity cultivated through the daily practices of growing and processing fruit. This was an environmental community—intimately tied to the seasons, which determined the calendar of fruit production. This sense of place is epistemological—based in the knowledge of seasons, soil, and fruit—and ontological—an identity intricately linked to land and understanding of the world based on the connection to earth. A collective sense of place was based on shared experiences of daily practice and seasonal change. Yvonne Jacobson continues: "The great masters of the farmer were still the weather, the markets, labor, and money. It would be wrong to think the beautiful blossoms reflected only tranquility. Rather, life seemed a series of conflicts and disasters tempered by endurance, patience, frugality, and hard work. Even so, the beauty of the landscape and being part of nature's unending cycle were among the highest rewards."[81] Jacobson weaves the threads of aesthetic and agricultural sense of place—that the appreciation of place is intricately tied to embodied agricultural practices. Seasons of fruit work cultivated an attachment to place marked by stewardship of the environment and community.

Environmental communication scholars have avowed the importance of a sense of place rooted in a connection to the environment. Donal Carbaugh reminds us that places themselves influence communication about environmental issues.[82] Cantrill and Senecah affirm that our sense of place and environmental self is socially constructed, based on our experience in that environment.[83] This history of place connects personal narratives and public discourse to reveal an inextricable connection between environment and community in the Santa Clara Valley. A collective sense of place built on environmental aesthetics and embodied practice demonstrates that an identification with place, while not always positive, nevertheless can cultivate a sense of environmental stewardship and community responsibility. Growth and development that gave rise to Silicon Valley dismantled the orchards, the locus of place meaning and belonging, and now memory sustains the anesthetic and material sense of place in the Valley of Heart's Delight. Rhetorical histories of place are an important way to explore a sense of place in community and environmental change.

HERITAGE DISCOURSE AS A RESPONSE TO PLACELESSNESS

In a world marked by placelessness, there remains a longing for place-based connection. Place changes the way we live. "Even as the power of place is diminished and often lost, it continues—as an absence—to define culture and identity. It also continues—as a presence—to change the way we live."[84] Renowned environmentalist and local author, Wallace Stegner attributes this missing connection to a lack of local history, "a simple inability to participate in the love of place that others seem to feel. We have gnawings and cravings for something we cannot name. We are uncertain where we belong, we have doubts about the adequacy of the present that has neither past nor future attached to it."[85] The memoirs and other personal discourse featured in this book attempt to memorialize the Santa Clara Valley's fruit community and culture. There is a "rich culture and heritage" of a group bound by the experience of "cuttin' cots" and picking prunes.[86] The orchards of the

Valley of Heart's Delight rooted residents to the valley as they cultivated the land season after season. In addition to memoirs and reflections, numerous activities promote the Santa Clara Valley's agricultural heritage: A performance of the San José Nutcracker in 2017 was set in the Valley of Heart's Delight; the plays *Valley of the Heart* and *Swift Justice* dramatize the history of the valley; and the annual Blossom Festival attracts hundreds of people interested in the agricultural history of the valley. "Communities develop their own occasions, rituals, archives and practices of remembering."[87]

Numerous *places*—physical locations such as parks and museums with interpretive exhibits—are designed to preserve various aspects of Santa Clara Valley's fruit history. The Cities of Los Altos, Saratoga, and Sunnyvale protect heritage orchards, and in San José, Emma Prusch Park and Martial Cottle Park feature working farms. The Campbell Historical Museum, Gilroy Museum, Morgan Hill Historical Society, and Sunnyvale Historical Society are a few of the museums that preserve records and ephemera of the valley. These historical resources offer opportunities for civic engagement. The Sunnyvale Orchard Heritage Project, like others, addresses questions about heritage and memory: "Will future generations know what an orchard looked like, and will anyone be left to remember The Valley of Heart's Delight? What can be done to preserve an important part of our culture and heritage?"[88] The park "offers us a glimpse of yesterday's demanding farm life, introduces us to many families who planted deep roots in this valley, reminds us of the high quality of the fruit produced from this rich soil and it urges us to ponder our own legacy."[89]

The Fruit Cocktail Club, a side project of several members of the California Pioneers of Santa Clara County, collects and archives newsreels and videos from the Santa Clara Valley's fruit industry. The group digitizes historical footage and hosts public screenings. At one movie night hosted by the Fruit Cocktail Club, the vaulted redwood ceilings of the Saratoga Foothill Club could not contain the buzz of conversation. The silver-haired crowd roared when Jim Zetterquist, the emcee, dedicated the night to a time when "canners were kings and fruit packers were queens."[90] The crowd of kings and queens stayed rowdy throughout the evening's screening. The Fruit Cocktail Club celebrates "a grand era" in the Santa Clara Valley.[91] Zetterquist describes this as "a time when people were a lot happier than they are now."[92] As noted throughout this book, the fruit worker experience was not always happy, and Stephanie Coontz cautions that such collective nostalgia can create romanticized myths that deflect historical realities and ignore social injustices. Coontz urges us to deploy nostalgia to "integrate the best values and ideas of the past into the improvements and advances" of the future.[93]

In this way, the Fruit Cocktail Club, museums, festivals, and the memoirs and personal reflections cited throughout this book, are important discursive responses to placelessness. Edward Casey notes that nostalgia "is not merely a matter of regret for lost times; it is also a pining for *lost places*. . . . Massive nostalgia is a speaking symptom of the profound placelessness of our times."[94] Charlie Olson's lament that children today may never taste a good apricot reflects a profound sense of loss. "One of the most eloquent testimonies to place's extraordinary memorability is found in nostalgia."[95] For example, many memoirs recall a sensual relationship to place: the smell of the fruit, the physical embodiment of fruit work. Carbaugh and Cerulli remind us that, places are "concrete and contingent circumstances [that] serve as the grounds of our existence, our experiences and lives. By losing sight—or touch, or feel, or smell—of our places, we risk being unsettled in our thoughts."[96] The sensual connection to place that marked the Valley of Heart's Delight is not found in social networks, they disrupted the material conditions of the fruit community that fostered an aesthetic and agricultural sense of place.

The rapid development of the Santa Clara Valley and the intense, forward thinking of Silicon Valley have diminished the integrity of a connection to place. Nostalgia is a response to such placelessness: when "people perceive that changes are occurring too rapidly, spinning out of control, nostalgia for an idyllic past waxes strong."[97] People are "drawn to images of the past, to times that seem slower and more peaceful, where life gives an appearance of being "richer" than what is offered in this contemporary fast-paced, highly mobile world."[98] We seek stronger connections to place as an archive of memory: "Place is an archive of fond memories and splendid achievements that inspire the present; place is permanent and hence reassuring [to humans], who [see] frailty in [themselves] and chance and flux everywhere."[99]

One response to placelessness is what Stephanie K. Hawke terms heritage discourse. Heritage discourse is historical discourse with a strong sense of the continuity of place, identity, and time that offers significant contribution to sense of place.[100] Heritage narratives "make a case for ordinary and everyday places to be included within . . . the significance of discursive processes in the construction of sense of place."[101] Heritage discourse offers a significant and hopeful response to disruptions to our sense of place. It allows us to study nostalgia from a critical lens—asking what loss heritage discourse seeks to stem. We must study this with care so as not to romanticize connections between people and place in rural communities.[102]

Romanticized versions of farming life serve to further distance the remembered intimate connection to the environment from the non-place of a tech-centered world. This does not invalidate heritage discourse, but it is incumbent on scholars to recognize the particular story it tells so as not to erase diverse experiences. Memory becomes a source of community identity that is not monolithic but diverse and intersectional. Evaluating heritage discourse is useful for understanding a response to changing place, the aspirations and values of the community, and the importance of environmental sense of place in that heritage discourse.

Keeping in mind Coontz's caveat about the "nostalgia trap,"[103] heritage discourse is important to study. Sense of place "is bound up intimately with a sense of heritage, as well as with a sense of culture."[104] Heritage discourse is rooted in place, which serves as a compass for the base of human relations. Scholars can look to heritage discourse to explore how environmental sense of place changed in other regions. This allows us to see the impact of industrialization, development, and environmental change on communities. In the Santa Clara Valley, we see a loss of community, of aesthetics, of emotional attachment to the land.

There is a proposal to establish Santa Clara County as a National Heritage Area (NHA). An NHA is a "landscape of national importance" designated by Congress.[105] The designation recognizes "places where natural, cultural, and historic resources combine to form a cohesive, nationally important landscape."[106] The County of Santa Clara established a National Heritage Task Force that developed a proposal for national recognition of the Santa Clara Valley's cultural diversity, historical achievements, and ecological features.[107] While the proposal for the NHA stalled due to lack of political support for the National Parks at the federal level, a National Heritage Area project is worthwhile, and would offer an opportunity to engage the community around agricultural heritage. "The historic environment has a resonance in creating a sense of place and cultural identity which contributes to the quality of the environment in which people live and work."[108] Heritage areas can contribute to community identity by establishing infrastructure for experiences and shared understanding of a history of place. Heritage discourse can amplify "memory of place [that] implaces us and thus empowers us."[109]

It is garlic planting day. Gusts of wind carry the pungent smell of green garlic across the field. I sit in the back of a van with Sam Thorp. Sam is tall; his feet rest easily on the ground, while mine swing freely with more than a foot of clearance. A shock of blond curly hair escapes from his baseball cap. His easy smile and candid conversation remind me of Andy Mariani. Both are doing what they love, bright blue eyes wide open to the challenges ahead. Sam and his brother Nick, along with their father, Mike, founded Spade & Plow Organics in 2015, and are farming forty acres in San Martin. The Thorps grow organic produce and personally deliver it at affordable prices. They offer "fresh, local and organic for all, not just the select few."[110] Sam emphasizes the family's mission to help Silicon Valley customers to develop a "direct connection to the grower."[111] He sees Spade & Plow as "a bridge to connect small businesses, restaurants, and individuals through good farming practices and good food."[112] This means not only making food more accessible, but also cultivating connections between the community and the farm.

Sam takes care not to romanticize farming life. The future of the farm depends on the Thorps holding on to their leases and, of course, the success of their crop. Sam is honest about the challenges: "The farmer has all the risks. There's the environment, there's your costs going into it, your seed costs, fertilizer costs, carton costs, gas costs, those are all things you can't control, and then you have the price of the market."[113] Like Andy, Sam is bemused that people still romanticize farming: "People tell me, 'Oh man, you're so lucky you get to work outside all day; you get to work on the farm.' Well, first off, I probably spend more time in the office than on the farm. Second off, sometimes it sucks to work outside when it's 100 degrees; I'd rather be inside your air-conditioned office. I'm working seven days a week every single day and I'm working at least ten hours a day if not more. And, I make very little money."[114] The quixotic farming ideal persists. The misconceptions of farm work reveal how detached we are from our food production. In the Valley of Heart's Delight, the community had intimate knowledge of the cultivation, harvesting, and preparation of fruit.

Today, as the country has "moved from a producer to consumer economy," low pay and long work make it hard to recruit workers.[115] Sam asks, "Who would want to go work for a farm for ten hours a day making twelve or fourteen bucks an hour when they can go work for a tech company, and make six figures and live a good life?"[116] Yvonne Jacobson puts it bluntly:

"Americans [have turned] their backs on manual labor."[117] Rarely today, she notes, "does an entire family work together for common ends," so the "social health developed by the family farm system" is lost.[118] Spade & Plow is a throwback—generations working together to change the food system. Sam concludes, "I enjoy farming. There are a lot of people that see the value of this.... I think it comes down to a lot of things as far as making a local food movement or creating a unique food culture here in the South Bay, and that is not easy to do, but there is a big payoff if we do it right."[119]

Andy's Orchard and Spade & Plow connect people with food and offer a link to the land and the community. The Spade & Plow farm box and Andy's summer fruit tastings forge relationships between people and their food, between people and the valley. Urban farms such as Veggielution in San José engage community through a variety of food programs, promoting a "sense of place" through community interaction and civic engagement."[120] As one article claims, in language familiar to Silicon Valley readers, "Urban ag startups plant the seed for a new Valley of Heart's Delight."[121]

Santa Clara County is making a commitment to preserving agricultural land. In 2018, the County of Santa Clara and the Santa Clara Valley Open Space Authority developed an Agricultural Plan to preserve twelve thousand acres of agricultural land. Strategies include reducing agricultural property taxes, funding for farm infrastructure, and zoning restrictions to reduce development.[122] Then County Supervisor Dave Cortese, from an orcharding family, champions the effort: "It's amazing that we still have this opportunity to save so much acreage. We must not squander it."[123] In January 2019, the Santa Clara County Board of Supervisors unanimously approved the Santa Clara Valley Agricultural Plan. The main objective of the plan is to purchase development rights so that farmers can keep farming, "protecting the local agricultural economy."[124] In November 2021, the San José City Council voted unanimously to rezone northern Coyote Valley for open space and agriculture. They also removed the "Urban Reserve" designation, signaling that the city has no intentions of annexing the valley for urban development. Whereas fancy cars of developers once drove up gravel roads to offer cash to farmers, today it's a white county van with members of the County Planning Department and the valley's Open Space Authority.[125] Karl Belser would be proud.

My scheduled meeting with Deborah Olson coincides with the news that she is closing C. J. Olson's Cherry Stand. At a Sunnyvale City Council meeting on a late August evening, Olson placed her hand on her heart as she fought back tears, her voice brimming with emotion. There were audible gasps from the audience when she announced: "I want you to know we will be closing our doors September 30, after more than 100 years of serving the community."[126] The news of the Olson's fruit stand came in the same week as the news that Orchard Supply Hardware would shutter. "Everything is closing. What's going on?" asked one longtime fruit stand customer. "It makes me sad. Some of my favorite haunts are closing. In a lot of these small places, you know who to ask for or they know you. It's the loss of a community feeling."[127] Another customer concurred: "The fruit stand helped connect us to the beauty of community, kindness and caring for the farming history of the Valley of Heart's Delight."[128]

Deborah tells me matter-of-factly, "I wanted to continue with this stand; it would always be my roots. Unfortunately, it didn't work out that way because of all the factors involved and what's going on today and today's climate, retail climate."[129] She explains the tough choice: "I don't want to personally continue doing what I've been doing because it's not working any longer in this environment. So, you know, I can either wither up and die or change gears and thrive."[130] Charlie Olson acknowledges the tough decision: "It's sad. All my life I've been in the fruit stand. . . . We talked it over. She was right. You can't keep running in the red. It's not one problem, but a bunch of problems. She did the right thing and honorable thing. You have to move on and do what you can."[131] Charlie Olson will still work the city of Sunnyvale's thirteen acres of cherry and apricot orchards. He says the hard-work ethic that his parents and grandparents ingrained in him keeps him going: "We keep it because it will take care of you. That's what it does. Why do I farm this orchard? Because I can. . . . When I stand here, where it's peaceful and quiet, I can forget about the crazy world of ours."[132]

RESEARCH NOTES

ARCHIVES

Bentley Historical Library, University of Michigan
    Karl A. Belser Papers
Martin Luther King Library, San José State University
    San José Mercury News Archive
Special Collections, San José State University
    John C. Gordon Collection
    Clyde Arbuckle Collection
    Glenna Matthews Collection
    Sourisseau Collection
    Edith C. Smith Postcard Collection
California Room, San José Public Library
    Collections of Santa Clara's Agricultural Past
    Silicon Valley History Online Collection
    San José Public Library Ephemera Collection
    Pioneer Papers
California History Center, DeAnza College
    Michelle Ann Jacobson Collection
    Agricultural History Collection
    Silicon Valley Documentation Project
History San José Research Library
    California Pioneers of Santa Clara County Records
    Loomis Collection
    Postcard Collection
    San José Chamber of Commerce Collection
    Periodicals and Newsletters
    Scrapbooks

Silicon Valley History Online, Santa Clara University
California Pioneers of Santa Clara Valley
  Pioneers Film Archive

LABELS

There are numerous sources of labels around the valley: History San José Research Library and California History Center, DeAnza College, have significant label collections. I was also fortunate enough to have access to private collections: particular thanks to Deb Wool for sharing his extensive collection with me.

BACKGROUND CONVERSATIONS

I am indebted to the following people who took the time to share their recollections and understanding of the Valley of Heart's Delight: Vicky Bosworth, Robin Chapman, Terry Christensen, David Cortese, Eric Goodrich, April Halberstadt, Mac Hamilton, Tori Hamilton, Mike Kutilek, Joanne Larsen, Andy Mariani, David Mariani, Mark Mariani, Patty MacDonald, Mike MacDonald, Jean McCorquodale, Joe Melehan, Betty Nygren, Charlie Olson, Deborah Olson, Barbara Pyle, John Pyle, Chad Raphael, Xavier Regli, Audrey Rust, Ruth Savage, Ted Smith, Brad Stapleton, Sam Thorp, Peter Coe Verbica, Bruce Wool, Deb Wool, Jennifer Wool, Jim Zetterquist.

MEMOIRS

Allen, Thomas. L. *Growing Up in the Santa Clara Valley: From Picking Prunes to Submarine Service*. Seattle, WA: Create Space, 2013.
Calles, Rudy. *Champion Prune Pickers: Migrant Worker's Dilemma*. Los Alamitos, CA: Hwong Publishing Company. 1979.
Chapman, Robin. *California Apricots: The Lost Orchards of Silicon Valley*. Mt. Pleasant, SC: Arcadia Publishing. 2013.
Downey, Carolyn Marie *Voices from the Orchards*. San José, CA: Anacaro Publications. 1997.
Garrod, Emma S. *One Life Mine*. Bloomington, IN: Xlibris. 2012.
Garrod, R. V. *A Saratoga Story*. 1962.
Garrod, Vince S. *Gulchin' Out*. Bloomington, IN: Xlibris. 2013.
Hendrix, Winifred Wool. *Recollections*. Wool Family Collection. 1956.
Jacobson, Yvonne. *Passing Farms, Enduring Values: California's Santa Clara Valley*. Los Altos, CA: William Kaufmann, Inc. 1984.
Mariani, David. *Poverty of Affluence*. Los Altos, CA: Griffith Press. 2019.

Olson, Deborah. *Life Is a Bowl of Olson's Cherries.* Santa Cruz, CA: Mission Printers, n.d.

Peck, Willys I. *Saratoga Stereopticon: A Magic Lantern of Memory.* Cupertino: California History Center and Foundation. 1997.

Stanley, Tim. *The Last of the Prune Pickers: A Pre-Silicon Valley Story.* Irvine, CA: Timothy Publishing. 2009.

Tower, Clarence Robert. *Seventy Years in the Silicon Valley: An Anecdotal History.* United States of America, James Stevenson. 2002.

Wool, Frederick Austin. *Memories of Frederick Austin Wool Sr.* Wool Family Collection. 1989/1990.

HISTORICAL RESEARCH

I'm indebted to many local historians. Clyde Arbuckle was San José's first official City Historian, a position he held for more than fifty years. He founded the San José Historical Museum (now History San José) and wrote the definitive *History of San José.* He was also a champion racer with the local bicycle club, Garden City Wheelmen, from 1920 to 1926.[1] Jack Douglas, archivist at San José State, wrote articles for local newsletters collected in "Historical Footnotes" (1993) and "Historical Highlights" (2005) of the Santa Clara Valley. He worked to preserve landmarks and secure significant collections of historical photographs.[2] Pat Loomis reported at the San José Mercury News for forty years. Her column, Signposts, featured historical vignettes from the lives of pioneers remembered in street names around San José. Leonard McKay, a printer by trade, was a local historian who ran a San José memorabilia shop. He was active in the Santa Clara County Pioneers, and History San José, and was on the board of the Sourisseau Academy for State and Local History. He published columns in the local electronic newspaper *San José Inside.*[3] Ralph Rambo, the label artist, published several books of drawing and historical vignettes.[4] Other historians and scholars have contributed to the history of San José: Terry Christensen, Mary Jo Ignoffo, April Halberstadt, and others.[5] Scott Herhold publishes semi-regular articles in the *San José Mercury News* on local and fruit history.[6] The California Pioneers of Santa Clara County publish the *Trailblazer* newsletters.

NOTES

INTRODUCTION

1. Sally Richards, *Silicon Valley Sand Dreams and Silicon Orchards* (Carlsbad, CA: Heritage Media Corp, 2000), 57.

2. Richards, *Silicon Valley Sand Dreams and Silicon Orchards*, 57.

3. Richards, *Silicon Valley Sand Dreams and Silicon Orchards*, 57–58.

4. Craig VonWaaden, *Million Dollar Dirt* (2003), documentary film, https://www.youtube.com/watch?v=_oKFtf2Twms; Christina Waters, "Cherry Condition," *Metro, Taste*, October 10–16, 1996.

5. Waters, "Cherry Condition."

6. Maria Alicia Guara, "Last Call for the Last Sunnyvale Orchard," *San Francisco Chronicle*, August 1, 1994.

7. Yvonne Jacobson, *Passing Farms, Enduring Values: California's Santa Clara Valley* (Los Altos, CA: William Kaufmann, 1984), 23.

8. Jacobson, *Passing Farms, Enduring Values.*

9. Glory Anne Laffey, "Historical Overview and Context for the City of San Jose," Planning Department of the City of San José, March 39, 1992, https://www.sanjoseca.gov/home/showpublisheddocument/78265/637697308303770000.

10. E. S. Harrison, *Central California, Santa Clara Valley. Its Resources, Advantages and Prospects. Homes for a Million* (San Jose: McNeil Brothers, 1887), 9.

11. R. C. Olson, Interview by Yvonne Jacobson, n.d.

12. Mark Robertson, "Looking Back: Canning in the Valley of Heart's Delight" San Jose Public Library, 2013, https://www.sjpl.org/blog/looking-back-canning-valley-hearts-delight.

13. Bob Johnson, "Agriculture," Silicon Valley History Online Project, 2004: 2, San José Public Library, California Room.

14. Harrison, *Central California, Santa Clara Valley*, 60.

15. Cecilia M. Tsu, *Garden of the World: Asian Immigrants and the Making of Agriculture in California's Santa Clara Valley* (New York: Oxford University Press, 2013), 17.

16. Johnson, "Agriculture," 2.

17. Patricia Zavella, *Women's Work and Chicano Families: Cannery Workers of the Santa Clara Valley* (Ithaca, NY: Cornell University Press, 1987), 34.

18. Vince S. Garrod, *Gulchin' Out* (Bloomington, IN: Xlibris, 2013), 106.

19. Garrod, *Gulchin' Out*, 106.

20. National Oceanic and Atmospheric Administration, "National Centers for Environmental Information," https://www.ncdc.noaa.gov/cdo-web/search;jsession id=A04E6D705544DA3F59F3D30C10C2635E.

21. *San Jose Mercury Herald*, "Loss Near Quarter of Crop," September 14, 1918.

22. *San Jose Mercury Herald*, "Storm Calamity for Santa Clara Valley—Heavy Loss for Growers," September 13, 1918.

23. *San Jose Mercury Herald*, "Plan Move to Lessen Loss Here," September 17, 1918; *San Jose Mercury Herald*, "Prune Pits Wanted by U.S.," September 18, 1918.

24. Andy Mariani, Interview with Anne Marie Todd, March 11, 2016.

25. *San Jose Mercury Herald*, "Fruit Administration Leader in Plea to Orchardists of Valley," September 16, 1918.

26. *San Jose Mercury Herald*, "Save Fruit for Our Boys!," September 12, 1918.

27. *San Jose Mercury Herald*, "Plan Move to Lessen Loss Here"; *San Jose Mercury Herald*, "Soldiers from Fremont Likely to Assist in Gathering Prunes," September 15, 1918.

28. *San Jose Mercury Herald*, "Plan Move to Lessen Loss Here."

29. *San Jose Mercury Herald*, "Fruit Men Hit Hard by Rain," September 15, 1918.

30. Robin Chapman, *California Apricots: The Lost Orchards of Silicon Valley* (Mt. Pleasant, SC: Arcadia Publishing, 2013), 109; Johnson, "Agriculture," 3.

31. Eugene T. Sawyer, *History of Santa Clara County* (Los Angeles, CA: Historic Record Company, 1922), http://www.usgwarchives.net/ca/santaclara/history.html; VonWaaden, "Million Dollar Dirt."

32. Sawyer, *History of Santa Clara County*.

33. George P. Clements, "Billion Dollar Agricultural Production State, 1929," *California Cultivator*, December 31, 1921, 1.

34. California Farm Bureau, "'It is Time to Do Something about It,' Say Santa Clara County Farmers," *Farm Bureau Monthly*, April 1934, 1.

35. Glenna Matthews, *Silicon Valley, Women, and the California Dream: Gender, Class, and Opportunity in the Twentieth Century* (Palo Alto, CA: Stanford University Press, 2002), 49.

36. Matthews, *Silicon Valley, Women, and the California Dream*, 49.

37. Robert Couchman, *The Sunsweet Story* (San Jose, CA: Sunsweet Growers, Inc., 1967), 37.

38. Glenna Matthews, "A California Middletown: The Social History of San Jose in the Depression" (PhD diss. Stanford, 1976), 216.

39. Matthews, "A California Middletown," 216; David N. Pellow and Lisa Sun-Hee Park, *The Silicon Valley of Dreams: Environmental Injustice, Immigrant Workers, and the High-Tech Global Economy* (New York: New York University Press, 2002), 55.

40. Joe Rodriguez, "Oral History: How World War II Changed Silicon Valley " *San Jose Mercury News,* August 12, 2010, https://www.mercurynews.com/2010/08 /12/oral-history-how-world-war-ii-changed-silicon-valley/. Quoting Chuck Darrah, professor of anthropology, San José State University.

41. Carl Nolte, "World War II Reshaped the Bay Area and Its People," *San Francisco Chronicle,* May 28, 2012, https://www.sfgate.com/bayarea/article/World -War-II-reshaped-the-Bay-Area-and-its-people–3589894.php.

42. Matthews, "A California Middletown," 216; Willys I. Peck, "Agriculture's Erosion: W.W. II Began a Shift to Industry," *San José Mercury News,* December 27, 1999.

43. Jacobson, *Passing Farms, Enduring Values,* 231.

44. Peck, "Agriculture's Erosion," 1A.

45. Karl Belser, "The Making of Slurban America," *Cry California: The Journal of California Tomorrow* 5, no. 4 (1970): 3.

46. Rebecca Conrad, "The Conservation of Local Autonomy: California's Agricultural Land Policies, 1900–1966," *California Legal History* 13 (2018).

47. Michael Cronk, "The Olsons' Last Stand," *San Jose Mercury News,* March 31, 1997.

48. Bruce Gardner, "U.S. Agriculture in the Twentieth Century," *EH.Net Encyclopedia,* ed. Robert Whaples, 2003, https://eh.net/encyclopedia/u-s-agriculture -in-the-twentieth-century/.

49. David Swenson, "Most of America's Rural Areas Are Doomed to Decline," *The Conversation* (May 7, 2019). https://theconversation.com/most-of-americas-rural -areas-are-doomed-to-decline–115343.

50. American Farmland Trust, *Farms under Threat: The State of America's Farmland* (Washington, DC: American Farmland Trust, 2018), 4, https://www.farmland info.org/sites/default/files/AFT_Farms_Under_Threat_ExecSum-min.pdf.

51. US Global Change Research Program, *National Climate Assessment* (Washington, DC: US Global Change Research Program, 2014), https://nca2014 .globalchange.gov/report.

52. Leonard Downie, *The Santa Clara Valley's Appointment with Destiny,* Alicia Patterson Foundation (1971), 1–2, http://aliciapatterson.org/stories/santa-clara -valley%E2%80%99s-%E2%80%9Cappointment-destiny%E2%80%9D.

53. Zavella, *Women's Work and Chicano Families,* 169.

54. Michael Tumolo, "On Useful Rhetorical History," *Journal of Contemporary Rhetoric* 1, no. 2 (2011): 60.

55. Yi-Fu Tuan, *Space and Place: The Perspective of Experience* (Minneapolis: University of Minnesota Press, 1977), 6.

56. Jacobson, *Passing Farms, Enduring Values,* 135.

57. James Zetterquist and Joe Melehan, Interview with Anne Marie Todd, February 29, 2016.

58. Matthews, "A California Middletown," 34–36.

59. Margo McBane, "Santa Clara Valley Women Cannery Workers," Sourisseau Academy, updated July 2017, https://www.sourisseauacademy.org/LADS /July2017LADS.pdf.

60. Elias Castillo, "Canning Industry Still Fruitful Here," *San Jose Mercury News*, August 24, 1980, 1C.

61. Chapman, *California Apricots*, 101.

62. Deborah Olson, Interview with Anne Marie Todd, September 6, 2018.

63. Terry Christensen and Philip J. Trounstine, "Flashback: A Short Political History of San Jose," In *Movers and Shakers* (New York: St. Martin's Press, 1982), 1, http://www.sjsu.edu/polisci/docs/faculty_links/Terry%20San%20Jose%20Political%20History%20%20to%201970-1.pdf.

64. Olson, interview.

65. Kenneth W. Brown, David H. Caldwell, and John T. Norgaard, *San Jose Sewage Treatment Study: Design Criteria, Preliminary Plans and Cost Estimates for Secondary Treatment of Sewage and Industrial Wastes. A Report Prepared for the City of San Jose, CA* (San Francisco: Brown and Caldwell, Civil and Chemical Engineers, December 1959), 14.

66. E. A. Torriero, "Fresh-Fruit Craze Puts Lid on Canneries," *San Jose Mercury News*, August 27, 1986, 1.

67. Carol Beddo quoted in Carolyn Marie Downey, *Voices from the Orchards* (San Jose, CA: Anacaro Publications, 1997), 70.

68. Dave Cortese, Interview with Anne Marie Todd, March 8, 2019.

69. Jacobson, *Passing Farms, Enduring Values*, 128.

70. Vince S. Garrod quoted in Downey, *Voices from the Orchards*, 34.

71. Vicky Bosworth, Interview with Anne Marie Todd, September 6, 2018.

72. Olson, interview.

73. Olson, interview.

74. Ruth Savage and Betty Nygren, Interview with Anne Marie Todd, October 22, 2018.

75. Chapman, *California Apricots*, 17.

76. Zetterquist and Melehan, interview.

77. Leonard McKay, "The Canning Industry in San Jose," *San Jose Inside*, February 20, 2006, http://www.sanjoseinside.com/2006/02/20/the_canning_industry_in_san_jose/.

78. Belser, "The Making of Slurban America," 3.

79. Anne Kearney, "Final Farms," *Peninsula Magazine*, 48.

80. Matthews, "A California Middletown," 34–36.

81. Matthews, "A California Middletown," 34–36.

82. Edward Relph, "Spirit of Place and Sense of Place in Virtual Realities," *Society for Philosophy and Technology Quarterly Electronic Journal* 10, no. 3 (2007): 1.

83. Donal Carbaugh and Tovar Cerulli, "Cultural Discourses of Dwelling: Investigating Environmental Communication as a Place-Based Practice," *Environmental Communication: A Journal of Nature and Culture* 7, no. 1 (2013): 6–7.

84. Casey, *Getting Back into Place: Toward a Renewed Understanding of the Place-World* (Bloomington: Indiana University Press, 1993), 15.

85. Tim Creswell, *Place: An Introduction*, 2nd ed. (West Sussex, UK: Wiley Blackwell, 2015), 18.

86. Jennifer D. Adams et al., "Sense of Place," in *Urban Environmental Education Review*, ed. Alex Russ and Marianne E. Krasney (Ithaca, NY: Cornell University Press, 2017); Keith H. Basso, "Wisdom Sits in Places: Notes on a Western Apache Landscape," in *Senses of Place*, ed. Steven Feld and Keith H. Basso (Santa Fe, NM: School of American Research Press, 1996).

87. Danielle Endres and Samantha Senda-Cook, "Location Matters: The Rhetoric of Place in Protest," *Quarterly Journal of Speech* 97, no. 3 (August 1, 2011): 258.

88. Gregory Clark, *Rhetorical Landscapes in America: Variations on a Theme from Kenneth Burke* (Columbia: University of South Carolina Press, 2004), 9, 13.

89. Relph, "Spirit of Place," 1.

90. Tim Creswell, "Place," in *International Encyclopedia of Human Geography*, ed. Nigel Thrift and Rob Kitchen (Oxford: Elsevier, 2009), 1.

91. Creswell, "Place," 1.

92. Daniel R. Williams, "Making Sense of 'Place': Reflections on Pluralism and Positionality in Place Research," *Landscape and Urban Planning* 131 (2014): 76, https://doi.org/10.1016/j.landurbplan.2014.08.002.

93. Adams et al., "Sense of Place,"; Alex Russ et al., "Development of Ecological Place Meaning in New York City," *The Journal of Environmental Education* 46, no. 2 (2015).

94. Relph, "Spirit of Place," 1.

95. Jeff Malpas, "New Media, Cultural Heritage and the Sense of Place: Mapping the Conceptual Ground," *International Journal of Heritage Studies* 14, no. 3 (2008): 199.

96. James G. Cantrill et al., "Exploring a Sense of Self-in-Place to Explain the Impulse for Urban Sprawl." *Environmental Communication: A Journal of Nature and Culture* 1, no. 2 (2007), 126.

97. James G. Cantrill and Susan L. Senecah, "Using the 'Sense of Self-in-Place' Construct in the Context of Environmental Policy-Making and Landscape Planning," *Environmental Science and Policy* 4 (2001): 187.

98. Carbaugh and Cerulli, "Cultural Discourses of Dwelling," 17.

99. Donal Carbaugh, "Naturalizing Communication and Culture," in *The Symbolic Earth: Discourse and Our Creation of the Environment*, ed. J. G. Cantrill and Christine L. Oravec (Lexington: University Press of Kentucky, 1996).

100. Carbaugh and Cerulli, "Cultural Discourses of Dwelling," 9.

101. Samantha Senda-Cook, "Materializing Tensions: How Maps and Trails Mediate Nature," *Environmental Communication* 7, no. 3 (2013): 356.

102. Cantrill and Senecah, "Using the 'Sense of Self-in-Place' Construct," 188.

103. Cantrill et al., "Exploring a Sense of Self-in-Place," 127.

104. Edward S. Casey, "How to Get from Space to Place in a Fairly Short Stretch of Time: Phenomenological Prolegomena," in *Sense of Place*, ed. Steven Feld and Keith H. Basso (Santa Fe, New Mexico: School of American Research Press, 1996), 26.

105. Elizabeth Dickinson, "Displaced in Nature: The Cultural Production of (Non-)Place in Place-Based Forest Conservation Pedagogy," *Environmental Communication* 5, no. 3 (2011): 315.

106. Barbara Allen, "Regional Studies in American Folklore Scholarship," in *Sense of Place: American Regional Cultures*, ed. Barbara Allen and Thomas J. Schlereth (Lexington: University of Kentucky Press, 1990), 2.

107. David Harvey, *Justice, Nature and the Geography of Difference* (Cambridge, MA: Blackwell, 1996), 45.

108. Steven M. Pedersen, "A Composed "Rhetoric" in Place: A Material-Epistemic Reading of Plato's Phaedrus," *Rhetoric Review* 36, no. 1 (January 2, 2017).

109. Endres and Senda-Cook, "Location Matters," 262.

110. Adams et al., "Sense of Place."

111. Maria Korusiewicz, "Places in Placelessness: Notes on the Aesthetic and the Strategies of Place-Making," *Argument* 5, no. 2 (2015): 410.

112. Creswell, "Place."

113. Endres and Senda-Cook, "Location Matters," 263.

114. Tuan, *Space and Place*, 183–84.

115. Harvey, *Justice, Nature and the Geography of Difference*, 316.

116. David Cooper, "Introduction," in *A Companion to Aesthetics*, ed. David Cooper (Malden, MA: Wiley-Blackwell, 1992), viii.

117. Allen Carlson, "Environmental Aesthetics," in *Routledge Companion to Aesthetics*, ed. B. Gaut and D. M. Lopes (London: Routledge, 2001), 428; Allen Carlson, *Aesthetics and the Environment: The Appreciation of Nature, Art and Architecture* (London: Routledge, 2002); Allen Carlson, *Nature and Landscape: An Introduction to Environmental Aesthetics* (New York: Columbia University Press, 2009).

118. Christine Oravec, "Conservationism vs. preservationism: The Public Interest in the Hetch Hetchy Controversy" *Quarterly Journal of Speech* 70, no. 4 (1984): 445.

119. Christine Oravec, "To Stand Outside Oneself: The Sublime in the Discourse of Natural Scenery," in *The Symbolic Earth*, ed. James Cantrill and Christine Oravec (Lexington: University Press of Kentucky, 1996), 64.

120. Oravec, "To Stand Outside Oneself," 67.

121. Oravec, "To Stand Outside Oneself," 59.

122. Oravec, "To Stand Outside Oneself," 58.

123. Victor Counted, "Making Sense of Place Attachment: Towards a Holistic Understanding of People-Place Relationships and Experiences," *Environment, Space, Place* 8, no. 1 (2016): 9.

124. Julia Corbett, *Communicating Nature: How We Create and Understand Environmental Messages* (Washington, DC: Island Press, 2006), 169.

125. Korusiewicz, "Places in Placelessness," 403.

126. John Agnew, "Space and Place," in *Handbook of Geographical Knowledge*, ed. John Agnew and D. Livingstone (London: Sage, 2011), 7–8.

127. Paul C. Adams and Astrid Gynnild, "Environmental Messages in Online Media: The Role of Place," *Environmental Communication* 7, no. 1 (March 1, 2013): 116.

128. Creswell, "Place," 8.

129. Creswell, "Place," 8.

130. David Storey, "Land, Territory and Identity," in *Making Sense of Place*, ed. Ian Convery, Gerard Corsane, and Peter Davis, Multidisciplinary Perspectives (Rochester, NY: Boydell & Brewer, 2012), 18.

131. Creswell, "Place," 7.

132. Patricia A. Stokowski, "Languages of Place and Discourses of Power: Constructing New Senses of Place," *Journal of Leisure Research* 34, no. 4 (December 1, 2002): 36.

133. Miriam Kahn, "Your Place and Mine: Sharing Emotional Landscapes in Wamira, Papua New Guinea," in *Senses of Place*, ed. Steven Feld and Keith H. Basso (Santa Fe, NM: School of American Research Press, 1996), 168.

134. Ian Convery, Gerard Corsane, and Peter Davis, "Introduction Making Sense of Place," in *Making Sense of Place*, ed. Ian Convery, Gerard Corsane, and Peter Davis, Multidisciplinary Perspectives (Rochester, NY: Boydell & Brewer, 2012), 1.

135. Gerard Kyle and Garry Chick, "The Social Construction of a Sense of Place," *Leisure Sciences* 29, no. 3 (2007): 212, https://doi.org/10.1080/01490400701257922.

136. Allen, "Regional Studies in American Folklore Scholarship," 1.

137. Casey, *Getting Back into Place*, 23.

138. Tuan, *Space and Place*, 33.

139. Jessica Leigh Thompson and James G. Cantrill, "The Symbolic Transformation of Space," *Environmental Communication* 7, no. 1 (2013): 1, https://doi.org/10.1080/17524032.2012.758650.

140. Adams et al., "Sense of Place."

141. Kenneth R. Olwig, "Landscape as a Contested Topos of Place, Community, and Self," in *Textures of Place*, ed. Paul C. Adams, Steven Hoelscher, and Karen E. Till, Exploring Humanist Geographies (Minneapolis: University of Minnesota Press, 2001), 93.

142. Harvey, *Justice, Nature and the Geography of Difference*, 306.

143. Daniel D. Arreola, "Introduction," in *Hispanic Spaces, Latino Places: Community and Cultural Diversity in Contemporary America*, ed. Daniel D. Arreola (Austin: University of Texas Press, 2004), 2.

144. Kathleen C. Stewart, "An Occupied Place," in *Senses of Place*, ed. Steven Feld and Keith H. Basso (Santa Fe, NM: School of American Research, 1996), 140.

145. Stokowski, "Languages of Place," 369.

146. Carbaugh and Cerulli, "Cultural Discourses of Dwelling," 7–8.

147. Tuan, *Space and Place*, 178.

148. Thomas L. Haskell, *Objectivity Is Not Neutrality: Explanatory Schemes in History* (Baltimore: Johns Hopkins University Press, 1998), 1–2.

149. Gerda Lerner, *Why History Matters: Life and Thought* (New York: Oxford University Press, 1997), 52.

150. William Cronon, ed., *Uncommon Ground: Rethinking the Human Place in Nature* (New York: W. W. Norton, 1995), 20, 25.

151. James G. Cantrill, "A Sense of Self-in-Place for Adaptive Management, Capacity Building, and Public Participation," in *Environmental Communication*

Yearbook I, ed. Susan L. Senecah (Mahwah, NJ: Lawrence Erlbaum Associates, 2004), 169.

152. Cantrill et al., "Exploring a Sense of Self-in-Place," 126.

153. Stokowski, "Languages of Place," 372.

154. Tarla Rai Peterson, "Environmental Communication: Tales of Life on Earth," *Quarterly Journal of Speech* 84 (1998): 385.

155. Stokowski, "Languages of Place," 372–74.

156. Endres and Senda-Cook, "Location Matters," 276.

157. Bruce E. Gronbeck, "The Rhetorics of the Past: History, Argument, and Collective Memory," in *Doing Rhetorical History: Concepts and Cases*, ed. Kathleen J. Turner (Tuscaloosa: University of Alabama Press, 1998), 2.

158. James Jasinski, "A Constitutive Framework for Rhetorical Historiography: Toward an Understanding of the Discursive (Re)Constituion of 'Constitution' in *The Federalist Papers*," in *Doing Rhetorical History: Concepts and Cases*, ed. Kathleen J. Turner (Tuscaloosa: University of Alabama Press, 1998), 75.

159. Kathleen J. Turner, "Introduction," in *Doing Rhetorical History: Concepts and Cases*, ed. Kathleen J. Turner, Studies in Rhetoric and Communication (Tuscaloosa: University of Alabama Press, 1998), 9.

160. Bruce E. Gronbeck, "Rhetorical History and Rhetorical Criticism: A Distinction," *The Speech Teacher* 24 (1975): 310.

161. David Zarefsky, "Four Senses of Rhetorical History," in *Doing Rhetorical History: Concepts and Cases*, ed. Kathleen J. Turner (Tuscaloosa: University of Alabama Press, 1998), 30.

162. Cara A. Finnegan, "Doing Rhetorical History of the Visual: The Photograph and the Archive," in *Defining Visual Rhetorics*, ed. Charles A. Hill and Marguerite Helmers (New York: Routledge, 2009), 200; Zarefsky, "Four Senses of Rhetorical History," 30.

163. Zarefsky, "Four Senses of Rhetorical History," 29; Kathleen J. Turner, ed., *Doing Rhetorical History: Concepts and Cases*, Studies in Rhetoric and Communication (Tuscaloosa: University of Alabama Press, 1998). 25–26

164. Kahn, "Your Place and Mine," 167.

165. Keith H. Basso, "Wisdom Sits in Places: Notes on a Western Apache Landscape," in *Senses of Place*, ed. Steven Feld and Keith H. Basso (Santa Fe, NM: School of American Research Press, 1996), 83.

166. Basso, "Wisdom Sits in Places," 55.

167. Kahn, "Your Place and Mine," 168.

168. Basso, "Wisdom Sits in Places," 84.

169. Philip Gardner, "Oral History," in *The Sage Dictionary of Social Research Methods*, ed. Victor Jupp (London: Sage Publications, 2006), 207.

170. Stokowski, "Languages of Place," 372–74.

171. Gardner, "Oral History," 208.

172. Donald A. Ritchie, *Doing Oral History: A Practical Guide* (New York: Oxford University Press, 2003), 19.

173. Kristin M. Langellier and Eric E. Peterson, *Storytelling in Daily Life: Performing Narrative* (Philadelphia: Temple University Press, 2004), 1.

174. Sidonie Smith and Julia Watson, *Reading Autobiography: A Guide for Interpreting Life Narratives*, 2nd ed. (Minneapolis: University of Minnesota Press, 2010), 63.

175. Danielle Endres, "Environmental Oral History," *Environmental Communication: A Journal of Nature and Culture* 5, no. 4 (December 2011): 485.

176. Turner, "Introduction," 5.

177. Tumolo, "On Useful Rhetorical History," 59.

178. Steven Feld and Keith H. Basso, "Introduction," in *Sense of Place*, ed. Steven Feld and Keith H. Basso (Santa Fe, NM: School of American Research Press, 1996), 5.

179. Feld and Basso, "Introducction," 5.

180. Endres, "Environmental Oral History," 485.

181. Turner, "Introduction," 5.

182. Andrea A. Lunsford, Kirt H. Wilson, and Rosa A. Eberly, "The Common Goods of Public Discourse," in *The Sage Handbook of Rhetorical Studies*, ed. Andrea A. Lunsford, Kirt H. Wilson, and Rosa A. Eberly (Thousand Oaks, CA: Sage Publications, 2009), 425.

183. Thomas W. Benson, "Series Editor's Preface," in *Vernacular Voices: The Rhetoric of Publics and Public Spheres* (Columbia: University of South Carolina Press, 1999), xii.

184. Gerard A. Hauser, *Vernacular Voices: The Rhetoric of Publics and Public Spheres* (Columbia: University of South Carolina Press, 1999).

185. Dean MacCannell, *The Tourist: A New Theory of the Leisure Class* (Berkeley: University of California Press, 1976), 45.

186. George Hughes, "Tourism and the Semiological Realization of Space," in *Desintations: Cultural Landscapes of Tourism*, ed. Gregory Ringer (London: Routledge, 1998).

187. Tema Milstein, "When Whales "Speak for Themselves": Communication as a Mediating Force in Wildlife Tourism," *Environmental Communication* 2, no. 2 (2008): 173.

188. Tracy Marafiote, "The American Dream: Technology, Tourism, and the Transformation of Wilderness," *Environmental Communication* 2, no. 2 (2008).

189. Lee Edwards, "Questions of Self-Interest, Agency, and the Rhetor," *Management Communication Quarterly* 25, no. 3 (2011): 532, https://doi.org/10.1177/0893318911409866.

190. Josh Boyd, "Corporate Rhetoric Participates in Public Dialogue: A Solution to the Public/Private Conundrum," *Southern Communication Journal* 66, no. 4 (2001): 290.

191. Nicholas S. Paliewicz, "The Country, the City, and the Corporation: Rio Tinto Kennecott and the Materiality of Corporate Rhetoric," *Environmental Communication* 12, no. 6 (2018): 747.

192. Judith Hoover, "Corporate Advocacy: A Powerful Persuasive Strategy," in *Corporate Advocacy: Rhetoric in the Information Age*, ed. Judith Hoover (Westport, CT: Quorum Books, 1997), 5, 8.

193. Paliewicz, "The Country, the City, and the Corporation," 748.

194. Karlyn Kohrs Campbell, *The Rhetorical Act* (Belmont, CA: Wadsworth Publishing, 1982), 4.

195. Smith and Watson, *Reading Autobiography*, 16.

196. Smith and Watson, *Reading Autobiography*, 13.

197. Stephanie Coontz, *The Way We Never Were: American Families and the Nostalgia Trap* (New York: Basic Books, 2016), 9.

198. Coontz, *The Way We Never Were*, 20, 374.

199. Lauret Edith Savoy, *Trace: Memory, History, Race, and the American Landscape* (Berkeley, CA: Counterpoint, 2015), 108.

200. Patricia Zavella, *Women's Work and Chicano Families*; Vicki L. Ruiz, *Cannery Women Cannery Lives: Mexican Women, Unionization, and the California Food Processing Industry, 1930–1950* (Albequerque: University of New Mexico Press, 1987).

201. Zarefsky, "Four Senses of Rhetorical History," 31–22.

202. Stokowski, "Languages of Place," 372–74.

203. Carbaugh and Cerulli, "Cultural Discourses of Dwelling," 17.

204. Stokowski, "Languages of Place," 372–74.

205. Doreen Massey, "Preface," in *Making Sense of Place*, ed. Ian Convery, Gerard Corsane, and Peter Davis, Multidisciplinary Perspectives (Rochester, NY: Boydell & Brewer, 2012), xiii–xiv.

206. Doreen Massey, *Space, Place, and Gender* (Minneapolis: University of Minnesota Press, 1994), 120.

207. Stewart, "An Occupied Place," 139.

208. Storey, "Land, Territory and Identity," 13.

209. Massey, *Space, Place, and Gender*, 183.

210. Stephen J. Pitti, *The Devil in Silicon Valley: Northern California, Race and Mexican Americans* (Princeton, NJ: Princeton University Press, 2003), 34.

211. Pitti, *The Devil in Silicon Valley*.

212. Ruiz, *Cannery Women Cannery Lives*; Zavella, *Women's Work and Chicano Families*.

213. Tsu, *Garden of the World*, 16, 25.

214. Robert Higgs, "Landless by Law: Japanese Immigrants in California Agriculture to 1941," *Journal of Economic History* 38, no. 1 (1978).

215. Timothy J. Lukes and Gary Y. Okihiro, *Japanese Legacy: Farming and Community Life in California's Santa Clara Valley* vol. 31, Local History Studies (Cuptertino: California History Center, DeAnza College, 1985), 4–5.

216. Lukes and Okihiro, *Japanese Legacy*, 31, 69.

217. Tsu, *Garden of the World*, 5.

218. Savoy, *Trace: Memory, History, Race*, 111.

219. Tsu, *Garden of the World*, 17; Richard Levy, "Costanoan," in *Handbook of North American Indians (California)*, ed. William C. Sturtevant and Robert F. Heizer

(Washington, DC: Smithsonian Institution, 1978); Sherburne F. Cook, *The Population of the California Indians, 1769–1970* (Berkeley: University of California Press, 1976).

220. Joan Irvine, "Native Oaks and Urban Sprawl," *Pacific Horticulture* (Spring 1982), https://www.pacifichorticulture.org/articles/native-oaks-and-urban-sprawl/.

221. Alan Leventhal et al., "The Ohlone Back from Extinction," in *The Ohlone Past and Present: Native Americans of the San Francisco Bay Region*, ed. Lowell John Bean (Menlo Park, CA: Ballena Press, 1994), 303.

222. Alan K. Brown, ed., *With Anza to California 1775–1776: The Journal of Pedro Font, O.F.M.*, vol. 1, Early California Commentaries (Norman, OK: The Arthur C. Clark Company, 2011), 292.

223. Harrison, *Central California, Santa Clara Valley*, 9.

224. Pellow and Park, *The Silicon Valley of Dreams*, 28.

225. Leventhal et al., "The Ohlone Back from Exctinction," 305–6.

226. Leventhal et al., "The Ohlone Back from Exctinction," 305.

227. Brendan C. Lindsay, *Murder State: California's Native American Genocide 1846–1873* (Omaha: University of Nebraska Press, 2012).

228. James J. Rawls, *Indians of California: The Changing Image* (Norman: University of Oklahoma Press, 1986), xiv.

229. Rawls, *Indians of California*, 186.

230. Edward D. Castillo, "Short Overview of California Indian History," State of California Native American Heritage Comission, 2021, http://nahc.ca.gov/resources/california-indian-history/.

231. Randall Milliken, Laurence H. Shoup, and Beverly R. Ortiz, *Ohlone/Costanoan Indians of the San Francisco Peninsula and Their Neighbors, Yesterday and Today*, ed. Archaeological and Historical Consultants (Oakland, CA: National Park Service 2009), 179. http://www.muwekma.org/images/Ohlone_Costanoan_Indians_of_SF_Peninsula_NPS_2009.pdf.

232. Leventhal et al., "The Ohlone Back from Extinction."

233. Monte Mills, "The Legacy of Federal Control in Indian Country," *Regulatory Review* (March 16, 2021), https://www.theregreview.org/2021/03/16/mills-legacy-federal-control-indian-country/.

234. *The Regulatory Review*, "Native Peoples, Tribal Sovereignty, and Regulation," March 15, 2021, https://www.theregreview.org/2021/03/15/native-tribal-regulation/.

235. Pellow and Park, *The Silicon Valley of Dreams*, 33.

236. Cantrill et al., "Exploring a Sense of Self-in-Place," 141.

237. Edward Relph, *Place and Placelessness (Research in Planning and Design)* (London: Pion, 1976), preface.

CHAPTER I. THE WORLD'S LARGEST ORCHARD

1. Peter Thomas and Donna Thomas, *Muir Ramble Route: Walking from San Francisco to Yosemite in the Footsteps of John Muir* (Madera, CA: Poetic Matrix Press, 2010), 4.

2. John Muir, "Rambles of a Botanist among the Plants and Climates of California," *Old and New* 5, no. 6 (June 1872): 768, https://scholarlycommons.pacific.edu/cgi /viewcontent.cgi?referer=https://www.google.com/&httpsredir=1&article=1015& context=jmb; Thomas and Thomas, *Muir Ramble Route*, 17; Donald Worster, *A Passion for Nature: The Life of John Muir* (Oxford: Oxford University Press, 2008), 150.

3. John Muir, *The Yosemite* (New York: The Century Co. , 1912). https://vault .sierraclub.org/john_muir_exhibit/writings/the_yosemite/; Muir, "Rambles of a Botanist Among the Plants and Climates of California."

4. Muir, *The Yosemite*; Muir, "Rambles of a Botanist."

5. Michael Brune, "Pulling Down Our Monuments," *Sierra Club* (July 22, 2020). https://www.sierraclub.org/michael-brune/2020/07/john-muir-early-history-sierra -club; Justin Nobel, "The Miseducation of John Muir," *Atlas Obscura* (July 26, 2016). https://www.atlasobscura.com/articles/the-miseducation-of-john-muir; Brian Melley, "Sierra Club Apologizes for Founder John Muir's Racist Views," *AP News*, July 22, 2020, https://apnews.com/article/national-parks-us-news-parks -environment-ca-state-wire-c52ccd3ac1c127289cf5b1a5c0dc070d.

6. Christine Oravec, "John Muir, Yosemite, and the Sublime Response: A Study in the Rhetoric of Preservationism," *Quarterly Journal of Speech* 67, no. 3 (1981): 254.

7. Michael Brune, "Pulling Down Our Monuments," *Sierra Club* (July 22, 2020). https://www.sierraclub.org/michael-brune/2020/07/john-muir-early-history-sierra -club.

8. Justin Nobel, "The Miseducation of John Muir," *Atlas Obscura* (July 26, 2016). https://www.atlasobscura.com/articles/the-miseducation-of-john-muir.

9. Muir, "Rambles of a Botanist," 768; Thomas and Thomas, *Muir Ramble Route*, 17; Worster, *A Passion for Nature*, 150.

10. Muir, *The Yosemite*; Muir, "Rambles of a Botanist."

11. Muir, "Rambles of a Botanist," 768; Thomas and Thomas, *Muir Ramble Route*, 17; Worster, *A Passion for Nature*, 150.

12. Downey, *Voices from the Orchards*, 19.

13. San Jose Chamber of Commerce, *The Valley of Heart's Delight: Where It Is, How to See It* [brochure] (San Jose: San Jose Chamber of Commerce 1910).

14. San Jose Chamber of Commerce, *The Valley of Heart's Delight*.

15. Charles S. McCaleb, *Tracks, Tires and Wires: Public Transportation in California's Santa Calra Valley* (Glendale, CA: Interurban Press, 1981).

16. San Jose Chamber of Commerce, *The Valley of Heart's Delight*; Judge Belden, *Santa Clara County, California* [brochure] (San Jose, CA: Board of Trade of San Jose, 1887), 35.

17. Downey, *Voices from the Orchards*, 19.

18. San Jose Chamber of Commerce, *San Jose (San Hosay) Santa Clara County California* [brochure] (San Jose: San Jose Chamber of Commerce,, 1904).

19. Harrison, *Central California, Santa Clara Valley*, 8–9.

20. The San Jose Mercury, *Sunshine Fruit and Flowers: Santa Clara County and its Resources: Historical Descriptive Statistical. A Souvenir* (San Jose, CA: Alfred C. Eaton, 1896).

21. Harrison, *Central California, Santa Clara Valley*, 142.

22. Malcolm Andrews, *The Search for the Picturesque: Landscape Aesthetics and Tourism in Britain, 1760–1800* (Stanford, CA: Stanford University Press, 1989), vii.

23. Oravec, "To Stand Outside Oneself," 59.

24. Corbett, *Communicating Nature*, 168.

25. Oravec, "To Stand Outside Oneself," 61.

26. Oravec, "To Stand Outside Oneself," 59.

27. Emily Brady, *The Sublime in Modern Philosophy : Aesthetics, Ethics, and Nature* (Cambridge: Cambridge University Press, 2013), 201.

28. Brady, *The Sublime in Modern Philosophy*, 205.

29. Brady, *The Sublime in Modern Philosophy*, 206.

30. F. Orvis, "Why Real Estate Pays in Santa Clara County," *Overland Monthly* 54, no. 3 (September 1909): 302.

31. Jacobson, *Passing Farms, Enduring Values*, 95.

32. Andrews, *The Search for the Picturesque*, vii.

33. David Mariani, Interview by Anne Marie Todd, July 19, 2018.

34. David Mariani, *Poverty of Affluence* (Los Altos: Griffith Press, 2019), 33.

35. David Mariani, interview.

36. Mariani, *Poverty of Affluence*, 100.

37. Rick Carroll, "How the Pears Got Bulldozed," *San Francisco Chronicle*, January 27, 1978.

38. Jacobson, *Passing Farms, Enduring Values*, 104.

39. Jacobson, *Passing Farms, Enduring Values*, 230.

40. Agnew, "Space and Place," 7.

41. Senda-Cook, "Materializing Tensions," 356–57.

42. Senda-Cook, "Materializing Tensions," 356–57.

43. Richmond Croom Beatty, *Bayard Taylor: Laureate of the Gilded Age* (Norman: University of Oklahoma Press, 1936); Liam Corley, *Bayard Taylor: Determined Dreamer of America's Rise, 1825–1878* (Lanham, MD: Bucknell University Press, 2014); James Todd Uhlman, "Geographies of Desire: Bayard Taylor and the Romance of Travel in Bourgeois American Culture, 1820–1880" (PhD diss., Rutgers University, 2007), https://rucore.libraries.rutgers.edu/rutgers-lib/23892/; Bayard Taylor, *El Dorado or Adventures in the Path of Empire* (New York: G.P. Putnam, 1850).

44. Harrison, *Central California, Santa Clara Valley*, 15.

45. San Jose Chamber of Commerce, *The Valley of Heart's Delight*.

46. San Jose Chamber of Commerce, *The Valley of Heart's Delight*; Leah Irvine, *Santa Clara County California* [brochure] (San Jose: San Jose Chamber of Commerce, 1915), 3.

47. San Jose Chamber of Commerce, *The Valley of Heart's Delight*.

48. Oravec, "To Stand Outside Oneself," 66.

49. Casey, *Getting Back into Place*, 25.

50. San Jose Chamber of Commerce, *Santa Clara County California* [brochure] (San Jose: San Jose Chamber of Commerce Publicity Department, 1930).

51. Harry L. Wells, "In Blossom Land: A Springtime Sketch of San Jose and Santa Clara County California," *Sunset Magazine*, May 1902, 47–48.

52. Wells, "In Blossom Land," 47–48.

53. Aaron Sachs, "Virtual Ecology: A Brief Environmental History of Silicon Valley," *World Watch* 12 (January/February 1999): 15.

54. Joanne Larsen, Interview with Anne Marie Todd, December 10, 2015.

55. Mark Mariani, Interview with Anne Marie Todd, January 28, 2016.

56. Tuan, *Space and Place*, 123.

57. Tuan, *Space and Place*, 123.

58. Belden, *Santa Clara County, California*, 3, 23.

59. Tuan, *Space and Place*, 124.

60. Chapman, *California Apricots*, 9.

61. Chapman, *California Apricots*, 89–90.

62. George H. Stipp, "The Valley of Santa Clara," *Out West*, November 1909, 925.

63. Stipp, "The Valley of Santa Clara," 925.

64. Oravec, "To Stand Outside Oneself," 64.

65. Stipp, "The Valley of Santa Clara," 925.

66. San Jose Chamber of Commerce, *San Jose (San Hosay)*, 4.

67. Santa Clara County Fruit Exchange, *How to Prepare Nature's Health Food: The California Prune* (San Jose, CA: Santa Clara County Fruit Exchange, 1905), 11.

68. Santa Clara County Fruit Exchange, *How to Prepare Nature's Health Food*, 11.

69. The San Jose Mercury, *Sunshine Fruit and Flowers*, 22.

70. The San Jose Mercury, *Sunshine Fruit and Flowers*, 22–24.

71. San Jose Chamber of Commerce, *Santa Clara County California*, 3.

72. The San Jose Mercury, *Sunshine Fruit and Flowers*, 232.

73. Irvine, *Santa Clara County California*.

74. The San Jose Mercury, *Sunshine Fruit and Flowers*, 32.

75. The San Jose Mercury, *Sunshine Fruit and Flowers*., 34.

76. The San Jose Mercury, *Sunshine Fruit and Flowers*, 35.

77. Oravec, "To Stand Outside Oneself," 64.

78. Spencer Winthrop, "The Spirit of Santa Clara Valley," *Overland Monthly* 54, no. 3 (1909): 315.

79. J. J. Owen, *Santa Clara Valley: Its Resources, Climate, Productions, River and Railroad Systems, Towns and Cities, Public Institutions and General Advantages as a Place of Residence with Pen-Sketches of Prominent Citizens* (San Jose, CA: Mercury, 1873).

80. Chapman, *California Apricots*, 69.

81. H. S. Foote and C. A. Woolfolk, *Picturesque San Jose and Environments* (San Jose, CA: Hulbert Brothers and Company, 1893), 3; Belden, *Santa Clara County, California*, 7.

82. W. S. Thorne, *Santa Clara County, California* [brochure] (San Jose, CA: Board of Trade of San Jose, 1887), 60.

83. San Jose Chamber of Commerce, *The Valley of Heart's Delight*.

84. Harrison, *Central California, Santa Clara Valley*, 11.

85. Thorne, *Santa Clara County, California*, 71.

86. Thorne, *Santa Clara County, California*, 71.

87. E. T. Brown and E. H. Overstreet, eds., *The San Jose Daily Herald Souvenir Publication: Horticulture, Viticulture, Agriculture: The Railroads, Manufacturing, Financial, Commercial, and Professional Representative Firms of Santa Clara County, California* [brochure] (San Jose, CA: San Jose Daily Herald, 1890), 1.

88. Harrison, *Central California, Santa Clara Valley*, 8.

89. San Jose Chamber of Commerce, *San Jose (San Hosay)*, 14–18.

90. Steven Stoll, *The Fruits of Natural Advantage: Making the Industrial Countryside in California* (Berkeley: University of California Press, 1998), 85.

91. William Braznell, *California's Finest: The History of the Del Monte Corporation and the Del Monte Brand* (San Francisco: Del Monte Corporation, 1982), 49.

92. Braznell, *California's Finest*, 49.

93. *Orchard and Farm*, "Fruit Growers and the Parcel Post; A Questionable Law," March 1910, 9.

94. KTEH, *The Valley That Was*, documentary film clip, Part 1 3:43, YouTube, 2011, https://www.youtube.com/watch?v=CMAdLRIlSGo.

95. Thomas Derdak, "Del Monte Foods," in *International Directory of Company Histories*, ed. Jay Pederson (Ann Arbor, MI: St. James Press, 1998).

96. Stoll, *The Fruits of Natural Advantage*, 85.

97. Stoll, *The Fruits of Natural Advantage*, 85.

98. Stoll, *The Fruits of Natural Advantage*, 85.

99. Tom Spellman, "The Citrus Label Era (1887–1955)," *Citrograph*, July–August 2011.

100. History San Jose, *Label Legacy: The Muirson Label Comapny*, https://historysanjose.org/exhibits-activities/online-exhibits/label-legacy-muirson-label-company-san-jose-calif/.

101. History San Jose, "People: Ralph Rambo," in *Label Legacy: The Muirson Label Comapny*, https://historysanjose.org/exhibits-activities/online-exhibits/label-legacy-muirson-label-company-san-jose-calif/.

102. History San Jose, "People: Ralph Rambo."

103. Nicole Porter, "'Single-Minded, Compelling, and unique': Visual Communications, Landscape, and the Calculated Aesthetic of Place Branding," *Environmental Communication* 7, no. 2 (June 1, 2013): 232.

104. Downey, *Voices from the Orchards*, 19.

105. Chapman, *California Apricots*, 91.

106. Downey, *Voices from the Orchards*, 19.

107. Downey, *Voices from the Orchards*, 19.

108. Chapman, *California Apricots*.

109. Chapman, *California Apricots*.

110. Cookie Curci, "Commentary: Early Residents of Santa Clara Valley Remember the Orchards and Canneries," *San Jose Mercury News*, June 28, 2012, https://www.mercurynews.com/2012/06/28/commentary-early-residents-of-santa-clara-valley-remember-the-orchards-and-canneries/.

111. Juliet Eilperin and Darryl Fears, "Deadly Air Pollutant 'Disproportionately and Systematically' Harms Americans of Color, Study Finds," *Washington Post*,

April 28, 2021, https://www.washingtonpost.com/climate-environment/2021/04
/28/environmental-justice-pollution/; Meredith Fowlie, Reed Walker, and David
Wooley, *Climate Policy, Environmental Justice, and Local Air Pollution* (Washington, DC: Brookings Institution, October 20, 2020), https://www.brookings
.edu/research/climate-policy-environmental-justice-and-local-air-pollution/; Marie
Lynn Miranda et al., "Making the Environmental Justice Grade: The Relative
Burden of Air Pollution Exposure in the United States," *International Journal of
Environmental Research and Public Health* 8 (2011).

113. Foote and Woolfolk, *Picturesque San Jose and Environments*, 13.

113. San Jose Chamber of Commerce, *Santa Clara County California*, 4.

114. Kevin Fish, "Organization for Water—Rise of Economic and Political
Interests," in *Water in the Santa Clara Valley: A History*, ed. Seonaid McArthur
(Cupertino: California History Center, 1981), 40.

115. Fish, "Organization for Water," 26.

116. Fish, "Organization for Water," 26–27.

117. Matthews, *Silicon Valley, Women, and the California Dream*, 37.

118. S. E. Ingebritsen and David R. Jones, "Santa Clara County, California: A
Case of Arrested Subsidence," in *Land Subsidence in the United States*, ed. Devin L.
Galloway, David Richard Jones, and S. E. Ingebritsen (Reston, VA: US Geological
Survey, 1999).

119. Ingebritsen and Jones, "Santa Clara County, California."

120. Ingebritsen and Jones, "Santa Clara County, California."

121. Matthews, *Silicon Valley, Women, and the California Dream*.

122. Brown, Caldwell, and Norgaard, *San Jose Sewage Treatment Study*, 143.

123. Ingebritsen and Jones, "Santa Clara County, California."

124. Marian J. Neal et al., "The Social-Environmental Justice of Groundwater
Governance," in *Integrated Groundwater Management: Concepts, Approaches and
Challenges*, ed. Anthony J. Jakeman et al. (Cham, Switzerland: Springer International Publishing, 2016); Amy Vanderwarker, "Water and Environmental Justice,"
in *A Twenty-First Century U.S. Water Policy*, ed. Juliet Christian-Smith and
Peter H. Gleick (Oakland, CA: Pacific Institute, 2013); Laurel A. Schaider et al.,
"Environmental Justice and Drinking Water Quality: Are There Socioeconomic
Disparities in Nitrate Levels in U.S. Drinking Water?," *Enviromental Health* 18,
no. 3 (2019), https://doi.org/10.1186/s12940-018-0442-6.

125. Brian Melley, "Sierra Club Apologizes for Founder John Muir's Racist
Views," AP News, July 22, 2020, https://apnews.com/article/national-parks-us
-news-parks-environment-ca-state-wire-c52ccd3ac1c127289cf5b1a5c0dc070d.

CHAPTER 2. PRUNE PICKERS AND 'COT CUTTERS

1. *Sacramento Daily Union*, "Railroad and Boat Timetable for Sacramento,",
March 14, 1874, https://cdnc.ucr.edu/?a=d&d=SDU18740314.2.43&e=-------en
--20--1--txt-txIN--------1.

2. "Brownell Biography Entries," Historical California Stone Carvers, Stone Cutters, & Monument Dealers, Quarries and Byond, updated January 13, 2012, https://quarriesandbeyond.org/states/ca/ca-stone_carvers/b-5_brownell_bios .html.

3. Winifred Wool Hendrix, Recollections, February 8 1956, Wool Family Collection, San Jose.

4. Harrison, *Central California, Santa Clara Valley*, 17.

5. Hendrix, Recollections, 2.

6. Frederick Austin Wool Sr., Memories of Frederick Austin Wool Sr., 1989/1999, Wool Family Collection.

7. Hendrix, Recollections, 3; Wool Family, Interview with Anne Marie Todd, February 13, 2016.

8. Hendrix, Recollections, 4.

9. Matthews, *Silicon Valley, Women, and the California Dream*, 27.

10. J. M. Guinn, *History of the State of California and Biographical Record of Coast Counties, California*, trans. Louise E. Shoemaker (Chicago: Chapman Publishing Company, 1904).

11. Guinn, *History of the State of California and Biographical Record*.

12. Michael Woods et al., "Rural People and the Land," in *Making Sense of Place: Multidisciplinary Perspectives*, ed. Ian Convery, Gerard Corsane, and Peter Davis (Woodbridge, UK: Boydell & Brewer, 2012), 62.

13. Curci, "Commentary: Early Residents of Santa Clara Valley."

14. Arto Haapala, "The Everyday, Building, and Architecture: Reflections on the Ethos and Beauty of Our Built Surroundings," *Cloud-Cuckoo-Land: International Journal of Architectural Theory* 22 (2017): 172.

15. Paliewicz, "The Country, the City, and the Corporation," 747.

16. Paliewicz, "The Country, the City, and the Corporation," 748.

17. San Jose Chamber of Commerce, *Valley of Heart's Delight*, 1948, 3:30.

18. San Jose Chamber of Commerce, *Valley of Heart's Delight*, 4:00.

19. San Jose Chamber of Commerce, *Valley of Heart's Delight*, 0:35.

20. San Jose Chamber of Commerce, *Valley of Heart's Delight*, 3:45.

21. Douglas Cazaux Sackman, *Orange Empire* (Berkeley: University of California Press, 2005), 236.

22. Taylor Brothers Farms, "FAQ: What Is a Prune?," https://www.taylor brothersfarms.com/pages/faq.

23. Rudy Calles, *Champion Prune Pickers: Migrant Worker's Dilemma* (Los Alamitos, CA: Hwong Publishing Company, 1979), v.

24. Matthews, "A California Middletown," 45.

25. Pellow and Park, *The Silicon Valley of Dreams*, 49.

26. Calles, *Champion Prune Pickers'*, 59.

27. Calles, *Champion Prune Pickers'*, viii.

28. Garrod, *Gulchin' Out*, 101.

29. Garrod, *Gulchin' Out*, 101; Pellow and Park, *The Silicon Valley of Dreams*, 50–51.

30. Curci, "Commentary: Early Residents of Santa Clara Valley."

31. Anthony J. Zerbo quoted in Downey, *Voices from the Orchards*, 68–69.

32. Garrod, *Gulchin' Out*, 100.

33. Debbie S. Dougherty, *The Reluctant Farmer: An Exploration of Work, Social Class, and the Production of Food*, ed. Omar Swartz (Leicester, UK: Troubador, 2011), 201.

34. Garrod, *Gulchin' Out*, 100.

35. Dougherty, *The Reluctant Farmer*, 201.

36. Andy Mariani, interview.

37. Anthony J. Zerbo quoted in Downey, *Voices from the Orchards*, 68–69.

38. Juan Manual Herrera quoted in Downey, *Voices from the Orchards*, 65.

39. Garrod, Emma Stolte. *One Life, Mine* (Bloomington, IN: Xlibris, 2012), 42.

40. Garrod, Vince S. *Gulchin' Out* (Bloomington, IN: Xlibris, 2013), 83.

41. Frank Preglascio quoted in Downey, 1997, 82.

42. Calles, *Champion Prune Pickers*, 69.

43. Creswell, "Place," 7.

44. Samantha Senda-Cook, "Rugged Practices: Embodying Authenticity in Outdoor Recreation," *Quarterly Journal of Speech* 98 (2013): 131.

45. Tim Stanley, *The Last of the Prune Pickers: A Pre-Silicon Valley Story* (Irvine, CA: Timothy Publishing, 2009), 133–34.

46. Gerrye Kee Wong quoted in Downey, *Voices from the Orchards*, 59.

47. Dorena Berryessa Penner quoted in Downey, *Voices from the Orchards*, 41.

48. Leslie Rose Takamoto quoted in Downey, *Voices from the Orchards*, 51.

49. Calles, *Champion Prune Pickers*, 47.

50. Dorena Berressa Penner quoted in Downey, *Voices from the Orchards*, 41.

51. Dougherty, *The Reluctant Farmer*, 19.

52. Downey, *Voices from the Orchards*, 49.

53. Calles, *Champion Prune Pickers*, 47.

54. Calles, *Champion Prune Pickers*, vii.

55. Stanley, *The Last of the Prune Pickers*, 133–34.

56. Garrod, *Gulchin' Out*, 96.

57. Margaret Martins Rendler quoted in Downey, *Voices from the Orchards*, 52.

58. Carol Beddo quoted in Downey, *Voices from the Orchards*, 76.

59. Gerrye Kee Wong quoted in Downey, *Voices from the Orchards*, 59.

60. Leslie Rose Takamoto quoted in Downey, *Voices from the Orchards*, 51.

61. History San Jose, "California Fruit Canners Assn.," in *Cannery Life: Del Monte in the Santa Clara Valley* (San Jose, CA: History San Jose, 2018), https://historysanjose.org/exhibits-activities/online-exhibits/cannery-life-del-monte-in-the-santa-clara-valley/.

62. History San Jose, "Plant Number 3 on Auzerais Ave.," in *Cannery Life: Del Monte in the Santa Clara Valley*, 2018, https://historysanjose.org/exhibits-activities/online-exhibits/cannery-life-del-monte-in-the-santa-clara-valley/.

63. History San Jose, "Plant Number 3 on Auzerais Ave."

64. "California Packing Corporation," in *Cannery Life: Del Monte in the Santa Clara Valley*, 2018, https://historysanjose.org/exhibits-activities/online-exhibits/cannery-life-del-monte-in-the-santa-clara-valley/.

65. History San Jose, "California Packing Corporation."

66. Todd Holmes, "Farmer's Market: Agribusiness and the Agrarian Imaginary in California and the Far West," *California History* 90, no. 2 (2013).

67. Zavella, *Women's Work and Chicano Families*, 51.

68. Ruiz, *Cannery Women Cannery Lives*, 24.

69. McBane, "Santa Clara Valley Women Cannery Workers," 4.

70. McBane, "Santa Clara Valley Women Cannery Workers," 6.

71. Ruiz, *Cannery Women Cannery Lives*, 15.

72. McBane, "Santa Clara Valley Women Cannery Workers," 6.

73. Jacobson, *Passing Farms*, 226.

74. Stephanie Statz, "California's Fruit Cocktail: A History of Industrial Food Production, the State, and the Environment of Northern California" (PhD diss., University of Houston, 2012), 85.

75. Statz, "California's Fruit Cocktail," 81–82.

76. McBane, "Santa Clara Valley Women Cannery Workers," 6.

77. Matthews, "A California Middletown," 47.

78. Statz, "California's Fruit Cocktail," 81–82.

79. Braznell, *California's Finest*, 59.

80. "Anderson Prune Dipper Company," Packing Houses of Santa Clara County, updated January 1, 2017, http://vasonabranch.com/packing_houses/index.php?title=Anderson_Prune_Dipper_Company.

81. The American Society of Mechanical Engineers, "The FMC Rotary Pressure Sterilizer, Introduced in 1920: An International Historic Mechanical Engineering Landmark," ASME Historic Engineering Landmark Program, 1982, 7, https://docplayer.net/13625337-The-fmc-rotary-pressure-sterilizer-introduced-in-1920-an-international-historic-mechanical-engineering-landmark.html.

82. "Anderson Prune Dipper Company."

83. The American Society of Mechanical Engineers, "The FMC Rotary Pressure Sterilizer," 7.

84. *Invention & Technology*, "FMC Sterilizer," Winter 2007, http://www.inventionandtech.com/content/fmc-sterilizer-0.

85. The American Society of Mechanical Engineers, The FMC Rotary Pressure Sterilizer, 3–6.

86. Jacobson, *Passing Farms, Enduring Values*, 225.

87. Jacobson, *Passing Farms, Enduring Values*; Stephen M. Payne, *Santa Clara County: Harvest of Change* (Northridge, CA: Windsor Publications, Inc., 1987), 145–46.

88. Robert James Claus, "The Fruit and Vegetable Canning Industry in the Santa Clara Valley" (master's thesis, San Jose State University, 1966), 46–47.

89. Wool Family, interview.

90. Zetterquist and Melehan, interview.

91. Wool Family, interview.

92. Zavella, *Women's Work and Chicano Families*, 34.

93. *Canning Age*, "Canning Peaches in Santa Clara Valley," August, 1921, 1.

94. Zavella, *Women's Work and Chicano Families*, 102.

95. Statz, "California's Fruit Cocktail," 81–82.

96. Zavella, *Women's Work and Chicano Families*, 103.

97. *Canning Age*, "Canning Peaches in Santa Clara Valley," 1.

98. Zavella, *Women's Work and Chicano Families*, 101.

99. Jennifer Wool and Bruce Wool, Interview with Anne Marie Todd, October 21, 2018.

100. Zetterquist and Melehan, interview.

101. Zetterquist and Melehan, interview.

102. Joan Jackson, "Cannery Season Can Be Life Long," *San Jose Mercury News*, August 11, 1974, 6S.

103. Zavella, *Women's Work and Chicano Families*, 104.

104. Zavella, *Women's Work and Chicano Families*, 102.

105. Zavella, *Women's Work and Chicano Families*, 104–5.

106. Zavella, *Women's Work and Chicano Families*, 104.

107. Margaret Martins Rendler quoted in Downey, *Voices from the Orchards*, 45.

108. Margaret Martins Rendler quoted in Downey, *Voices from the Orchards*, 45.

109. Matthews, "A California Middletown," 47.

110. Ruiz, *Cannery Women Cannery Lives*, 36.

111. Ruiz, *Cannery Women Cannery Lives*, 36.

112. McBane, "Santa Clara Valley Women Cannery Workers," 6.

113. Matthews, "A California Middletown," 47–48; McBane, "Santa Clara Valley Women Cannery Workers," 6.

114. Margaret Martins Rendler quoted in Downey, *Voices from the Orchards*, 45.

115. Matthews, "A California Middletown," 47–48.

116. Ruiz, *Cannery Women Cannery Lives*, 33.

117. Zetterquist and Melehan, interview.

118. Zavella, *Women's Work and Chicano Families*, 102.

119. Wool Family, interview.

120. Jackson, "Cannery Season Can Be Life Long," 6S.

121. Zetterquist and Melehan, interview.

122. Calles, *Champion Prune Pickers*.

123. Ruiz, *Cannery Women Cannery Lives*, 72.

124. Ruiz, *Cannery Women Cannery Lives*, 72.

125. Ruiz, *Cannery Women Cannery Lives*, 72.

126. Zavella, *Women's Work and Chicano Families*, 38.

127. Zavella, *Women's Work and Chicano Families*, 105.

128. Matthews, "A California Middletown," 48.

129. Clarke A. Chambers, *California Farm Organizations: A Historical Study of the Grange, the Farm Bureau, and the Associated Farmers, 1929–1941* (Berkeley: University of California Press, 1952), 5.

130. David Vaught, *Cultivating California: Growers, Specialty Crops, and Labor, 1875–1920* (Baltimore, MD: Johns Hopkins University Press, 1999); Carey McWilliams, *Factories in the Field: The Story of Migratory Farm Labor in California* (Berkeley, California: University of California Press, 1939).

131. Cletus E. Daniel, *Bitter Harvest: A History of California Farmworkers, 1870–1941* (Berkeley: University of California Press, 1982), 72.

132. Chambers, *California Farm Organizations*, 31.

133. Tarla Rai Peterson, "Telling the Farmers' Story: Competing Responses to Soil Conservation Rhetoric," *Quarterly Journal of Speech* 77 (1991): 289.

134. Chambers, *California Farm Organizations*, 5.

135. Daniel, *Bitter Harvest*, 72.

136. Pellow and Park, *The Silicon Valley of Dreams*, 49.

137. Kate Brofenbrenner, "California Farmworkers' Strikes of 1933," in *Labor Conflict in the United States: An Encyclopedia*, ed. R. L. Filippelli (New York: Garland Publishing, Inc., 1990), 80.

138. Brofenbrenner, "California Farmworkers' Strikes of 1933," 79.

139. Brofenbrenner, "California Farmworkers' Strikes of 1933," 80.

140. Herbert W. Free, "California Apricot Growers Union" (master's thesis, University of California, 1941), 38.

141. Glenna Matthews, "The Apricot War: A Study of the Changing Fruit Industry during the 1930s," *Agricultural History* 59, no. 1 (January 1985): 34.

142. Glenna Matthews, "The Fruit Workers of the Santa Clara Valley: Alternative Paths to Union Organization during the 1930s," *Pacific Historical Review* 54, no. 1 (February 1985): 57.

143. California Farm Bureau, "'It Is Time to Do Something about It.'"

144. Chambers, *California Farm Organizations*, 6.

145. Jacobson, *Passing Farms, Enduring Values*, 226.

146. Daniel, *Bitter Harvest*, 39.

147. Creswell, "Place," 1.

148. Jacobson, *Passing Farms, Enduring Values*, 231.

149. Garrod, *Gulchin' Out*, 103.

150. Garrod, *Gulchin' Out*, 103.

151. Dominic Cirone quoted in Downey, *Voices from the Orchards*, 28.

152. April Lynch, "Valley's Hidden Pesticide Risk," *San Jose Mercury News*, October 18, 2007, https://www.mercurynews.com/2007/10/18/valleys-hidden-pesticide-risk/.

153. See, for example, Christos A. Damalas and Spyridon D. Koutroubas, "Farmers' Exposure to Pesticides: Toxicity Types and Ways of Prevention," *Toxics* 4, no. 1 (2016), https://www.ncbi.nlm.nih.gov/pmc/articles/PMC5606636/; Srishti Shrestha et al., "High Pesticide Exposure Events and Olfactory Impairment among

U.S. Farmers," *Environmental Health Perspectives* 127, no. 1 (2019), https://ehp.niehs .nih.gov/doi/10.1289/ehp3713; Christos A. Damalas and Ilias G. Eleftherohorinos, "Pesticide Exposure, Safety Issues, and Risk Assessment Indicators," *International Journal of Environmental Research and Public Health* 8, no. 4 (2011), https://www .ncbi.nlm.nih.gov/pmc/articles/PMC3108117/.

154. Calles, *Champion Prune Pickers*, 75.

155. Calles, *Champion Prune Pickers*, 75.

156. Lynch, "Valley's Hidden Pesticide Risk."

157. Garrod, *Gulchin' Out*, 103.

158. Jill Lindsey Harrison, *Pesticide Drift and the Pursuit of Environmental Justice* (Cambridge, MA: MIT Press, 2011); Joan D. Flocks, "The Environmental and Social Injustice of Farmworker Pesticide Exposure," *Georgetown Journal on Poverty Law and Policy* 19, no. 2 (2012); David B. Donald et al., "Agricultural Pesticides Threaten the Ecological Integrity of Northern Prairie Wetlands," *Science of the Total Environment* 231, no. 2 (1999/07/01/ 1999), https://doi.org/https://doi.org/10 .1016/S0048-9697(99)00091-1, https://www.sciencedirect.com/science/article/pii /S0048969799000911.

159. Leonard McKay, "Dutch Hamman Part 1," *San Jose Inside*, January 16 2006, http://www.sanJoseinside.com/2006/01/16/dutch_hamann/.

160. Pellow and Park, *The Silicon Valley of Dreams*, 55.

161. Pellow and Park, *The Silicon Valley of Dreams*, 56.

162. City Planning Commission, *San Jose: Design for Tomorrow* (San Jose, CA, 1961), 47.

163. Brown et al., *San Jose Sewage Treatment Study*,142.

164. Jim Larimore, "Valley Losing Its No. 1 Position," *San Jose Mercury News*, January 28, 1968.

165. San Jose Mercury News, "S.J. Increases Sewer Fees," March 3, 1976, 29.

166. Pellow and Park, *The Silicon Valley of Dreams*, 56.

167. Marita Hernandez, "Orchards Long Gone, Valley Canneries Still Big Industry," *San Jose Mercury News*, August 15, 1977.

168. Jack Sirica, "Sealing the Fate of a Dying Trade," *San Jose Mercury*, August 22, 1982.

169. Sirica, "Sealing the Fate of a Dying Trade."

170. Storey, "Land, Territory and Identity," 12.

171. Storey, "Land, Territory and Identity," 12.

172. Jeff Motter and Ross Singer, "Review Essay: Cultivating a Rhetoric of Agrarianism," *Quarterly Journal of Speech* 98, no. 4 (2012): 446.

173. Motter and Singer, "Review Essay: Cultivating a Rhetoric of Agrarianism," 446.

174. Edward S. Casey, *Remembering: A Phenomological Study* (Bloomington: Indiana University Press, 1987), 182.

175. Dougherty, *The Reluctant Farmer*, 198–99.

176. Dougherty, *The Reluctant Farmer*, 201–2.

177. Zavella, *Women's Work and Chicano Families*; Ruiz, *Cannery Women Cannery Lives*.

CHAPTER 3. FROM FARMLAND TO METROPOLIS

1. History San Jose, "Welcome Key to San Jose," 2017, http://historysanjose.org /wp/welcome-key-to-san-jose/.

2. IBM, "San Jose Card Plant," IBM Archives, 2018, https://www.ibm.com/ibm /history/exhibits/supplies/supplies_5404PH06.html.

3. Harry McCracken, "IBM Goes West: A 73-Year-Long Saga, from Punch Cards to Watson, *Fast Company*, October 28, 2016. https://www.fastcompany.com /3064902/ibm-goes-west-a-73-year-long-saga-from-punch-cards-to-watson.

4. Philip J. Trounstine and Terry Christensen, *Movers and Shakers: The Study of Community Power* (New York: St. Martin's Press, 1982), 86.

5. Glenna Matthews, "The Los Angeles of the North: San Jose's Transition from Fruit Capital to High-Tech Metropolis." *Journal of Urban History* 25, no. 4 (May 1999): 461.

6. Trounstine and Christensen, *Movers and Shakers*, 87.

7. Matthews, "The Los Angeles of the North."

8. Trounstine and Christensen, *Movers and Shakers*, 87; Stanford Environmental Law Society, *San José: Sprawling City: A Study of the Causes and Effects of Urban Sprawl, in San José, California* (Stanford, CA: Stanford Environmental Law Society, 1971), 16.

9. *Gilroy Dispatch*, "San Jose Chamber of Commerce Opens Big Campaign for New Industry with Magazine Advertising," November 8, 1943.

10. Harrison, *Central California, Santa Clara Valley*, 142.

11. Stanley, *The Last of the Prune Pickers*, 107.

12. Conrad, "The Conservation of Local Autonomy," 119.

13. Matthews, "The Los Angeles of the North,"461.

14. *San Francisco Examiner*, "San Jose Chamber of Commerce Lures 2000 Industries," March 8, 1953.

15. Stokowski, "Languages of Place and Discourses of Power," 36.

16. *San Jose News*, "'City That Dutch Built' Salutes Its A. P. Hamann," Special A. P. Hamann Edition, November 21, 1969; Scott Herhold, "San Jose Moves to Correct Hamann Legacy," *San Jose Mercury News*, April 13, 1987, 1B.

17. Trounstine and Christensen, *Movers and Shakers*, 89.

18. Leonard McKay, "Dutch Hamann, Part 2," *San Jose Inside*, January 23, 2006, http://www.sanjoseinside.com/2006/01/23/dutch_hamann1/.

19. Matthews, "The Los Angeles of the North,"461.

20. Conrad, "The Conservation of Local Autonomy."

21. Conrad, "The Conservation of Local Autonomy," 127.

22. *San Jose Mercury*, "300,000 in SJ within 18 Months," August 24, 1961.

23. Conrad, "The Conservation of Local Autonomy," 127.

24. Conrad, "The Conservation of Local Autonomy," 127.

25. Norman Bowman, "Over 10,000 New Homes in a Year," *San Jose Mercury News*, December 29, 1958.

26. Sunnyvale Chamber of Commerce, *Sunnyvale, U.S.A: The City with the Built in Future* (Sunnyvale, CA: Sunnyvale Chamber of Commerce, 1955).

27. Opportunities for development and settlement were foreclosed for one group of residents returning to the Santa Clara Valley after the war. Executive Order 9066 authorized internment of citizen and noncitizen residents of Japanese ancestry, which affected the more than 1,152 Japanese Americans who called the Santa Clara Valley home, of whom 882 worked in agriculture. As Japanese residents were preparing to be deported to internment camps, the Wartime Civil Control Administration sought non-Japanese growers to assume stewardship of Japanese farms. Many Japanese-Americans attempted to make private arrangements in hopes of securing their farms for their hoped return. After the war, Japanese farmers faced often insurmountable economic losses. Japanese farmers returned to find "their homes and barns were ransacked . . . their fields were covered with weeds." Most Japanese farmers, even those who owned their land, were unable to reclaim land they had "leased or otherwise entrusted to neighbors." In many cases, those who committed to safeguard the land were later unwilling to part with lucrative farms, "often going through deceitful means to prevent returning Japanese from reclaiming their land." The war had "transformed the valley's economy, making the pre-war Japanese farming community obsolete.". See Timothy J. Lukes and Gary Y. Okihiro, *Japanese Legacy: Farming and Community Life in California's Santa Clara Valley* vol. 31, Local History Studies (Cuptertino: California History Center, DeAnza College, 1985), 118; and *Mercury Herald*, "Tenants for Lands Vacated by Japanese Sought by WCCA Here," April 2, 1942.

28. Scott Herhold, "How San Jose Grew in a Topsy Turvy Way," *San Jose Mercury News*, August 12, 2015, https://www.mercurynews.com/2015/08/12/herhold-how-san-Jose-grew-in-a-topsy-turvy-way/.

29. Herhold, "How San Jose Grew in a Topsy Turvy Way."

30. Herhold, "San Jose Moves to Correct Hamann Legacy," 1B/3B.

31. Joanne Grant, "S.J. Recall Effort in '64 Only a Dim Memory," *San Jose Mercury News*, April 4, 1994.

32. Trounstine and Christensen, *Movers and Shakers*, 124.

33. Trounstine and Christensen, *Movers and Shakers*, 96.

34. Mary Jo Ignoffo, "A Change of Seasons," in *Reflections of the Past: An Anthology of San Jose*, ed. Judith Henderson (Encinatas, CA: Heritage Media Corporation, 1996), 186.

35. Downie, *The Santa Clara Valley's Appointment with Destiny*, 11; Dennis Rockstroh, "San Jose Secret—until Now," *Dennis Rockstroh's California*, June 11, 2013, https://drockstroh.wordpress.com/2013/06/11/san-jose-secret-until-now/.

36. Downie, *The Santa Clara Valley's Appointment with Destiny*.

37. Herhold, "How San Jose Grew in a Topsy Turvy Way."

38. History San Jose, "The *Mercury News* Changes Along with San Jose," 750 Ridder Park Drive: Documenting the Former Headquarters of the Mercury News, 2016, http://mercurynews.historysanjose.org/750-ridder-park-drive-the-mercury -news-changes-along-with-san-jose/.

39. Stanley, *The Last of the Prune Pickers*, 107–8.

40. Matthews, "The Los Angeles of the North," 461.

41. Herhold, "How San Jose Grew in a Topsy Turvy Way."

42. Paul Rogers, "Hamann: San Jose's Growth Guru," *San Jose Mercury News*, February 28, 2002, https://web.archive.org/web/20050223144311/http://www .siliconvalley.com/mld/siliconvalley/living/2765036.htm; McKay, "Dutch Hamman Part 1."

43. Stanley, *The Last of the Prune Pickers*, 107–8.

44. Matthews, "The Los Angeles of the North," 465.

45. Jacobson, *Passing Farms, Enduring Values*, 235.

46. Cortese, interview.

47. Ignoffo, "A Change of Seasons," 183.

48. Ignoffo, "A Change of Seasons," 183.

49. Trounstine and Christensen, *Movers and Shakers*, 93.

50. Stanford Environmental Law Society, *San José: Sprawling City*, 5; *Business Week*, "Correcting San Jose's Boomtime Mistake," September 19, 1970, 74.

51. Downie, *The Santa Clara Valley's Appointment with Destiny*, 13.

52. Matthews, "The Los Angeles of the North," 461.

53. Trounstine and Christensen, *Movers and Shakers*, 89.

54. *New York Times*, "Joseph B. Ridder, 68, Publisher in San Jose," January 26, 1989, https://www.nytimes.com/1989/01/26/obituaries/joseph-b-ridder -68-publisher-in-san-jose.html.

55. Stanford Environmental Law Society, *San José: Sprawling City*, 17; Reinhardt, "Joe Ridder's San Jose," 68.

56. San Jose Newspaper Guild, *4th Annual Gridiron Dinner Program*, San Jose Newspaper Guild, April 30, 1955, 1. California History Center Silicon Valley History Online, De Anza College, California History Center, https://calisphere.org /item/ark:/13030/kt0779p8zg/.

57. San Jose Newspaper Guild, *4th Annual Gridiron Dinner Program*, 1.

58. Willys I. Peck, *Saratoga Stereoopticon: A Magic Lantern of Memory* (Cupertino: California History Center and Foundation, 1997), 14.

59. *San Jose Mercury News*, "City Grew by 7,200 Persons, 500 Acres," October 8, 1967.

60. *San Jose Mercury News*, "City Grew by 7,200 Persons," 3F.

61. Reinhardt, "Joe Ridder's San Jose," 46.

62. Philip Hamburger, "Notes for a Gazetteer," *New Yorker*, May 4, 1963, 148.

63. Trounstine and Christensen, *Movers and Shakers*, 93; Ignoffo, "A Change of Seasons," 183.

64. Downie, *The Santa Clara Valley's Appointment with Destiny*, 13.

65. *San Jose Mercury*, "San Jose Named All-America City," *San Jose Mercury*, March 16, 1961.

66. John Spalding, "San Jose's Growth Shaped by A. P. Hamann," *San Jose News*, March 29, 1977.

67. *San Jose News*, "'City That Dutch Built' Salutes Its A. P. Hamann."

68. *San Jose Mercury*, "From Farmland to Metropolis, Hamann Guided San Jose During Spectacular Boom,", March 24, 1977, 1C.

69. Hamburger, "Notes for a Gazetteer," 148.

70. San Jose Chamber of Commerce, *It's Happening Downtown San Jose* (San Jose: San Jose Chamber of Commerce, 1973), https://historysanjose.pastperfect online.com/library/901E8A31-218A-4208-9991-144394401980.

71. Downie, *The Santa Clara Valley's Appointment with Destiny*, 10.

72. Downie, *The Santa Clara Valley's Appointment with Destiny*, 10.

73. Downie, *The Santa Clara Valley's Appointment with Destiny*, 10.

74. Belser, "The Making of Slurban America," 8.

75. Jacobson, *Passing Farms, Enduring Values*, 231.

76. Jacobson, *Passing Farms, Enduring Values*, 233.

77. Belser, "The Making of Slurban America," 5–6.

78. Downie, *The Santa Clara Valley's Appointment with Destiny*, 9.

79. Robert C. Fellmeth, *Politics of Land: Ralph Nader's Study Group Report on Land Use in California* (New York: Grossman Publishers, 1973), 31, https://archive .org/details/politicsoflandra00fell.

80. Wallace Turner, "Idyllic Valley Now Urban Anthill, Planner Charges," *New York Times*, September 7, 1970, https://www.nytimes.com/1970/09/07/archives /idyllic-valley-now-urban-anthill-planner-charges-county-in.html.

81. John Hart, *Farming on the Edge: Saving Family Farms in Marin County, California* (Berkeley: University of California Press, 1991), 9.

82. San Jose Chamber of Commerce, *This Is San Jose* (San Jose, CA: San Jose Chamber of Commerce, 1977), https://historysanjose.pastperfectonline.com/library /6D4AF6E7-D0D0-42ED-A042-320187703217.

83. Edward A. Williams, *Open Space: The Choices before California; the Urban Metropolitan Open Space Study* (San Francisco: Diablo Press, 1969), 13. //catalog .hathitrust.org/Record/001322839.

http://hdl.handle.net/2027/mdp.39015007262333.

84. Motter and Singer, "Review Essay: Cultivating a Rhetoric of Agrarianism," 446.

85. *Sacramento Business Journal*, "Mariani Packing Co. Moves to Vacaville," Sepbemter 7, 2000, https://www.bizjournals.com/sacramento/stories/2000/09/04 /daily14.html.

86. Jacobson, *Passing Farms, Enduring Values*, 232.

87. Conrad, "The Conservation of Local Autonomy," 44.

88. Conrad, "The Conservation of Local Autonomy," 30.

89. Conrad, "The Conservation of Local Autonomy," 46.

90. Conrad, "The Conservation of Local Autonomy," 30.

91. Downie, *The Santa Clara Valley's Appointment with Destiny*, 11.

92. Fellmeth, *Politics of Land*, 369.

93. Downie, *The Santa Clara Valley's Appointment with Destiny*, 15.

94. Downie, *The Santa Clara Valley's Appointment with Destiny*, 15.

95. Downie, *The Santa Clara Valley's Appointment with Destiny*, 9.

96. Downie, *The Santa Clara Valley's Appointment with Destiny*, 9.

97. Belser, "The Making of Slurban America," 9.

98. Downie, *The Santa Clara Valley's Appointment with Destiny*, 11.

99. Conrad, "The Conservation of Local Autonomy," 117.

100. Belser, "The Making of Slurban America," 11.

101. Race M. Davies, *Preserving Agricultural and Open-Space Lands: Legislative Policymaking in California* (Davis: University of California, Institute of Governmental Affairs, 1972), 18, 384. https://digitalcommons.law.ggu.edu/cgi/viewcontent.cgi?article=1383&context=caldocs_agencies.

102. Robert Woolley, "Tracts Replacing Orchards," *San Francisco Chronicle*, March 13, 1955, 1.

103. Davies, *Preserving Agricultural and Open-Space Lands*.

104. Belser, "The Making of Slurban America," 11.

105. Fellmeth, *Politics of Land*, 374.

106. Conrad, "The Conservation of Local Autonomy," 114.

107. Davies, *Preserving Agricultural and Open-Space Lands*, 12.

108. Davies, *Preserving Agricultural and Open-Space Lands*, 74; California Assembly Subcommittee on Planning and Zoning, *State Greenbelt Legislation and the Problem of Urban Encroachment in California Agriculture*, Assembly Interim Committee Reports vol. 13, no. 14 (Sacramento: Assembly of the State of California, 1957).

109. Subcommittee on Planning and Zoning, "State Greenbelt Legislation and the Problem of Urban Encroachment on California Agriculture," *Journal of the Assembly of the State of California*, Sacramento, May 1957.

110. Subcommittee on Planning and Zoning, *Journal of the Assembly of the State of California*, 30.

111. Downie, *The Santa Clara Valley's Appointment with Destiny*, 10.

112. Stanford Environmental Law Society, *San José: Sprawling City*, 122.

113. Downie, *The Santa Clara Valley's Appointment with Destiny*, 11.

114. Downie, *The Santa Clara Valley's Appointment with Destiny*, 10.

115. Matthews, "The Los Angeles of the North," 465.

116. Turner, "Idyllic Valley Now Urban Anthill, Planner Charges."

117. Olson, interview.

118. Jacobson, *Passing Farms, Enduring Values*, 233.

119. Olson, interview.

120. Tom Philip, "Sign of Spring: Long-Lived Sunnyvale Orchard Faces Its Toughest Challenge," *San Jose Mercury News*, May 21, 1986.

121. Jacobson, *Passing Farms, Enduring Values*, ii.

122. Wallace Stegner, "The Frontier Spirit," *Span Magazine*, December 1981, 11–12.

123. Jacobson, *Passing Farms, Enduring Values*, 234.

124. *Sunnyvale Standard*, "Editorial," October 20, 1965.

125. Olson, interview.

126. Olson, interview.

127. David Kline, "The Embattled Family Farm," *This World*, December 13, 1981, 15.

128. Mike Lassiter, "End of an Era for Bay Area Farms," *San Francisco Examiner*, September 22, 1980.

129. *San Francisco Examiner*, "Let's Conserve the Vanishing Farmland," December 25, 1981.

130. Karl Belser, "The Planning Fiasco in California," *Cry California: The Journal of California Tomorrow* 2, no. 3 (Summer 1967): 10.

131. Fellmeth, *Politics of Land*, 383; Belser, "The Planning Fiasco in California," 13.

132. Karl Belser, "The Santa Clara Valley: A Case Study in Land Use, Rural vrs. Urban" (paper presented at the Natural Environment Studies, University California Berkeley, June 28, 1970), 4.

133. Matthews, "The Los Angeles of the North," 465.

134. Downie, *The Santa Clara Valley's Appointment with Destiny*, 20; Stanford Environmental Law Society, *San José: Sprawling City*; Belser, "The Making of Slurban America"; Fellmeth, *Politics of Land*.

135. Fellmeth, *Politics of Land*.

136. *Newsweek*, "Boom Town," September 14, 1970; Stanford Environmental Law Society, *San José: Sprawling City*, 2.

137. *Business Week*, "Correcting San Jose's Boomtime Mistake"; Stanford Environmental Law Society, *San José: Sprawling City*, 5.

138. Turner, "Idyllic Valley Now Urban Anthill, Planner Charges."

139. Belser, "The Santa Clara Valley," 6.

140. Downie, *The Santa Clara Valley's Appointment with Destiny*, 9.

141. Belser, "The Making of Slurban America," 2.

142. Barbara French, "Time Runs Out on Once-Thriving Pear Industry," *San Jose Mercury News*, January 24, 1978.

143. Dick Flood, "Bleak Summer for 'Cot Growers," *San Jose Mercury*, July 10, 1965, 21.

144. Downie, *The Santa Clara Valley's Appointment with Destiny*, 9.

145. French, "Time Runs Out on Once-Thriving Pear Industry."

146. Carroll, "How the Pears Got Bulldozed."

147. Carroll, "How the Pears Got Bulldozed."

148. Philip, "Sign of Spring."

149. Kirstin Downey, "Sunnyvale's Rural Oasis Urban Farm May Not Be Around Long," *San Jose Mercury News*, January 13, 1988.

150. Mike Cassidy, "Rain Was the Pits for Olson Orchard: Cherry Grower Suffers Huge Losses," *San Jose Mercury News*, May 30, 1990.

151. Dyan Chan, "Sunnyvale's Last Orchard Slated for Development," *Valley Journal*, May 1, 1991.

152. Mike Cassidy, "Olsons Know the Dirty Truth about Shrinking," *San Jose Mercury News*, May 8, 1994.

153. Guara, "Last Call for the Last Sunnyvale Orchard," A17.

154. Joyce Gemperlein, "For Growers, Life Can't Be Called a Bowl of Cherries," *San Jose Mercury News*, May 11, 1996.

155. Gemperlein, "For Growers, Life Can't Be Called a Bowl of Cherries."

156. Michael Cronk, "The Olsons' Last Stand Sunnyvale's Famed Cherrypicking Family May Be Calling It Quits After 60 Years of Offering Customers Fruit of Their Labors," *San Jose Mercury News*, March 31, 1997; Michael Cronk, "Target Won't Build at Sunnyvale Site of Cherry Orchard," *San Jose Mercury News*, July 24, 1997.

157. Carolyn Jung, "Cherries," *San Jose Mercury News*, April 21, 1999.

158. Cronk, "The Olsons' Last Stand."

159. Debby Morse, "Olson's Takes a Stand," *San Francisco Examiner*, July 9, 1999, https://www.sfgate.com/bayarea/article/Olson-s-takes-a-stand-3076897.php.

160. Charlie Olson, interview with Anne Marie Todd, March 10, 2016.

161. Jacobson, *Passing Farms, Enduring Values*, 231.

162. Belser, "The Making of Slurban America," 8.

163. Richards, *Silicon Valley*, 57.

164. Wool Family, interview.

165. Wool and Wool, interview.

166. Wool and Wool, interview.

167. Wool and Wool, interview.

168. Mariani, *Poverty of Affluence*, 100.

169. David Matsumoto, *Epitaph for a Peach: Four Seasons on My Family Farm* (San Francisco: HarperOne, 1996), ix–xii.

170. Robert Dawson and Gray Brechin, *Farewell, Promised Land: Waking from the California Dream* (Berkeley: University of California Press, 1999), 79; Matsumoto, *Epitaph for a Peach*, ix–xii.

171. Matsumoto, *Epitaph for a Peach*, ix–xii.

172. Hamburger, "Notes for a Gazetteer," 148.

173. Claus, "The Fruit and Vegetable Canning Industry in the Santa Clara Valley," 105.

174. Stanley, *The Last of the Prune Pickers*, 108.

175. Matthews, *Silicon Valley, Women, and the California Dream*, 137.

176. Hernandez, "Orchards Long Gone."

177. Hernandez, "Orchards Long Gone."

178. Creswell, *Place: An Introduction*, 74.

179. Wool Family, interview.

180. Julia Prodis Sulek, "Valley's Last Packing Plant for Dried Fruit Is Moving," *San Jose Mercury News*, April 24, 2001, 8a.

181. Torriero, "Fresh-Fruit Craze Puts Lid on Canneries."

182. Zavella, *Women's Work and Chicano Families*, 53.

183. Torriero, "Fresh-Fruit Craze Puts Lid on Canneries."

184. Wool Family, interview.

185. Payne, *Santa Clara County: Harvest of Change*, 98.

186. Zavella, *Women's Work and Chicano Families*, 164.

187. Torriero, "Fresh-Fruit Craze Puts Lid on Canneries."

188. Dick Cox, "There Was a Time When the Working Class Had Jobs," *San Jose Mercury News*, August 19, 1992.

189. Torriero, "Fresh-Fruit Craze Puts Lid on Canneries."

190. Maya Suryaraman, "Valley Packers Wither on the Vine," *San Jose Mercury News*, July 22, 1990.

191. Geoffrey Tomb, "As the Final Harvest Ends, a Tech Fortune Begins," *San Jose Mercury News*, December 18, 1999, 31A.

192. Tomb, "As the Final Harvest Ends, a Tech Fortune Begins," 31A.

193. Tomb, "As the Final Harvest Ends, a Tech Fortune Begins," 1.

194. Tomb, "As the Final Harvest Ends, a Tech Fortune Begins," 1.

195. Matthews, "A California Middletown," 34–36; San Jose Chamber of Commerce, *Valley of Heart's Delight*, film, at 0:15.

196. San Jose Chamber of Commerce, *Valley of Heart's Delight*, film, at 6:00.

197. San Jose Chamber of Commerce, *An Aerial View of Progressive, San Jose, Calif.* (San Jose, CA: San Jose Chamber of Commerce, 1952), https://historysanjose.pastperfectonline.com/archive/AFE7BA6A-1115-429B-9A96-807341316437.

198. *The Resident*, "It's Blossom Time again in Santa Clara Valley," March 31, 1953.

199. *San Jose News*, "1,000 Tour Blooming Valley," *San Jose News*, March 21, 1955; *San Jose News*, "99 Tour Blossom Land on 22 Busses," *San Jose News*, March 14, 1955.

200. Ignoffo, "A Change of Seasons," 186.

201. Stanford Environmental Law Society, *San José: Sprawling City*, 18–19.

202. Stanford Environmental Law Society, *San José: Sprawling City*, 18–19.

203. Carl Heintz, "Fruit Trees Displaced by Homes," *San Jose Mercury News*, March 26, 1953.

204. *San Jose Mercury*, "Booming, Blooming—That's Santa Clara County Now!," March 7, 1953.

205. *San Jose Mercury*, "Progress Edition," January 19, 1958; Matthews, "The Los Angeles of the North," 465.

206. Conrad, "The Conservation of Local Autonomy," 125.

207. Mark Mariani, interview.

208. Mark Mariani, interview.

209. Sunnyvale Historical Society and Museum Association, *Orchard Heritage Park* (Sunnyvale, CA: Sunnyvale Historical Society and Museum Association, 2001), 22.

210. Woods et al., "Rural People and the Land," 62.

211. Cindy M. Spurlock, "Performing and Sustaining (Agri)Culture and Place: The Cultivation of Environmental Subjectivity on the Piedmont Farm Tour," *Text and Performance Quarterly* 29, no. 1 (2009): 12.

212. Spurlock, "Performing and Sustaining (Agri)Culture and Place," 10.

213. Sunnyvale Historical Society and Museum Association, *Orchard Heritage Park*, 15.

CHAPTER 4. CONCLUSION

1. *Gilroy Dispatch*, "A Road Runs Through It," August 13, 2004, http://gilroy dispatch.com/2004/08/13/a-road-runs-through-it/.

2. *Gilroy Dispatch*, "A Road Runs Through It."

3. Andy Mariani, interview.

4. Susan Hathaway, "Andy's Orchard Maverick Orchardist Demystifies Heirloom Stone Fruit and Shares Tips for Selection," *Bay Area Bites*, KQED, July 15, 2014, https://www.kqed.org/bayareabites/84874/andys-orchard-maverick -orchardist-andy-mariani-demystifies-heirloom-stone-fruit-and-shares-tips-for -selection.

5. Melissa Hansen, "Flavor Reigns at Andy's Orchard," *Good Fruit Grower*, February 17, 2015. http://www.goodfruit.com/flavor-reigns-at-andys-orchard/.

6. David Karp, "Orchard of Dreams," *Gourmet*, July 2005, http://www.gourmet .com/magazine/2000s/2005/07/marianica16.html?printable=true&currentPage=2.

7. Rachel Myrow, "To Survive as a Fruit Farmer in Silicon Valley, You Need to Grow Tastier Fruit," *California Report*, KQED, June 24, 2018, https://www.kqed .org/news/11676561/to-survive-as-a-fruit-farmer-in-silicon-valley-you-need-to-grow -tastier-fruit.

8. Andy Mariani, interview.

9. Andy Mariani, interview.

10. Andy Mariani, interview.

11. Fellmeth, *Politics of Land*, 31.

12. Fellmeth, *Politics of Land*, 31.

13. Andy Mariani, interview.

14. Andy Mariani, interview.

15. Andy Mariani, interview.

16. Andy Mariani, interview.

17. Waters, "Cherry Condition."

18. Olson, interview.

19. Andy Mariani, interview.

20. Andy Mariani, interview.

21. Scott Budman, "Highway 101: The Tech Industry's Madison Avenue," NBC Bay Area, August 4, 2009, https://www.nbcbayarea.com/news/local/The-Tech -Industrys-Madison-Avenue-52443607.html.

22. Allison Arieff, "One Thing Silicon Valley Can't Seem to Fix," *New York Times*, July 9, 2017, Week in Review, 6.

23. Ashlee Vance, "36 Hours in Silicon Valley," *New York Times*, September 5, 2010, https://www.nytimes.com/2010/09/05/travel/05hours.html.

24. Trip Advisor, "Silicon Valley, California," 2019, https://www.tripadvisor.com/Attraction_Review-g28926-d142401-Reviews-Silicon_Valley-California.html.

25. Trip Advisor, "Silicon Valley, California."

26. Arieff, "One Thing Silicon Valley Can't Seem to Fix," 6.

27. Joshua Kwan, "How the Valley Found Its Future in the Chips Area's Generations of Bold Fortune-Seekers Have Turned Self-Confidence and Arrogance into a Tradition of Innovation and Success," *San Jose Mercury News*, June 10. 2001.

28. Relph, *Place and Placelessness*, preface.

29. Relph, *Place and Placelessness*.

30. Marc Augé, *Non-Places: Introduction to an Anthropology of Supermodernity*, trans. John Howe (London: Verso, 1995), 94.

31. Creswell, "Place," 6.

32. Paul Graham, "How to Be Silicon Valley," May 2006, http://www.paulgraham.com/siliconvalley.html.

33. Agnew, "Space and Place," 7–8.

34. Evelyn Nieves, "The Superfund Sites of Silicon Valley," *New York Times*, March 26. 2018, https://www.nytimes.com/2018/03/26/lens/the-superfund-sites-of-silicon-valley.html.

35. Dawson and Brechin, *Farewell, Promised Land*, 149; Bob Frost, "Norman Mailer," *West*, November 17, 1991.

36. Relph, *Place and Placelessness*, ii.

37. Creswell, "Place," 6.

38. Joshua Meyrowitz, *No Sense of Place: The Impact of Electronic Media on Social Behavior* (New York: Oxford University Press, 1985), 308.

39. Pellow and Park, *The Silicon Valley of Dreams*, 217.

40. Relph, *Place and Placelessness*, 87.

41. Relph, *Place and Placelessness*, 92.

42. Augé, *Non-Places*, 103–4.

43. Augé, *Non-Places*, 103–4.

44. Meyrowitz, *No Sense of Place*, 7.

45. Intel Corporation, *Don't Be Encumbered by Past History—Go Off and Do Something Wonderful*, Intel Museum, 1992, http://www.oac.cdlib.org/ark:/13030/kt8s2022mq/?order=1.

46. Daniel Harris, "What's in a Name? San Jose Needs to Know," *San Jose Mercury News*, February 22, 2017, https://www.mercurynews.com/2017/02/22/opinion-whats-in-a-name-san-jose-needs-to-know/.

47. Malpas, "New Media, Cultural Heritage and the Sense of Place," 198.

48. Relph, *Place and Placelessness*, 143.

49. Jan A. English-Lueck, *Cultures@Silicon Valley* (Stanford, CA: Stanford University Press, 2002), 179.

50. Thanks to Emily Schwing.

51. Creswell, "Place," 9.

52. Basso, "Wisdom Sits in Places," 83.

53. Arto Haapala, "Aesthetics, Ethics, and the Meaning of Place," *Filozofski vestnik* 20, no. 2 (1999): 262–63.

54. Stanford Environmental Law Society, *San José: Sprawling City*, 9.

55. Downie, *The Santa Clara Valley's Appointment with Destiny*, 1.

56. Downie, *The Santa Clara Valley's Appointment with Destiny*, 5.

57. Stanford Environmental Law Society, *San José: Sprawling City*, 9.

58. Stanford Environmental Law Society, *San José: Sprawling City*, 9.

59. Fellmeth, *Politics of Land*, 30.

60. Cantrill, "A Sense of Self-in-Place," 169.

61. Cantrill and Senecah, "Using the 'Sense of Self-in-Place' Construct," 185.

62. US Global Change Research Program, *National Climate Assessment*.

63. Ted Smith, David A. Sonnenfeld, and David Naguib Pellow, eds., *Challenging the Chip: Labor Rights and Environmental Justice in the Global Electronics Industry* (Philadelphia: Temple University Press, 2006); David N. Pellow, *Resisting Global Toxics: Transnational Movements for Environmental Justice* (Cambridge, MA: MIT Press, 2007); Lisa Sun-Hee Park and David N. Pellow, "Racial Formation, Environmental Racism, and the Emergence of Silicon Valley," *Ethnicities* 4, no. 3 (2004); Andrew Szasz and Michael Meuser, "Unintended, Inexorable: The Production of Environmental Inequalities in Santa Clara County, California," *American Behavioral Scientist* 43, no. 4 (2000); T. Smith, C. Wilmsen, and B.L.R.O. History, *Pioneer Activist for Environmental Justice in Silicon Valley, 1967–2000: Oral History Transcript/2003* (Charleston, SC: BiblioBazaar, 2016)..

64. Pellow and Park, *The Silicon Valley of Dreams*, 80.

65. Pellow and Park, *The Silicon Valley of Dreams*, 82.

66. Pitti, *The Devil in Silicon Valley*, 173.

67. Wool Family, interview.

68. Guara, "Last Call for the Last Sunnyvale Orchard," A17.

69. Basso, "Wisdom Sits in Places," 85.

70. Mark Mariani, interview.

71. Ralph Rambo, *Rembmer when . . . : A Boy's Eye View of an Old Valley* (San Jose, CA: The Rosicrucian Press, 1965), 9.

72. Creswell, "Place," 8.

73. Daniel D. Arreola, "Hispanic American Legacy, Latino American Diaspora," in *Hispanic Spaces, Latino Places: Community and Cultural Diversity in Contemporary America*, ed. Daniel D. Arreola (Austin: University of Texas Press, 2004), 34.

74. Katherine McKittrick, "On Plantations, Prisons, and a Black Sense of Place," *Social and Cultural Geography* 12, no. 8 (2011): 960.

75. Mark Mariani, interview.

76. Andy Mariani, interview.

77. Wool and Wool, interview.

78. Geoffrey Tomb, "Valley Once Was Ripe with Fruit, Nuts, Canneries," *San Jose Mercury News*, December 18, 1999, 31A.

79. Zetterquist and Melehan, interview.

80. Jacobson, *Passing Farms, Enduring Values*, 230.

81. Jacobson, *Passing Farms, Enduring Values*, 189.

82. Carbaugh, "Naturalizing Communication and Culture."

83. Cantrill and Senecah, "Using the 'Sense of Self-in-Place' Construct."

84. Creswell, *Place*, 85.

85. Wallace Stegner, "Forward," in *Passing Farms, Enduring Values: California's Santa Clara Valley*, ed. Yvonne Jacobson (Los Altos, CA: William Kaufman Inc., 1984), ix.

86. Khalida Sarwai, "Fruit Cocktail Club Stirs Up Historical Views of Saratoga," *San Jose Mercury News*, January 18, 2018, https://www.mercurynews.com/2018/01/18/fruit-cocktail-club-to-stir-up-historical-views-of-saratoga/.

87. Smith and Watson, *Reading Autobiography*, 25.

88. Sunnyvale Historical Society and Museum Association, *Orchard Heritage Park*, 5.

89. Sunnyvale Historical Society and Museum Association, *Orchard Heritage Park*, 13.

90. James Zetterquist, "Fruit Cocktail Club Movie Night" (paper presented at the Fruit Cocktail Club, Saratoga Foothill Club, January 27, 2016).

91. Carroll, "How the Pears Got Bulldozed."

92. Zetterquist, "Fruit Cocktail Club Movie Night."

93. Stephanie Coontz, "The Nostalgia Trap," *Harvard Business Review*, April 10, 2018, https://hbr.org/2018/04/the-nostalgia-trap.

94. Casey, *Getting Back into Place*, 37–38.

95. Casey, *Remembering: A Phenomological Study*, 201.

96. Carbaugh and Cerulli, "Cultural Discourses of Dwelling," 6.

97. Tuan, *Space and Place*, 195.

98. Stokowski, "Languages of Place and Discourses of Power," 368–69.

99. Tuan, *Space and Place*, 154.

100. Stephanie K. Hawke, "Heritage and Sense of Place: Amplifying Local Voice and Co-constructing Meaning," in *Making Sense of Place*, ed. Ian Convery, Gerard Corsane, and Peter Davis, Multidisciplinary Perspectives (Woodbridge, UK: Boydell & Brewer, 2012), 239.

101. Hawke, "Heritage and Sense of Place," 240.

102. Storey, "Land, Territory and Identity," 12.

103. Coontz, *The Way We Never Were*.

104. Malpas, "New Media, Cultural Heritage and the Sense of Place," 198.

105. National Park System Advisory Board. *Charting a Future for National Heritage Areas*, 2006, https://www.nps.gov/resources/upload/NHAreport.pdf.

106. National Park Service, Heritage Areas: Community-Led Conservation and Development. National Park Service, 2011. https://www.nps.gov/subjects/heritageareas/index.htm.

107. Santa Clara Valley National Heritage Area Task Force Special Meeting, National Heritage Area Task Force (2016).

108. Christin Dameria, Roos Akbar, and Petrus Natalivan Indradjati, "Whose Sense of Place? Re-thinking Place Concept and Urban Heritage Conservation in Social Media Era" (IOP Conference Series: Earth and Environmental Science, 2018).

109. Casey, *Remembering: A Phenomological Study*, 215.

110. Yvonne Cornell, "The Heart and Hustle of a Generational Farm Meant to Be Shared," *Edible Silicon Valley*, May 30, 2018, http://ediblesiliconvalley.edible communities.com/eat/spade-and-plow-generational-farm.

111. Sam Thorp, Interview by Anne Marie Todd, October 29, 2018.

112. Marianna Zavala, "Spade & Plow Organics: Continuing the Legacy of Santa Clara Valley Farmers," Pacific Coast Farmers' Market Association, December 27, 2017, https://www.pcfma.org/blog/spade-plow-organics-continuing-legacy -santa-clara-valley-farmers.

113. Thorp, interview.

114. Thorp, interview.

115. Jacobson, *Passing Farms, Enduring Values*, 231.

116. Thorp, interview.

117. Jacobson, *Passing Farms, Enduring Values*, 231.

118. Jacobson, *Passing Farms, Enduring Values*, 227.

119. Thorp, interview.

120. Leeta-Rose Ballester, "A Sense of Place," *San Jose Mercury News* March 7, 2015, B, B1.

121. Jennifer Wadsworth, "Fresh Choice," *Metro*, March 19–25, 2014, 13.

122. Silicon Valley Newsroom, "Ag Plan Aims to Preserve Santa Clara County Farms, Rangeland, *San José Inside,* January 29, 2019, https://www.sanjoseinside .com/news/ag-plan-aims-to-preserve-santa-clara-county-farms-rangeland/.

123. Cortese, "County Agricultural Future Looking Bright."

124. Silicon Valley Newsroom, "Ag Plan Aims to Preserve."

125. Sam Whiting, "Ag Plan Strives to Preserve Silicon Valley's Farming Heritage," *San Francisco Chronicle*, February 18, 2018, https://www.sfchronicle.com /bayarea/article/Ag-Plan-strives-to-preserves-Silicon-Valley-s-12623666.php.

126. Julia Prodis Sulek, "Sunnyvale: Landmark C.J. Olson's Cherries Fruit Stand to Close Sept. 30," *San Jose Mercury News*, August 29, 2018, https://www.mercurynews .com/2018/08/29/sunnyvale-landmark-c-j-olsons-cherries-fruit-stand-to-close-sept-30/.

127. Sulek, "Sunnyvale: Landmark C.J. Olson's Cherries Fruit Stand to Close Sept. 30."

128. Sulek, "Sunnyvale: Landmark C.J. Olson's Cherries Fruit Stand to Close Sept. 30."

129. Olson, interview.

130. Olson, interview.

131. Sulek, "Sunnyvale: Landmark C.J. Olson's Cherries Fruit Stand to Close Sept. 30."

132. Olson, interview; Sam Gugino, "No High-Tech Contraptions at this Sunnyvale Company. Olson Family Cherry Business Hasn't Changed Much Sinc 1902," *San Jose Mercury News*, May 27, 1992.

RESEARCH NOTES

1. Ralph Pearce, "Looking Back: Clyde Arbuckle, San José's First City Historian," San Jose Public Library, March 15, 2014, https://www.sjpl.org/blog/looking-back-clyde-arbuckle-san-Joses-first-city-historian.

2. Jack Douglas, *Historical Footnotes of the Santa Clara Valley* (San Jose: San Jose Historical Museum Association, 1993).

3. McKay, "Dutch Hamman Part 1."; McKay, "Dutch Hamann, Part 2"; Leonard McKay, "The 1906 Earthquake, Part III," *San Jose Inside*, April 3 2006, https://www.sanjoseinside.com/2006/04/03/the_1906_earthquake2/; Leonard McKay, "Louis Pellier," *San Jose Inside*, September 25 2006, http://www.sanjoseinside.com/2006/09/25/louis_pellier/; McKay, "The Canning Industry in San Jose"; Leonard McKay, "The Faith Davies Story," *San Jose Inside*, December 5 2005, http://www.sanjoseinside.com/2005/12/05/the_faith_davies_story/.

4. Ralph Rambo, *Almost Forgotten: Cartoon Pen and Inklings of the Old Santa Clara Valley by a Native* (San Jose, CA: The Rosecrucian Press, 1964); Rambo, *Rembmer when . . . : A Boy's Eye View of an Old Valley*; Ralph Rambo, *Pioneer Blue Book of the Old Santa Clara Valley* (San Jose: Rosicrucian Press, 1973).

5. Terry Christensen and Philip J. Trounstine, *Movers and Shakers: The Study of Community Power* (New York: St. Martin's Press, 1982); Mary Jo Ignoffo, *Gold Rush Politics: California's First Legislature* (Sacramento: California State Senate, 1999).

6. Scott Herhold, "Hello, Google. Goodbye, Patty's Inn," *San Jose Mercury News*, June 25, 2017, https://www.mercurynews.com/2017/06/25/hello-google-goodbye-pattys-inn/; Scott Herhold, "Visiting 1933 San José Lynching Sites It's the 25th Anniversary of the Publication of Harry Farrell's Book, *Swift Justice*," *San Jose Mercury News*, September 24, 2017, https://www.mercurynews.com/2017/09/24/san-joses-1933-lynching-a-guide-to-historic-sites/; Scott Herhold, "James Lick: An Eccentric's Legacy," *San Jose Mercury News*, June 12, 2017, https://www.mercurynews.com/2017/06/12/james-lick-an-eccentrics-legacy/; Scott Herhold, "Pellier Park Closer to Reincarnation," *San Jose Mercury News*, March 26, 2016, http://www.mercurynews.com/scott-herhold/ci_29689017/herhold-pellier-park-closer-reincarnation; Scott Herhold, "The Woman Behind San Jose's Hayes Mansion," *San Jose Mercury News*, June 14, 2016, https://www.mercurynews.com/2016/06/14/herhold-the-woman-behind-san-joses-hayes-mansion/; Herhold, "How San Jose Grew in a Topsy Turvy Way"; Scott Herhold, "The Mman for Whom a New San Jose Park Is Named," *San Jose Mercurty News*, February 12, 2014, https://www.mercurynews.com/2014/02/12/the-man-for-whom-a-new-san-jose-park-is-named/; Scott Herhold, "The Origins of Beer in Santa Clara County," *San Jose Mercury News*, July 30, 2014, https://www.mercurynews.com/2014/07/30/herhold-the-origins-of-beer-in-santa-clara-county/;

Scott Herhold, "When the Communists Held Sway in San Jose," *San Jose Mercury News*, June 27 2012, https://www.mercurynews.com/2012/06/27/herhold-when-the-communists-held-sway-in-san-jose/; Scott Herhold, "Two McKinley Statues. Two Very Different Towns," *San Jose Mercury News*, September 4 2009, https://www.mercurynews.com/2009/09/04/herhold-two-mckinley-statues-two-very-different-towns/; Scott Herhold, "Call It San Jose's Messiest Divorce," *San Jose Mercury News*, October 12, 1997; Herhold, "San Jose Moves to Correct Hamann Legacy."

REFERENCES

Adams, Jennifer D., David Greenwood, Mitchell Thomasshow, and Alex Russ. "Sense of Place." In *Urban Environmental Education Review*, edited by Alex Russ and Marianne E. Krasney, 68–75. Ithaca, NY: Cornell University Press, 2017.

Adams, Paul C., and Astrid Gynnild. "Environmental Messages in Online Media: The Role of Place." *Environmental Communication* 7, no. 1 (March 1, 2013): 113–30.

Agnew, John. "Space and Place." In *Handbook of Geographical Knowledge*, edited by John Agnew and D. Livingstone, 316–30. London: Sage, 2011.

Allen, Barbara. "Regional Studies in American Folklore Scholarship." In *Sense of Place: American Regional Cultures*, edited by Barbara Allen and Thomas J. Schlereth, 1–13. Lexington: University of Kentucky Press, 1990.

American Farmland Trust. *Farms under Threat: The State of America's Farmland.* American Farmland Trust. Washington, DC: 2018. https://www.farmlandinfo .org/sites/default/files/AFT_Farms_Under_Threat_ExecSum-min.pdf.

The American Society of Mechanical Engineers, "The FMC Rotary Pressure Sterilizer. Introduced in 1920." ASME Historic Mechanical Engineering Landmark Program, 1982. https://docplayer.net/13625337-The-fmc-rotary-pressure-sterilizer -introduced-in-1920-an-international-historic-mechanical-engineering-landmark .html.

"Anderson Prune Dipper Company." Packing Houses of Santa Clara County. Updated January 1, 2017, http://vasonabranch.com/packing_houses/index.php ?title=Anderson_Prune_Dipper_Company.

Andrews, Malcolm. *The Search for the Picturesque: Landscape Aesthetics and Tourism in Britain, 1760–1800.* Stanford, CA: Stanford University Press, 1989.

Arreola, Daniel D. "Hispanic American Legacy, Latino American Diaspora." In *Hispanic Spaces, Latino Places: Community and Cultural Diversity in Contemporary America*, edited by Daniel D. Arreola. Austin: University of Texas Press, 2004.

———. "Introduction." In *Hispanic Spaces, Latino Places: Community and Cultural Diversity in Contemporary America*, edited by Daniel D. Arreola, 1–12. Austin: University of Texas Press, 2004.

Arieff, Allison. "One Thing Silicon Valley Can't Seem to Fix." *New York Times*, July 9, 2017, Week in Review, 6.

Augé, Marc. *Non-Places: Introduction to an Anthropology of Supermodernity*. Translated by John Howe. London: Verso, 1995.

Ballester, Leeta-Rose. "A Sense of Place." *San Jose Mercury News*, March 7, 2015, B, B1-B2.

Basso, Keith H. "Wisdom Sits in Places: Notes on a Western Apache Landscape." In *Senses of Place*, edited by Steven Feld and Keith H. Basso, 53–90. Santa Fe, NM: School of American Research Press, 1996.

Beatty, Richmond Croom. *Bayard Taylor: Laureate of the Gilded Age*. Norman: University of Oklahoma Press, 1936.

Belden, Judge. *Santa Clara County, California*. Brochure. San Jose, CA, Board of Trade of San Jose, 1887.

Belser, Karl. "The Making of Slurban America." *Cry California: The Journal of California Tomorrow* 5, no. 4 (1970): 1–21.

———. "The Planning Fiasco in California." *Cry California: The Journal of California Tomorrow* 2, no. 3 (Summer 1967): 10–13.

———. "The Santa Clara Valley: A Case Study in Land Use, Rural vrs. Urban." Paper presented at the Natural Environment Studies, University California Berkeley, June 28, 1970.

Benson, Thomas W. "Series Editor's Preface." In *Vernacular Voices: The Rhetoric of Publics and Public Spheres*. Columbia: University of South Carolina Press, 1999, xi–xii.

Bowman, Norman. "Over 10,000 New Homes in a Year." *San Jose Mercury News*, December 29, 1958.

Boyd, Josh. "Corporate Rhetoric Participates in Public Dialogue: A Solution to the Public/Private Conundrum." *Southern Communication Journal* 66, no. 4 (2001): 279–92.

Brady, Emily. *The Sublime in Modern Philosophy : Aesthetics, Ethics, and Nature*. Cambridge: Cambridge University Press, 2013.

Braznell, William. *California's Finest: The History of the Del Monte Corporation and the Del Monte Brand*. San Francisco: Del Monte Corporation, 1982.

Brofenbrenner, Kate. "California Farmworkers' Strikes of 1933." In *Labor Conflict in the United States: An Encyclopedia*, edited by R. L. Filippelli. New York: Garland Publishing, Inc., 1990.

Brown, Alan K., ed. *With Anza to California 1775–1776: The Journal of Pedro Font, O.F.M.* Edited by Rose Marie Beebe and Robert M. Senkewicz. Vol. 1, Early California Commentaries. Norman, OK: The Arthur C. Clark Company, 2011.

Brown, E. T., and E. H. Overstreet, eds. *The San Jose Daily Herald Souvenir Publication: Horticulture, Viticulture, Agriculture: The Railroads, Manufacturing, Financial, Commercial, and Professional Representative Firms of Santa Clara County, California*. Brochure. San Jose, CA: San Jose Daily Herald, 1890.

Brown, Kenneth W., David H. Caldwell, and John T. Norgaard. *San Jose Sewage Treatment Study: Design Criteria, Preliminary Plans and Cost Estimates for*

Secondary Treatment of Sewage and Industrial Wastes. A Report Prepared for the City of San Jose, Ca. San Francisco: Brown and Caldwell, Civil and Chemical Engineers, December 1959.

"Brownell Biography Entries." Historical California Stone Carvers, Stone Cutters, & Monument Dealers. Quarries and Beyond. Updated January 13, 2012. https://quarriesandbeyond.org/states/ca/ca-stone_carvers/b-5_brownell_bios.html.

Brune, Michael. "Pulling Down Our Monuments." *Sierra Club* (July 22, 2020). https://www.sierraclub.org/michael-brune/2020/07/john-muir-early-history-sierra-club.

Budman, Scott. "Highway 101: The Tech Industry's Madison Avenue." NBC Bay Area, August 4, 2009. https://www.nbcbayarea.com/news/local/The-Tech-Industrys-Madison-Avenue-52443607.html.

Business Week. "Correcting San Jose's Boomtime Mistake." *Business Week*, September 19, 1970, 74.

California Assembly Subcommittee on Planning and Zoning. *State Greenbelt Legislation and the Problem of Urban Encroachment in California Agriculture,* Assembly Interim Committee Reports vol. 13, no. 14 (Sacramento: Assembly of the State of California, 1957).

California Farm Bureau. "'It Is Time to Do Something About It,' Say Santa Clara County Farmers." *Farm Bureau Monthly*, April 1934.

Calles, Rudy. *Champion Prune Pickers: Migrant Worker's Dilemma.* Los Alamitos, CA: Hwong Publishing Company, 1979.

Campbell, Karlyn Kohrs *The Rhetorical Act.* Belmont, CA: Wadsworth Publishing, 1982.

Canning Age. "Canning Peaches in Santa Clara Valley." *Canning Age*, August 1921, 1.

Cantrill, James G. "A Sense of Self-in-Place for Adaptive Management, Capacity Building, and Public Participation." In *Environmental Communication Yearbook I*, edited by Susan L. Senecah, 165–85. Mahwah, NJ: Lawrence Erlbaum Associates, 2004.

Cantrill, James G., and Susan L. Senecah. "Using the 'Sense of Self-in-Place' Construct in the Context of Environmental Policy-Making and Landscape Planning." *Environmental Science and Policy* 4 (2001): 185–203.

Cantrill, James G., J. L. Thompson, E. Garrett, and G. Rochester. "Exploring a Sense of Self-in-Place to Explain the Impulse for Urban Sprawl." *Environmental Communication: A Journal of Nature and Culture* 1, no. 2 (2007): 123–45.

Carbaugh, Donal. "Naturalizing Communication and Culture." In *The Symbolic Earth: Discourse and Our Creation of the Environment*, edited by J. G. Cantrill and Christine L. Oravec, 38–57. Lexington: University Press of Kentucky, 1996.

Carbaugh, Donal, and Tovar Cerulli. "Cultural Discourses of Dwelling: Investigating Environmental Communication as a Place-Based Practice." *Environmental Communication: A Journal of Nature and Culture* 7, no. 1 (2013): 4–23.

Carlson, Allen. *Aesthetics and the Environment: The Appreciation of Nature, Art and Architecture.* London: Routledge, 2002.

———. "Environmental Aesthetics." In *Routledge Companion to Aesthetics*, edited by B. Gaut and D. M. Lopes, 423–36. London: Routledge, 2001.

———. *Nature and Landscape: An Introduction to Environmental Aesthetics.* New York: Columbia University Press, 2009.

Carroll, Rick. "How the Pears Got Bulldozed." *San Francisco Chronicle*, January 27, 1978.

Casey, Edward S. *Getting Back into Place: Toward a Renewed Understanding of the Place-World.* Bloomington: Indiana University Press, 1993.

———. "How to Get from Space to Place in a Fairly Short Stretch of Time: Phenomenological Prolegomena." In *Sense of Place*, edited by Steven Feld and Keith H. Basso, 13–52. Santa Fe, New Mexico: School of American Research Press, 1996.

———. *Remembering: A Phenomological Study.* Bloomington: Indiana University Press, 1987.

Cassidy, Mike. "Olsons Know the Dirty Truth about Shrinking." *San Jose Mercury News*, May 8, 1994, 1B.

———. "Rain Was the Pits for Olson Orchard: Cherry Grower Suffers Huge Losses." *San Jose Mercury News*, May 30, 1990.

Castillo, Edward D. "Short Overview of California Indian History." *State of California Native American Heritage Comission.* (2021). http://nahc.ca.gov/resources /california-indian-history/.

Castillo, Elias. "Canning Industry Still Fruitful Here." *San Jose Mercury News*, August 24, 1980.

Chambers, Clarke A. *California Farm Organizations: A Historical Study of the Grange, the Farm Bureau, and the Associated Farmers, 1929–1941.* Berkeley: University of California Press, 1952.

Chan, Dyan. "Sunnyvale's Last Orchard Slated for Development." *Valley Journal*, May 1, 1991.

Chapman, Robin. *California Apricots: The Lost Orchards of Silicon Valley.* Mt Pleasant, SC: Arcadia Publishing, 2013.

Christensen, Terry, and Philip J. Trounstine. "Flashback: A Short Political History of San Jose." In *Movers and Shakers* New York: St. Martin's Press, 1982. http:// www.sjsu.edu/polisci/docs/faculty_links/Terry%20San%20Jose%20Political %20History%20to%201970–1.pdf.

———. *Movers and Shakers: The Study of Community Power.* New York: St. Martin's Press, 1982.

City Planning Commission. *San Jose: Design for Tomorrow.* San Jose, California: 1961.

Clark, Gregory. *Rhetorical Landscapes in America: Variations on a Theme from Kenneth Burke.* Columbia: University of South Carolina Press, 2004.

Claus, Robert James. "The Fruit and Vegetable Canning Industry in the Santa Clara Valley." Master's thesis, San Jose State University, 1966.

Clements, Geo P. "Billion Dollar Agricultural Production State, 1929." *California Cultivator*, December 31, 1921.

Conrad, Rebecca. "The Conservation of Local Autonomy: California's Agricultural Land Policies, 1900–1966." *California Legal History* 13 (2018): 113–51.

Convery, Ian, Gerard Corsane, and Peter Davis. "Introduction Making Sense of Place." In *Making Sense of Place*, edited by Ian Convery, Gerard Corsane and Peter Davis. Multidisciplinary Perspectives, 1–8. Rochester, NY: Boydell & Brewer, 2012.

Cook, Sherburne F. *The Population of the California Indians, 1769–1970*. Berkeley: University of California Press, 1976.

Coontz, Stephanie. "The Nostalgia Trap." *Harvard Business Review*, April 10, 2018. https://hbr.org/2018/04/the-nostalgia-trap.

———. *The Way We Never Were: American Families and the Nostalgia Trap*. New York: Basic Books, 2016.

Cooper, David. "Introduction." In *A Companion to Aesthetics*, edited by David Cooper, vii–ix. Malden, MA: Wiley-Blackwell, 1992.

Corbett, Julia. *Communicating Nature: How We Create and Understand Environmental Messages*. Washington, DC: Island Press, 2006.

Corley, Liam. *Bayard Taylor: Determined Dreamer of America's Rise, 1825–1878*. Lanham, MD: Bucknell University Press, 2014.

Cornell, Yvonne. "The Heart and Hustle of a Generational Farm Meant to Be Shared." *Edible Silicon Valley*, May 30, 2018. http://ediblesiliconvalley.ediblecommunities .com/eat/spade-and-plow-generational-farm.

Cortese, Dave. "County Agricultural Future Looking Bright as Task Force Wraps Up." Santa Clara County news release, 2019, https://www.sccgov.org/sites/d3 /Documents/Ag%20final%20report%20press%20release%20FINAL.pdf.

Couchman, Robert. *The Sunsweet Story*. San Jose: Sunsweet Growers, 1967.

Counted, Victor. "Making Sense of Place Attachment: Towards a Holistic Understanding of People-Place Relationships and Experiences." *Environment, Space, Place* 8, no. 1 (2016): 7–32.

Cox, Dick. "There Was a Time When the Working Class Had Jobs." *San Jose Mercury News*, August 19, 1992.

Creswell, Tim. "Place." In *International Encyclopedia of Human Geography*, edited by Nigel Thrift and Rob Kitchen, 169–77. Oxford: Elsevier, 2009.

———. *Place: An Introduction*. 2nd ed. West Sussex, UK: Wiley Blackwell, 2015.

Cronk, Michael. "The Olsons' Last Stand: Sunnyvale's Famed Cherrypicking Family May Be Calling It Quits after 60 Years of Offering Customers Fruit of Their Labors." *San Jose Mercury News*, March 31, 1997, 1A.

———. "Target Won't Build at Sunnyvale Site of Cherry Orchard." *San Jose Mercury News* (San Jose), July 24, 1997, 1B.

Cronon, William, ed. *Uncommon Ground: Rethinking the Human Place in Nature*. New York: W. W. Norton & Co., 1995.

Curci, Cookie. "Commentary: Early Residents of Santa Clara Valley Remember the Orchards and Canneries " *San Jose Mercury News*, June 28, 2012. https:// www.mercurynews.com/2012/06/28/commentary-early-residents-of-santa-clara -valley-remember-the-orchards-and-canneries/.

Damalas, Christos A., and Ilias G. Eleftherohorinos. "Pesticide Exposure, Safety Issues, and Risk Assessment Indicators." *International Journal of Environmental*

Research and Public Health 8, no. 4 (2011): 1402–19. https://www.ncbi.nlm.nih .gov/pmc/articles/PMC3108117/.

Damalas, Christos A., and Spyridon D. Koutroubas. "Farmers' Exposure to Pesticides: Toxicity Types and Ways of Prevention." *Toxics* 4, no. 1 (2016). https://www .ncbi.nlm.nih.gov/pmc/articles/PMC5606636/.

Dameria, Christin, Roos Akbar, and Petrus Natalivan Indradjati. "Whose Sense of Place? Re-Thinking Place Concept and Urban Heritage Conservation in Social Media Era." IOP Conference Series: Earth and Environmental Science, 2018.

Daniel, Cletus E. *Bitter Harvest: A History of California Farmworkers, 1870–1941.* Berkeley: University of California Press, 1982.

Davies, Race M. *Preserving Agricultural and Open-Space Lands: Legislative Policy-making in California.* Davis: University of California Institute of Governmental Affairs, 1972. https://digitalcommons.law.ggu.edu/cgi/viewcontent.cgi?article= 1383&context=caldocs_agencies.

Dawson, Robert, and Gray Brechin. *Farewell, Promised Land: Waking from the California Dream.* Berkeley: University of California Press, 1999.

Derdak, Thomas, ed. "Del Monte Foods." In *International Directory of Company Histories*, edited by Jay Pederson Ann Arbor, MI: St. James Press, 1998.

Dickinson, Elizabeth. "Displaced in Nature: The Cultural Production of (Non-) Place in Place-Based Forest Conservation Pedagogy." *Environmental Communication* 5, no. 3 (2011): 300–319.

Donald, David B., Jim Syrgiannis, Fraser Hunter, and Gary Weiss. "Agricultural Pesticides Threaten the Ecological Integrity of Northern Prairie Wetlands." *Science of the Total Environment* 231, no. 2 (1999/07/01/ 1999): 173–81. https://doi.org /https://doi.org/10.1016/S0048-9697(99)00091-1. https://www.sciencedirect .com/science/article/pii/S0048969799000911.

Dougherty, Debbie S. *The Reluctant Farmer: An Exploration of Work, Social Class, and the Production of Food.* Edited by Omar Swartz. Leicester, UK: Troubador, 2011.

Douglas, Jack. *Historical Footnotes of the Santa Clara Valley.* San Jose: San Jose Historical Museum Association, 1993.

Downey, Carolyn Marie. *Voices from the Orchards.* San Jose, CA: Anacaro Publications, 1997.

Downey, Kirstin. "Sunnyvale's Rural Oasis Urban Farm May Not Be Around Long." *San Jose Mercury News*, January 13, 1988, A1.

Downie, Leonard. *The Santa Clara Valley's Appointment with Destiny.* Alicia Patterson Foundation (1971). http://aliciapatterson.org/stories/santa-clara-valley%E2 %80%99s-%E2%80%9Cappointment-destiny%E2%80%9D.

Edwards, Lee. "Questions of Self-Interest, Agency, and the Rhetor." *Management Communication Quarterly* 25, no. 3 (2011): 531–40. https://doi.org/10.1177 /0893318911409866.

Eilperin, Juliet, and Darryl Fears. "Deadly Air Pollutant 'Disproportionately and Systematically' Harms Americans of Color, Study Finds." *Washington Post*, April 28,

2021. https://www.washingtonpost.com/climate-environment/2021/04/28
/environmental-justice-pollution/.

Endres, Danielle. "Environmental Oral History." *Environmental Communication: A Journal of Nature and Culture* 5, no. 4 (December 2011): 485–98.

Endres, Danielle, and Samantha Senda-Cook. "Location Matters: The Rhetoric of Place in Protest." *Quarterly Journal of Speech* 97, no. 3 (August 1, 2011): 257–82.

English-Lueck, Jan A. *Cultures@Silicon Valley*. Stanford, CA: Stanford University Press, 2002.

Feld, Steven, and Keith H. Basso. "Introduction." In *Sense of Place*, edited by Steven Feld and Keith H. Basso, 3–12. Santa Fe, New Mexico: School of American Research Press, 1996.

Fellmeth, Robert C. *Politics of Land: Ralph Nader's Study Group Report on Land Use in California*. New York: Grossman Publishers, 1973. https://archive.org/details/politicsoflandra00fell.

Finnegan, Cara A. "Doing Rhetorical History of the Visual: The Photograph and the Archive." In *Defining Visual Rhetorics*, edited by Charles A. Hill and Marguerite Helmers, 195–214. New York: Routledge, 2009.

Fish, Kevin. "Organization for Water—Rise of Economic and Political Interests." In *Water in the Santa Clara Valley: A History*, edited by Seonaid McArthur, 21–44. Cupertino: California History Center, 1981.

Flocks, Joan D. "The Environmental and Social Injustice of Farmworker Pesticide Exposure." *Georgetown Journal on Poverty Law and Policy* 19, no. 2 (2012): 255–82.

Flood, Dick. "Bleak Summer for 'Cot Growers." *San Jose Mercury*, July 10, 1965.

Foote, H. S., and C. A. Woolfolk. *Picturesque San Jose and Environments*. San Jose, CA: Hulbert Brothers and Company, 1893.

Fowlie, Meredith, Reed Walker, and David Wooley. *Climate Policy, Environmental Justice, and Local Air Pollution*. Washington, DC: Brookings Institution, October 20, 2020. https://www.brookings.edu/research/climate-policy-environmental-justice-and-local-air-pollution/.

Free, Herbert W. "California Apricot Growers Union." Master's thesis, University of California, 1941.

French, Barbara. "Time Runs out on Once-Thriving Pear Industry." *San Jose Mercury News* (San Jose), January 24, 1978.

Frost, Bob. "Norman Mailer." *West*, November 17, 1991.

Gardner, Bruce. "U.S. Agriculture in the Twentieth Century." In *EH.Net Encyclopedia*, edited by Robert Whaples2003https://eh.net/encyclopedia/u-s-agriculture-in-the-twentieth-century/.

Gardner, Philip. "Oral History." In *The Sage Dictionary of Social Research Methods*, edited by Victor Jupp, 207–9. London: Sage Publications, 2006.

Garrod, Vince S. *Gulchin' Out*. Bloomington, Indiana: Xlibris, 2013.

Garrod, Emma Stolte. *One Life, Mine*. Bloomington, Indiana: Xlibris, 2012.

Gemperlein, Joyce. "For Growers, Life Can't Be Called a Bowl of Cherries." *San Jose Mercury News*, May 11, 1996, 1A.

Gilroy Dispatch. "A Road Runs through It." *Gilroy (CA) Dispatch,* August 13, 2004. http://gilroydispatch.com/2004/08/13/a-road-runs-through-it/.

———. "San Jose Chamber of Commerce Opens Big Campaign for New Industry with Magazine Advertising." *Gilroy (CA) Dispatch,* November 8, 1943.

Graham, Paul. "How to Be Silicon Valley." May 2006. http://www.paulgraham.com /siliconvalley.html.

Grant, Joanne. "S.J. Recall Effort in '64 Only a Dim Memory." *San Jose Mercury News,* April 4, 1994.

Gronbeck, Bruce E. "Rhetorical History and Rhetorical Criticism: A Distinction." *The Speech Teacher* 24 (1975): 309–20.

———. "The Rhetorics of the Past: History, Argument, and Collective Memory." In *Doing Rhetorical History: Concepts and Cases,* edited by Kathleen J. Turner, 47–60. Tuscaloosa: University of Alabama Press, 1998.

Guara, Maria Alicia. "Last Call for the Last Sunnyvale Orchard." *San Francisco Chronicle,* August 1, 1994, 1.

Gugino, Sam. "No High-Tech Contraptions at this Sunnyvale Company. Olson Family Cherry Business Hasn't Changed Much Sinc 1902," *San Jose Mercury News,* May 27, 1992.

Guinn, J. M. *History of the State of California and Biographical Record of Coast Counties, California.* Translated by Louise E. Shoemaker. Chicago: Chapman Publishing Company, 1904.

Haapala, Arto. "Aesthetics, Ethics, and the Meaning of Place." *Filozofski vestnik* 20, no. 2 (1999): 253–64.

———. "The Everyday, Building, and Architecture: Reflections on the Ethos and Beauty of Our Built Surroundings." *Cloud-Cuckoo-Land: International Journal of Architectural Theory* 22 (2017): 169–82.

Hamburger, Philip. "Notes for a Gazetteer." *New Yorker,* May 4, 1963.

Hansen, Melissa. "Flavor Reigns at Andy's Orchard." *Good Fruit Grower,* February 17, 2015. http://www.goodfruit.com/flavor-reigns-at-andys-orchard/.

Harris, Daniel. "What's in a Name? San Jose Needs to Know." *San Jose Mercury News,* February 22, 2017. https://www.mercurynews.com/2017/02/22/opinion-whats -in-a-name-san-jose-needs-to-know/.

Harrison, E. S. *Central California, Santa Clara Valley: Its Resources, Advantages and Prospects. Homes for a Million.* San Jose, CA: McNeil Brothers, 1887.

Harrison, Jill Lindsey. *Pesticide Drift and the Pursuit of Environmental Justice.* Cambridge, MA: MIT Press, 2011.

Hart, John. *Farming on the Edge: Saving Family Farms in Marin County, California.* Berkeley: University of California Press, 1991.

Harvey, David. *Justice, Nature and the Geography of Difference.* Cambridge, MA: Blackwell, 1996.

Haskell, Thomas L. *Objectivity Is Not Neutrality: Explanatory Schemes in History.* Baltimore: Johns Hopkins University Press, 1998.

Hathaway, Susan, "Andy's Orchard Maverick Orchardist Demystifies Heirloom Stone Fruit and Shares Tips for Selection," *Bay Area Bites,* KQED, July 15, 2014,

https://www.kqed.org/bayareabites/84874/andys-orchard-maverick-orchardist
-andy-mariani-demystifies-heirloom-stone-fruit-and-shares-tips-for-selection.

Hauser, Gerard A. *Vernacular Voices: The Rhetoric of Publics and Public Spheres.*
Columbia: University of South Carolina Press, 1999.

Hawke, Stephanie K. "Heritage and Sense of Place: Amplifying Local Voice and Co-
Constructing Meaning." In *Making Sense of Place*, edited by Ian Convery, Gerard
Corsane and Peter Davis. Multidisciplinary Perspectives, 235–46. Woodbridge,
UK: Boydell & Brewer, 2012.

Heintz, Carl. "Fruit Trees Displaced by Homes." *San Jose Mercury News*, March 26, 1953.

Hendrix, Winifred Wool. Recollections. February 8, 1956. Wool Family Collection,
San Jose.

Herhold, Scott. "Call It San Jose's Messiest Divorce." *San Jose Mercury News*, October 12, 1997.

———. "Hello, Google. Goodbye, Patty's Inn." *San Jose Mercury News*, June 25, 2017.
https://www.mercurynews.com/2017/06/25/hello-google-goodbye-pattys-inn/.

———. "How San Jose Grew in a Topsy Turvy Way." *San Jose Mercury News*,
August 12, 2015. https://www.mercurynews.com/2015/08/12/herhold-how-san
-Jose-grew-in-a-topsy-turvy-way/.

———. "James Lick: An Eccentric's Legacy." *San Jose Mercury News*, June 12, 2017.
https://www.mercurynews.com/2017/06/12/james-lick-an-eccentrics-legacy/.

———. "The Man for Whom a New San Jose Park Is Named." *San Jose Mercurty
News*, February 12, 2014. https://www.mercurynews.com/2014/02/12/the-man
-for-whom-a-new-san-jose-park-is-named/.

———. "The Origins of Beer in Santa Clara County." *San Jose Mercury News*, July 30,
2014. https://www.mercurynews.com/2014/07/30/herhold-the-origins-of-beer
-in-santa-clara-county/.

———. "Pellier Park Closer to Reincarnation." *San Jose Mercury News*, March 26,
2016. http://www.mercurynews.com/scott-herhold/ci_29689017/herhold
-pellier-park-closer-reincarnation.

———. "San Jose Moves to Correct Hamann Legacy." *San Jose Mercury News*,
April 13, 1987.

———. "Two Mckinley Statues. Two Very Different Towns." *San Jose Mercury News*,
September 4, 2009. https://www.mercurynews.com/2009/09/04/herhold-two
-mckinley-statues-two-very-different-towns/

———. "Visiting 1933 San José Lynching Sites It's the 25th Anniversary of the Publication of Harry Farrell's Book, *Swift Justice*." *San Jose Mercury News*, September 24, 2017. https://www.mercurynews.com/2017/09/24/san-joses–1933-lynch
ing-a-guide-to-historic-sites/.

———. "When the Communists Held Sway in San Jose." *San Jose Mercury News*,
June 27, 2012. https://www.mercurynews.com/2012/06/27/herhold-when-the
-communists-held-sway-in-san-jose/.

———. "The Woman Behind San Jose's Hayes Mansion." *San Jose Mercury News*,
June 14, 2016. https://www.mercurynews.com/2016/06/14/herhold-the-woman
-behind-san-joses-hayes-mansion/.

Hernandez, Marita. "Orchards Long Gone, Valley Canneries Still Big Industry." *San Jose Mercury News*, August 15, 1977.

Higgs, Robert. "Landless by Law: Japanese Immigrants in California Agriculture to 1941." *Journal of Economic History* 38, no. 1 (1978): 205–25.

History San Jose. California Fruit Canners Assn. In *Cannery Life: Del Monte in the Santa Clara Valley*, San Jose, CA: History San Jose, 2018. https://historysanjose.org/exhibits-activities/online-exhibits/cannery-life-del-monte-in-the-santa-clara-valley/.

———. "California Packing Corporation." In *Cannery Life: Del Monte in the Santa Clara Valley*, 2018.https://historysanjose.org/exhibits-activities/online-exhibits/cannery-life-del-monte-in-the-santa-clara-valley/.

———. *Label Legacy: The Muirson Label Comapny.* https://historysanjose.org/exhibits-activities/online-exhibits/label-legacy-muirson-label-company-san-jose-calif/.

———. "The Mercury News Changes Along with San Jose." 750 Ridder Park Drive: Documenting the Former Headquarters of the Mercury News, 2016, https://historysanjose.org/exhibits-activities/online-exhibits/750-ridder-park-drive-documenting-the-former-headquarters-of-the-mercury-news/3/.

———. "People: Ralph Rambo." In *Label Legacy, History San Jose*, 2016, accessed June 7, 2016, https://historysanjose.org/exhibits-activities/online-exhibits/label-legacy-muirson-label-company-san-jose-calif/.

———. "Plant Number 3 on Auzerais Ave." Cannery Life: Del Monte in the Santa Clara Valley, 2018, http://onlineexhibits.historysanjose.org/cannerylife/through-the-years/1917–1966/cal-pak/plant-number–3.html.

———. "Welcome Key to San Jose." 2017, http://historysanjose.org/wp/welcome-key-to-san-jose/.

Holmes, Todd. "Farmer's Market: Agribusiness and the Agrarian Imaginary in California and the Far West ". *California History* 90, no. 2 (2013): 24–74.

Hoover, Judith. "Corporate Advocacy: A Powerful Persuasive Strategy." In *Corporate Advocacy: Rhetoric in the Information Age*, edited by Judith Hoover, 3–16. Westport, CT: Quorum Books, 1997.

Hughes, George. "Tourism and the Semiological Realization of Space." In *Desinations: Cultural Landscapes of Tourism*, edited by Gregory Ringer, 17–32. London: Routledge, 1998.

IBM. "San Jose Card Plant." IBM Archives, 2018, https://www.ibm.com/ibm/history/exhibits/supplies/supplies_5404PH06.html.

Ignoffo, Mary Jo. "A Change of Seasons." In *Reflections of the Past: An Anthology of San Jose*, edited by Judith Henderson, 182–203. Encinatas, CA: Heritage Media Corporation, 1996.

———. *Gold Rush Politics: California's First Legislature.* Sacramento: California State Senate, 1999.

Ingebritsen, S. E., and David R. Jones. "Santa Clara County, California: A Case of Arrested Subsidence." In *Land Subsidence in the United States*, edited by Devin L.

Galloway, David Richard Jones and S. E. Ingebritsen, 15–22. Reston, VA: US Geological Survey, 1999.

Intel Corporation. *Don't Be Encumbered by Past History—Go Off and Do Something Wonderful.* Santa Clara, CA: Intel Museum, 1992.

Invention & Technology. "FMC Sterilizer." *Invention & Technology: The Magazine of Innovation*, Winter 2007. http://www.inventionandtech.com/content/fmc -sterilizer–0.

Irvine, Joan. "Native Oaks and Urban Sprawl." *Pacific Horticulture* (Spring 1982). https://www.pacifichorticulture.org/articles/native-oaks-and-urban-sprawl/.

Irvine, Leah. *Santa Clara County California.* Brochure. San Jose: San Jose Chamber of Commerce, 1915.

Jackson, Joan. "Cannery Season Can Be Life Long." *San Jose Mercury News*, August 11, 1974, S2.

Jacobson, Yvonne. *Passing Farms, Enduring Values: California's Santa Clara Valley.* Los Altos, CA: William Kaufmann, Inc., 1984.

Jasinski, James. "A Constitutive Framework for Rhetorical Historiography: Toward an Understanding of the Discursive (Re)Constitiuon of 'Constitution' in *the Federalist Papers*." In *Doing Rhetorical History: Concepts and Cases*, edited by Kathleen J. Turner, 72–94. Tuscaloosa: University of Alabama Press, 1998.

Johnson, Bob. "Agriculture," Silicon Valley History Online Project. 2004, San José Public Library, California Room.

Jung, Carolyn. "Cherries." *San Jose Mercury News* (San Jose), April 21, 1999.

Kahn, Miriam. "Your Place and Mine: Sharing Emotional Landscapes in Wamira, Papua New Guinea." In *Senses of Place*, edited by Steven Feld and Keith H. Basso, 167–96. Santa Fe, NM: School of American Research Press, 1996.

Karp, David. "Orchard of Dreams." *Gourmet*, July 2005. http://www.gourmet .com/magazine/2000s/2005/07/marianica16.html?printable=true&current Page=2.

Kearney, Anne. "Final Farms." *Peninsula Magazine.*

Kline, David. "The Embattled Family Farm." *This World*, December 13, 1981.

Korusiewicz, Maria. "Places in Placelessness: Notes on the Aesthetic and the Strategies of Place-Making." *Argument* 5, no. 2 (2015): 399–413.

KTEH. *The Valley That Was.* Documentary film clip. YouTube, 2011. https://www .youtube.com/watch?v=CMAdLRIlSGo.

Kwan, Joshua. "How the Valley Found Its Future in the Chips Area's Generations of Bold Fortune-Seekers Have Turned Self-Confidence and Arrogance into a Tradition of Innovation and Success." *San Jose Mercury News*, June 10, 2001, 33S.

Kyle, Gerard, and Garry Chick. "The Social Construction of a Sense of Place." *Leisure Sciences* 29, no. 3 (2007/05/10 2007): 209–25. https://doi.org/10.1080 /01490400701257922.

Laffey, Glory Anne. "Historical Overview and Context for the City of San Jose" Planning Department of the City of San José, March 39, 1992, https://www .sanjoseca.gov/home/showpublisheddocument/78265/637697308303770000

Langellier, Kristin M., and Eric E. Peterson. *Storytelling in Daily Life: Performing Narrative.* Philadelphia: Temple University Press, 2004.

Larimore, Jim. "Valley Losing Its No. 1 Position." *San Jose Mercury News*, January 28, 1968.

Larsen, Joanne. By Anne Marie Todd. December 10, 2015.

Lassiter, Mike. "End of an Era for Bay Area Farms." *San Francisco Examiner*, September 22, 1980.

Lerner, Gerda. *Why History Matters: Life and Thought.* New York: Oxford University Press, 1997.

Leventhal, Alan, Rosemary Cambra, Les Field, and Hank Alvarez. "The Ohlone Back from Extinction." In *The Ohlone Past and Present: Native Americans of the San Francisco Bay Region*, edited by Lowell John Bean. Menlo Park, CA: Ballena Press, 1994.

Levy, Richard. "Costanoan." In *Handbook of North American Indians (California)*, edited by William C. Sturtevant and Robert F. Heizer. Washington, DC: Smithsonian Institution, 1978.

Lindsay, Brendan C. *Murder State: California's Native American Genocide 1846–1873.* Omaha: University of Nebraska Press, 2012.

Lukes, Timothy J., and Gary Y. Okihiro. *Japanese Legacy: Farming and Community Life in California's Santa Clara Valley.* Local History Studies. Vol. 31, Cuptertino: California History Center, DeAnza College, 1985.

Lunsford, Andrea A., Kirt H. Wilson, and Rosa A. Eberly. "The Common Goods of Public Discourse." In *The Sage Handbook of Rhetorical Studies*, edited by Andrea A. Lunsford, Kirt H. Wilson and Rosa A. Eberly, 424–31. Thousand Oaks, CA: Sage Publications, 2009.

Lynch, April. "Valley's Hidden Pesticide Risk." *San Jose Mercury News*, October 18, 2007. https://www.mercurynews.com/2007/10/18/valleys-hidden-pesticide -risk/.

MacCannell, Dean. *The Tourist: A New Theory of the Leisure Class.* Berkeley: University of California Press, 1976.

Malpas, Jeff. "New Media, Cultural Heritage and the Sense of Place: Mapping the Conceptual Ground." *International Journal of Heritage Studies* 14, no. 3 (2008): 197–209.

Marafiote, Tracy. "The American Dream: Technology, Tourism, and the Transformation of Wilderness." *Environmental Communication* 2, no. 2 (2008): 154–72.

Mariani, David. *Poverty of Affluence.* Los Altos: Griffith Press, 2019.

Massey, Doreen. *Space, Place, and Gender.* Minneapolis: University of Minnesota Press, 1994.

———. "Preface." In *Making Sense of Place*, edited by Ian Convery, Gerard Corsane and Peter Davis. Multidisciplinary Perspectives, xiii-xiv. Rochester, NY: Boydell & Brewer, 2012.

Matsumoto, David. *Epitaph for a Peach: Four Seasons on My Family Farm.* San Francisco: HarperOne, 1996.

Matthews, Glenna. "The Apricot War: A Study of the Changing Fruit Industry During the 1930s." *Agricultural History* 59, no. 1 (January 1985): 25–39.

———. "A California Middletown: The Social History of San Jose in the Depression." PhD, Stanford, 1976.

———. "The Fruit Workers of the Santa Clara Valley: Alternative Paths to Union Organization During the 1930s." *Pacific Historical Review* 54, no. 1 (February 1985): 51–70.

———. "The Los Angeles of the North: San Jose's Transition from Fruit Capital to High-Tech Metropolis." *Journal of Urban History* 25, no. 4 (May 1999): 459–76.

———. *Silicon Valley, Women, and the California Dream: Gender, Class, and Opportunity in the Twentieth Century*. Palo Alto, CA: Stanford University Press, 2002.

McBane, Margo, "Santa Clara Valley Women Cannery Workers," Sourisseau Academy, updated July 2017, https://www.sourisseauacademy.org/LADS/July 2017LADS.pdf.

McCaleb, Charles S. *Tracks, Tires and Wires: Public Transportation in California's Santa Calra Valley*. Glendale, CA: Interurban Press, 1981.

Harry McCracken, "IBM Goes West: A 73-Year-Long Saga, From Punch Cards to Watson, *Fast Company*, October 28, 2016. https://www.fastcompany.com /3064902/ibm-goes-west-a-73-year-long-saga-from-punch-cards-to-watson.

McKay, Leonard. "The Canning Industry in San Jose." *San Jose Inside*, February 20, 2006. http://www.sanjoseinside.com/2006/02/20/the_canning_industry_in_san_jose/.

———. "Dutch Hamman Part 1." *San Jose Inside*, January 16, 2006. http://www .sanJoseinside.com/2006/01/16/dutch_hamann/.

———. "Dutch Hamann, Part 2." *San Jose Inside*, January 23, 2006. http://www .sanJoseinside.com/2006/01/23/dutch_hamann1/.

———. "The Faith Davies Story." *San Jose Inside*, December 5, 2005. http://www .sanjoseinside.com/2005/12/05/the_faith_davies_story/.

———. "Louis Pellier." *San Jose Inside*, September 25, 2006. http://www.sanjoseinside .com/2006/09/25/louis_pellier/.

———. "The 1906 Earthquake, Part III." *San Jose Inside*, April 3, 2006. https://www .sanjoseinside.com/2006/04/03/the_1906_earthquake2/.

McKittrick, Katherine. "On Plantations, Prisons, and a Black Sense of Place." *Social and Cultural Geography* 12, no. 8 (2011): 947–63.

McWilliams, Carey. *Factories in the Field: The Story of Migratory Farm Labor in California*. Berkeley: University of California Press, 1939.

Melley, Brian. "Sierra Club Apologizes for Founder John Muir's Racist Views." AP News, July 22, 2020. https://apnews.com/article/national-parks-us-news-parks -environment-ca-state-wire-c52ccd3ac1c127289cf5b1a5c0dc070d.

Meyrowitz, Joshua. *No Sense of Place: The Impact of Electronic Media on Social Behavior*. New York: Oxford University Press, 1985.

Milliken, Randall, Laurence H. Shoup, and Beverly R. Ortiz. *Ohlone/Costanoan Indians of the San Francisco Peninsula and Their Neighbors, Yesterday and Today*. Edited by Archaeological and Historical Consultants. Oakland, CA: National

Park Service 2009. http://www.muwekma.org/images/Ohlone_Costanoan_Indians_of_SF_Peninsula_NPS_2009.pdf.

Mills, Monte. "The Legacy of Federal Control in Indian Country." *Regulatory Review*, March 16, 2021. https://www.theregreview.org/2021/03/16/mills-legacy-federal-control-indian-country/.

Milstein, Tema. "When Whales "Speak for Themselves": Communication as a Mediating Force in Wildlife Tourism." *Environmental Communication* 2, no. 2 (2008): 173–92.

Miranda, Marie Lynn, Sharon E. Edwards, Martha H. Keating, and Christopher J. Paul. "Making the Environmental Justice Grade: The Relative Burden of Air Pollution Exposure in the United States." *International Journal of Environmental Research and Public Health* 8 (2011): 1755–71.

Morse, Debby. "Olson's Takes a Stand." *San Francisco Examiner*, July 9, 1999. https://www.sfgate.com/bayarea/article/Olson-s-takes-a-stand-3076897.php.

Motter, Jeff, and Ross Singer. "Review Essay: Cultivating a Rhetoric of Agrarianism." *Quarterly Journal of Speech* 98, no. 4 (2012): 439–54.

Muir, John. "Rambles of a Botanist among the Plants and Climates of California." *Old and New* 5, no. 6 (June 1872): 767–72. https://scholarlycommons.pacific.edu/cgi/viewcontent.cgi?referer=https://www.google.com/&httpsredir=1&article=1015&context=jmb.

———. *The Yosemite*. New York: The Century Co., 1912. https://vault.sierraclub.org/john_muir_exhibit/writings/the_yosemite/.

Myrow, Rachel. "To Survive as a Fruit Farmer in Silicon Valley, You Need to Grow Tastier Fruit." *California Report*, KQED, June 24, 2018. https://www.kqed.org/news/11676561/to-survive-as-a-fruit-farmer-in-silicon-valley-you-need-to-grow-tastier-fruit.

National Heritage Area Task Force. Special Meeting. Santa Clara Valley National Heritage Area Task Force (2016).

National Oceanic and Atmospheric Administration. "National Centers for Environmental Information." https://www.ncdc.noaa.gov/cdo-web/search;jsessionid=A04E6D705544DA3F59F3D30C10C2635E.

National Park Service. National Heritage Areas: Community-Led Conservation and Development. National Park Service, 2011. https://www.nps.gov/subjects/heritageareas/index.htm.

National Park System Advisory Board. *Charting a Future for National Heritage Areas*. https://www.nps.gov/resources/upload/NHAreport.pdf

Neal, Marian J., Francesca Greco, Daniel Connell, and Julian Conrad. "The Social-Environmental Justice of Groundwater Governance." In *Integrated Groundwater Management: Concepts, Approaches and Challenges*, edited by Anthony J. Jakeman, Olivier Barreteau, Randall J. Hunt, Jean-Daniel Rinaudo and Andrew Ross, 253–72. Cham, Switzerland: Springer International Publishing, 2016.

New York Times. "Joseph B. Ridder, 68, Publisher in San Jose." *The New York Times*, January 26, 1989. https://www.nytimes.com/1989/01/26/obituaries/joseph-b-ridder-68-publisher-in-san-jose.html.

Newsweek. "Boom Town." *Newsweek,* September 14, 1970, 68.

Nieves, Evelyn. "The Superfund Sites of Silicon Valley." *New York Times,* March 26, 2018. https://www.nytimes.com/2018/03/26/lens/the-superfund-sites-of-silicon -valley.html.

Nobel, Justin. "The Miseducation of John Muir." *Atlas Obscura* (July 26, 2016). https://www.atlasobscura.com/articles/the-miseducation-of-john-muir.

Nolte, Carl. "World War II Reshaped the Bay Area and Its People " *San Francisco Chronicle,* May 28, 2012 2012. https://www.sfgate.com/bayarea/article/World -War-II-reshaped-the-Bay-Area-and-its-people–3589894.php.

Olson, Deborah. *Life Is a Bowl of Olson's Cherries.* Santa Cruz, CA: Mission Printers, n.d.

Olwig, Kenneth R. "Landscape as a Contested Topos of Place, Community, and Self." In *Textures of Place,* edited by Paul C. Adams, Steven Hoelscher and Karen E. Till. Exploring Humanist Geographies, 93–118. Minneapolis: University of Minnesota Press, 2001.

Oravec, Christine. "Conservationism vs. Preservationism: The Public Interest in the Hetch Hetchy Controversy." *Quarterly Journal of Speech* 70, no. 4 (1984): 444–58.

———. "John Muir, Yosemite, and the Sublime Response: A Study in the Rhetoric of Preservationism." *Quarterly Journal of Speech* 67, no. 3 (1981): 245–58.

———. "To Stand Outside Oneself: The Sublime in the Discourse of Natural Scenery." In *The Symbolic Earth,* edited by James Cantrill and Christine Oravec, 58–75. Lexington: University Press of Kentucky, 1996.

Orchard and Farm. "Fruit Growers and the Parcel Post; a Questionable Law." *Orchard and Farm,* March 1910.

Orvis, F. "Why Real Estate Pays in Santa Clara County." *Overland Monthly* 54, no. 3 (September 1909): 302–8.

Owen, J. J. *Santa Clara Valley: Its Resources, Climate, Productions, River and Railroad Systems, Towns and Cities, Public Institutions and General Advantages as a Place of Residence with Pen-Sketches of Prominent Citizens.* San Jose, Mercury, 1873.

Paliewicz, Nicholas S. "The Country, the City, and the Corporation: Rio Tinto Kennecott and the Materiality of Corporate Rhetoric." *Environmental Communication* 12, no. 6 (2018): 744–62.

Park, Lisa Sun-Hee, and David N. Pellow. "Racial Formation, Environmental Racism, and the Emergence of Silicon Valley." *Ethnicities* 4, no. 3 (2004): 403–24.

Payne, Stephen M. *Santa Clara County: Harvest of Change.* Northridge, CA: Windsor Publications, Inc., 1987.

Pearce, Ralph. "Looking Back: Clyde Arbuckle, San José's First City Historian." San Jose Public Library, March 15, 2014. Accessed March 15, 2014. https://www.sjpl .org/blog/looking-back-clyde-arbuckle-san-Joses-first-city-historian.

Peck, Willys I. "Agriculture's Erosion: W.W.II Began a Shift to Industry." *San José Mercury News,* December 27, 1999 1999, 1A.

―――. *Saratoga Stereoopticon: A Magic Lantern of Memory*. Cupertino: California History Center and Foundation, 1997.

Pedersen, Steven M. "A Composed "Rhetoric" in Place: A Material-Epistemic Reading of Plato's Phaedrus." *Rhetoric Review* 36, no. 1 (January 2, 2017): 1–14.

Pellow, David N. *Resisting Global Toxics: Transnational Movements for Environmental Justice*. Cambridge, MA: MIT Press, 2007.

Pellow, David N., and Lisa Sun-Hee Park. *The Silicon Valley of Dreams: Environmental Injustice, Immigrant Workers, and the High-Tech Global Economy*. New York: New York University Press, 2002.

Peterson, Tarla Rai. "Environmental Communication: Tales of Life on Earth." *Quarterly Journal of Speech* 84 (1998): 371–93.

―――. "Telling the Farmers' Story: Competing Responses to Soil Conservation Rhetoric." *Quarterly Journal of Speech* 77 (1991): 289–308.

Philip, Tom. "Sign of Spring: Long-Lived Sunnyvale Orchard Faces Its Toughest Challenge." *San Jose Mercury News*, May 21, 1986, 1.

Pitti, Stephen J. *The Devil in Silicon Valley: Northern California, Race and Mexican Americans*. Princeton, NJ: Princeton University Press, 2003.

Porter, Nicole. "'Single-Minded, Compelling, and Unique': Visual Communications, Landscape, and the Calculated Aesthetic of Place Branding." *Environmental Communication* 7, no. 2 (June 1, 2013): 231–54.

Rambo, Ralph. *Almost Forgotten: Cartoon Pen and Inklings of the Old Santa Clara Valley by a Native*. San Jose, CA: The Rosecrucian Press, 1964.

―――. *Pioneer Blue Book of the Old Santa Clara Valley*. San Jose: Rosicrucian Press, 1973.

―――. *Rembmer When . . . : A Boy's Eye View of an Old Valley*. San Jose, CA: The Rosicrucian Press, Ltd., 1965.

Rawls, James J. *Indians of California: The Changing Image*. Norman: University of Oklahoma Press, 1986.

The Regulatory Review. "Native Peoples, Tribal Sovereignty, and Regulation." *The Regulatory Review*, March 15, 2021. https://www.theregreview.org/2021/03/15/native-tribal-regulation/.

Reinhardt, Richard. "Joe Ridder's San Jose." *San Francisco Magazine*, November 1965, 45–48, 66–71. http://mercurynews.historysanjose.org/wp-content/uploads/2016/07/joe_ridders_san_jose_1965.pdf.

Relph, Edward. *Place and Placelessness*. Research in Planning and Design. London: Pion, 1976.

―――. "Spirit of Place and Sense of Place in Virtual Realities." *Society for Philosophy and Technology Quarterly Electronic Journal* 10, no. 3 (2007).

The Resident. "It's Blossom Time again in Santa Clara Valley." *The Resident*, March 31, 1953.

Richards, Sally. *Silicon Valley Sand Dreams and Silicon Orchards*. Carlsbad, CA: Heritage Media Corp, 2000.

Ritchie, Donald A. *Doing Oral History: A Practical Guide*. New York: Oxford University Press, 2003.

Robertson, Mark. "Looking Back: Canning in the Valley of Heart's Delight." San Jose Public Lbrary, o13. https://www.sjpl.org/blog/looking-back-canning-valley-hearts-delight.

Rockstroh, Dennis, "San Jose Secret—until Now," *Dennis Rockstroh's California*, June 11, 2013, https://drockstroh.wordpress.com/2013/06/11/san-jose-secret-until-now/

Rodriguez, Joe. "Oral History: How World War Ii Changed Silicon Valley " *San Jose Mercury News*, August 12, 2010. https://www.mercurynews.com/2010/08/12/oral-history-how-world-war-ii-changed-silicon-valley/.

Rogers, Paul. "Hamann: San Jose's Growth Guru." *San Jose Mercury News*, February 28, 2002. https://web.archive.org/web/20050223144311/http://www.siliconvalley.com/mld/siliconvalley/living/2765036.htm.

Ruiz, Vicki L. *Cannery Women Cannery Lives: Mexican Women, Unionization, and the California Food Processing Industry, 1930–1950*. Albequerque: University of New Mexico Press, 1987.

Russ, Alex, Scott J. Peters, Marianne E. Krasny, and Richard C. Stedman. "Development of Ecological Place Meaning in New York City." *Journal of Environmental Education* 46, no. 2 (2015): 73–93.

Sachs, Aaron. "Virtual Ecology: A Brief Environmental History of Silicon Valley." *World Watch* 12, (January/February 1999).

Sackman, Douglas Cazaux. *Orange Empire*. Berkeley: University of California Press, 2005.

Sacramento Business Journal. "Mariani Packing Co. Moves to Vacaville." *Sacramento Business Journal*, Sepbemter 7, 2000. https://www.bizjournals.com/sacramento/stories/2000/09/04/daily14.html.

Sacramento Daily Union. "Railroad and Boat Timetable for Sacramento." *Sacramento Daily Union*, March 14, 1874. https://cdnc.ucr.edu/?a=d&d=SDU18740314.2.43&e=-------en--20--1--txt-txIN--------1.

San Francisco Examiner. "Let's Conserve the Vanishing Farmland." *San Francisco Examiner*, December 25, 1981.

———. "San Jose Chamber of Commerce Lures 2000 Industries." *San Francisco Examiner*, March 8, 1953.

San Jose Chamber of Commerce. *An Aerial View of Progressive, San Jose, Calif.* San Jose, CA: San Jose Chamber of Commerce, 1952.

———. *It's Happening Downtown San Jose*. San Jose, CA: San Jose Chamber of Commerce, 1973.

———. *San Jose (San Hosay) Santa Clara County California*. Brochure. San Jose: San Jose Chamber of Commerce, 1904.

———. *Santa Clara County California*. Brochure. San Jose, CA: San Jose Chamber of Commerce Publicity Department, 1930.

———. *This Is San Jose*. San Jose, CA: San Jose Chamber of Commerce, 1977.

———. *Valley of Heart's Delight*. Film. 18:00. Three Crowns Productions, 1948. https://archive.org/details/valley_of_hearts_delight.

———. *The Valley of Heart's Delight: Where It Is, How to See It*. Brochure. San Jose, CA: San Jose Chamber of Commerce 1910.

San Jose Mercury. "Booming, Blooming—That's Santa Clara County Now!" *San Jose Mercury*, March 7, 1953.

———. "From Farmland to Metropolis, Hamann Guided San Jose During Spectacular Boom." *San Jose Mercury*, March 24, 1977.

———. "Progress Edition." *San Jose Mercury*, January 19, 1958.

———. "San Jose Named All-America City." *San Jose Mercury*, March 16, 1961.

———. "300,000 in SJ within 18 Months." *San Jose Mercury News*, August 24, 1961.

San Jose Mercury Herald. "Fruit Administration Leader in Plea to Orchardists of Valley." *San Jose Mercury Herald*, September 16, 1918, 1.

———. "Fruit Men Hit Hard by Rain." *San Jose Mercury Herald*, September 15, 1918, 1.

———. "Loss near Quarter of Crop." *San Jose Mercury Herald*, September 14, 1918, 1.

———. "Plan Move to Lessen Loss Here." *San Jose Mercury Herald*, September 17, 1918, 1.

———. "Prune Pits Wanted by U.S." *San Jose Mercury Herald*, September 18, 1918, 1.

———. "Save Fruit for Our Boys!" *San Jose Mercury Herald*, September 12, 1918, 1.

———. "Soldiers from Fremont Likely to Assist in Gathering Prunes." *San Jose Mercury Herald*, September 15, 1918, 1.

———. "Storm Calamity for Santa Clara Valley—Heavy Loss for Growers." September 13, 1918, 1.

———. "Tenants for Lands Vacated by Japanese Sought by WCCA Here." *Mercury Herald*, April 2, 1942.

San Jose Mercury News. "City Grew by 7,200 Persons, 500 Acres." *San Jose Mercury News*, October 8, 1967.

———. "S.J. Increases Sewer Fees." *San Jose Mercury News*, March 3, 1976.

———. *Sunshine Fruit and Flowers: Santa Clara County and Its Resources: Historical Descriptive Statistical. A Souvenir.* San Jose CA: Alfred C. Eaton, 1896.

San Jose News. "'City That Dutch Built' Salutes Its A. P. Hamann." *San Jose Mercury News*, Special A. P. Hamann Edition, November 21, 1969.

———. "99 Tour Blossom Land on 22 Busses." *San Jose News*, March 14, 1955.

———. "1,000 Tour Blooming Valley." *San Jose News*, March 21, 1955.

San Jose Newspaper Guild. *4th Annual Gridiron Dinner Program.* San Jose Newspaper Guild, April 30, 1955. California History Center Silicon Valley History Online. De Anza College, California History Center. https://calisphere.org/item/ark:/13030/kt0779p8zg/.

Santa Clara County Fruit Exchange. *How to Prepare Nature's Health Food: The California Prune.* San Jose, CA, Santa Clara County Fruit Exchange, 1905.

Sarwai, Khalida. "Fruit Cocktail Club Stirs Up Historical Views of Saratoga." *San Jose Mercury News*, January 18, 2018. https://www.mercurynews.com/2018/01/18/fruit-cocktail-club-to-stir-up-historical-views-of-saratoga/.

Savoy, Lauret Edith. *Trace: Memory, History, Race, and the American Landscape.* Berkeley, CA: Counterpoint, 2015.

Sawyer, Eugene T. *History of Santa Clara County.* Los Angeles, CA: Historic Record Company, 1922. http://www.usgwarchives.net/ca/santaclara/history.html.

Senda-Cook, Samantha. "Materializing Tensions: How Maps and Trails Mediate Nature." *Environmental Communication* 7, no. 3 (2013): 355–71.

———. "Rugged Practices: Embodying Authenticity in Outdoor Recreation." *Quarterly Journal of Speech* 98 (2013): 129–52.

Schaider, Laurel A., Lucien Swetschinski, Christopher Campbell, and Ruthann A. Rudel. "Environmental Justice and Drinking Water Quality: Are There Socioeconomic Disparities in Nitrate Levels in U.S. Drinking Water?" *Enviromental Health* 18, no. 3 (2019). https://doi.org/10.1186/s12940-018-0442-6.

Shrestha, Srishti, Freya Kamel, David M. Umbach, Laura E. Beane Freeman, Stella Koutros, Michael Alavanja, Aaron Blair, Dale P. Sandler, and Honglei Chen. "High Pesticide Exposure Events and Olfactory Impairment among U.S. Farmers." *Environmental Health Perspectives* 127, no. 1 (2019). https://ehp.niehs.nih.gov/doi/10.1289/ehp3713.

Silicon Valley Newsroom. "Ag Plan Aims to Preserve Santa Clara County Farms, Rangeland." *San Jose Inside*, January 29, 2019. http://www.sanjoseinside.com/2019/01/29/ag-plan-aims-to-preserve-santa-clara-county-farms-rangeland/.

Sirica, Jack. "Sealing the Fate of a Dying Trade." *San Jose Mercury*, August 22, 1982, 1A, 2A.

Smith, Sidonie, and Julia Watson. *Reading Autobiography: A Guide for Interpreting Life Narratives.* 2nd ed. Minneapolis: University of Minnesota Press, 2010.

Smith, T., C. Wilmsen, and Bancroft Library Research Organization. History. *Pioneer Activist for Environmental Justice in Silicon Valley, 1967–2000: Oral History Transcript/2003.* Charleston, SC: BiblioBazaar, 2016..

Smith, Ted, David A. Sonnenfeld, and David Naguib Pellow, eds. *Challenging the Chip: Labor Rights and Environmental Justice in the Global Electronics Industry.* Philadelphia, PA: Temple University Press, 2006.

Spalding, John. "San Jose's Growth Shaped by A. P. Hamann." *San Jose News*, March 29, 1977.

Spellman, Tom. "The Citrus Label Era (1887–1955)." *Citrograph*, July–August 2011, 21–23.

Spurlock, Cindy M. "Performing and Sustaining (Agri)Culture and Place: The Cultivation of Environmental Subjectivity on the Piedmont Farm Tour." *Text and Performance Quarterly* 29, no. 1 (2009): 5–21.

Stanford Environmental Law Society. *San José: Sprawling City: A Study of the Causes and Effects of Urban Sprawl, in San José, California.* Stanford, CA: Stanford Environmental Law Society, 1971.

Stanley, Tim. *The Last of the Prune Pickers: A Pre-Silicon Valley Story.* Irvine, CA: Timothy Publishing, 2009.

Statz, Stephanie. "California's Fruit Cocktail: A History of Industrial Food Production, the State, and the Environment of Northern California." PhD dissertation, University of Houston, 2012.

Stegner, Wallace. "Forward." In *Passing Farms, Enduring Values: California's Santa Clara Valley*, edited by Yvonne Jacobson, viii–xi. Los Altos, CA: William Kaufman Inc., 1984.

———. "The Frontier Spirit." *Span Magazine*, December 1981.

Stewart, Kathleen C. "An Occupied Place." In *Senses of Place*, edited by Steven Feld and Keith H. Basso, 137–65. Santa Fe, NM: School of American Research, 1996.

Stipp, George H. "The Valley of Santa Clara." *Out West*, November 1909, 923–36.

Stokowski, Patricia A. "Languages of Place and Discourses of Power: Constructing New Senses of Place." *Journal of Leisure Research* 34, no. 4 (December 1, 2002): 368–82.

Stoll, Steven. *The Fruits of Natural Advantage: Making the Industrial Countryside in California*. Berkeley: University of California Press, 1998.

Storey, David. "Land, Territory and Identity." In *Making Sense of Place*, edited by Ian Convery, Gerard Corsane and Peter Davis. Multidisciplinary Perspectives, 11–22. Rochester, NY: Boydell & Brewer, 2012.

Subcommittee on Planning and Zoning, "State Greenbelt Legislation and the Problem of Urban Encroachment on California Agriculture", *Journal of the Assembly of the State of California*, Sacramento May 1957.

Sulek, Julia Prodis. "Sunnyvale: Landmark C.J. Olson's Cherries Fruit Stand to Close Sept. 30." *San Jose Mercury News*, August 29, 2018. https://www.mercurynews .com/2018/08/29/sunnyvale-landmark-c-j-olsons-cherries-fruit-stand-to-close -sept–30/.

———. "Valley's Last Packing Plant for Dried Fruit Is Moving." *San Jose Mercury News*, April 24, 2001.

Sunnyvale Chamber of Commerce. *Sunnyvale, U.S.A: The City with the Built in Future*. Sunnyvale, CA, Sunnyvale Chamber of Commerce, 1955.

Sunnyvale Historical Society and Museum Association. *Orchard Heritage Park*. Sunnyvale, CA: Sunnyvale Historical Society and Museum Association, 2001.

Sunnyvale Standard. "Editorial." *Sunnyvale Standard*, October 20, 1965.

Suryaraman, Maya. "Valley Packers Wither on the Vine." *San Jose Mercury News*, July 22, 1990.

Swenson, David. "Most of America's Rural Areas Are Doomed to Decline." *The Conversation* (May 7, 2019). Accessed October 11, 2020. https://theconversation.com /most-of-americas-rural-areas-are-doomed-to-decline–115343.

Szasz, Andrew, and Michael Meuser. "Unintended, Inexorable: The Production of Environmental Inequalities in Santa Clara County, California." *American Behavioral Scientist* 43, no. 4 (2000): 602–32.

Taylor, Bayard. *El Dorado or Adventures in the Path of Empire*. New York: G.P. Putnam, 1850.

Taylor Brothers Farms. "FAQ: What Is a Prune?" https://www.taylorbrothersfarms .com/pages/faq.

Thomas, Peter, and Donna Thomas. *Muir Ramble Route: Walking from San Francisco to Yosemite in the Footsteps of John Muir*. Madera, CA: Poetic Matrix Press, 2010.

Thompson, Jessica Leigh, and James G. Cantrill. "The Symbolic Transformation of Space." *Environmental Communication* 7, no. 1 (2013): 1–3. https://doi.org/10 .1080/17524032.2012.758650.

Thorne, W. S. *Santa Clara County, California*. Brochure. San Jose, CA: Board of Trade of San Jose, 1887.

Tomb, Geoffrey. "As the Final Harvest Ends, a Tech Fortune Begins." *San Jose Mercury News*, December 18, 1999, 1.

———. "Valley Once Was Ripe with Fruit, Nuts, Canneries." *San Jose Mercury News*, December 18, 1999.

Torriero, E. A. "Fresh-Fruit Craze Puts Lid on Canneries." *San Jose Mercury News*, August 27, 1986.

Trip Advisor. "Silicon Valley, California." 2019, https://www.tripadvisor.com/Attraction_Review-g28926-d142401-Reviews-Silicon_Valley-California.html.

Trounstine, Philip J., and Terry Christensen. *Movers and Shakers: The Study of Community Power*. New York: St. Martin's Press, 1982.

Tsu, Cecilia M. *Garden of the World: Asian Immigrants and the Making of Agriculture in California's Santa Clara Valley*. New York: Oxford University Press, 2013.

Tuan, Yi-Fu. *Space and Place: The Perspective of Experience*. Minneapolis: University of Minnesota Press, 1977.

Tumolo, Michael. "On Useful Rhetorical History." *Journal of Contemporary Rhetoric* 1, no. 2 (2011): 55–62.

Turner, Kathleen J. "Introduction." In *Doing Rhetorical History: Concepts and Cases*, edited by Kathleen J. Turner. Studies in Rhetoric and Communication, 1–18. Tuscaloosa: The University of Alabama Press, 1998.

———, ed. *Doing Rhetorical History: Concepts and Cases*. Studies in Rhetoric and Communication. Tuscaloosa: The University of Alabama Press, 1998.

Turner, Wallace. "Idyllic Valley Now Urban Anthill, Planner Charges." *New York Times*, September 7, 1970. https://www.nytimes.com/1970/09/07/archives/idyllic-valley-now-urban-anthill-planner-charges-county-in.html.

US Global Change Research Program. *National Climate Assessment*. Washington DC: US Global Change Research Program, 2014. https://nca2014.globalchange.gov/report.

Uhlman, James Todd. "Geographies of Desire: Bayard Taylor and the Romance of Travel in Bourgeois American Culture, 1820–1880." PhD dissertaion. Rutgers University, 2007. https://rucore.libraries.rutgers.edu/rutgers-lib/23892/.

Vance, Ashlee. "36 Hours in Silicon Valley." *New York Times*, 2010. https://www.nytimes.com/2010/09/05/travel/05hours.html.

Vanderwarker, Amy. "Water and Environmental Justice." In *A Twenty-First Century U.S. Water Policy*, edited by Juliet Christian-Smith and Peter H. Gleick, 52–89. Oakland, CA: Pacific Institute, 2013.

Vaught, David. *Cultivating California: Growers, Specialty Crops, and Labor, 1875–1920*. Baltimore, MD: Johns Hopkins University Press, 1999.

VonWaaden, Craig. *Million Dollar Dirt*. 2003. Documentary film. https://www.youtube.com/watch?v=_oKFtf2Twms.

Wadsworth, Jennifer. "Fresh Choice." *Metro*, March 19–25, 2014, 14–19.

Waters, Christina. "Cherry Condition." *Metro, Taste*, October 10–16, 1996, 35.

Wells, Harry L. . "In Blossom Land: A Springtime Sketch of San Jose and Santa Clara County California." *Sunset Magazine*, May 1902.

Whiting, Sam. "Ag Plan Strives to Preserve Silicon Valley's Farming Heritage." *San Francisco Chronicle*, February 18, 2018. https://www.sfchronicle.com/bayarea /article/Ag-Plan-strives-to-preserves-Silicon-Valley-s-12623666.php.

Williams, Daniel R. "Making Sense of 'Place': Reflections on Pluralism and Positionality in Place Research." *Landscape and Urban Planning* 131 (2014): 74–82. https://doi.org/10.1016/j.landurbplan.2014.08.002.

Williams, Edward A., . *Open Space: The Choices before California; the Urban Metropolitan Open Space Study.* San Francisco: Diablo Press, 1969.

Winthrop, Spencer. "The Spirit of Santa Clara Valley." *Overland Monthly* 54, no. 3 (1909): 309–15.

Woods, Michael, Jesse Heley, Carol Richards, and Suzie Watkin. "Rural People and the Land." In *Making Sense of Place: Multidisciplinary Perspectives*, edited by Ian Convery, Gerard Corsane and Peter Davis, 57–66. Woodbridge, UK: Boydell & Brewer, 2012.

Woolley, Robert. "Tracts Replacing Orchards." *San Francisco Chronicle*, March 13, 1955.

Worster, Donald. *A Passion for Nature: The Life of John Muir.* Oxford: Oxford University Press, 2008.

Zarefsky, David. "Four Senses of Rhetorical History." In *Doing Rhetorical History: Concepts and Cases*, edited by Kathleen J. Turner, 19–32. Tuscaloosa: University of Alabama Press, 1998.

Zavala, Marianna, "Spade and Plow Organics: Continuing the Legacy of Santa Clara Valley Farmers." Pacific Coast Farmers' Market Association, December 27, 2017, https://www.pcfma.org/blog/spade-plow-organics-continuing-legacy-santa -clara-valley-farmers.

Zavella, Patricia. *Women's Work and Chicano Families: Cannery Workers of the Santa Clara Valley.* Ithaca, NY: Cornell University Press, 1987.

Zetterquist, James. "Fruit Cocktail Club Movie Night." Paper presented at the Fruit Cocktail Club, Saratoga Foothill Club, January 27, 2016.

INDEX

fruit work, 7–8, 29, 58; cannery work, 70–79; orchard, 59–69
fruit workers, 8, 21, 24, 27, 61–79, 61*fig.*, 65*fig.*, 67*fig.*, 69*fig.*, 72*fig.*, 76*fig.*, 81, 82,
fruit workers (*continued*)
    85, 125. *See also* cutting shed; prune(s), dipper; prune(s), pickers

Garrod, Emma Stolte, 63
Garrod, R. V., 62
Garrod, Vince S., 9, 62, 63, 68, 82
Gold Rush, 28–29
Great Depression, 4, 67, 86
greenbelt, 97, 100

Hamann, Dutch, 88–94, 89*fig.*, 97, 100, 102, 107, 112
Hamilton, Mac, 106
Hamilton, Tori, 109, 121
Heart's Delight (brand), 51, 52*fig.*
heritage discourse, 124–27
housing, 1, 5–6, 7, 95, 98, 100, 103, 103*fig.*, 105–7, 110–12, 115

IBM, 86, 87, 90
immigrants, 24, 25, 27, 30, 37, 62, 80, 121–22. *See also* migrant workers
indigenous peoples, 28–29, 32–33
Intel Corporation, 118

Jacobson, Yvonne, 1, 7, 37–38, 43, 56, 101, 105–6, 123, 128

labor: discourse of, 27; division of, 70; indigenous, 28; manual, 64, 73, 76, 129; seasonal, 61, 71; strikes, 80. *See also* cannery workers; cutting shed; fruit work; fruit workers; prune(s), picking; mechanization; migrant workers
land speculation, 94–96
Los Altos, California, 93, 125

machine(s), 9, 58, 59, 62, 70–81, 84–85. *See also* conveyor belt; mechanization; prune(s), dipper; Sterilmatic
Mariani, Andy, 63, 113–15, 122, 128
Mariani, David, 24, 37, 63, 106, 107
Mariani, Mark, 24, 37, 63, 111, 122

Mariani Packing Company, 24, 37
Martial Cottle Agricultural Park, 125
mechanization, 4, 31, 71, 72–74, 78, 79–85. *See also* conveyor belt; machine(s); Sterilmatic
Melehan, Joe, 24, 75
memoirs, 23–25, 36, 56, 59, 63, 66, 68, 69, 124, 126
migrant workers, 24, 27, 60, 61, 62, 66. *See also* immigrants; labor, seasonal
mobility, 16, 30, 118, 119
Morgan Hill, California, 63, 93, 113–14, 125
Muir, John, 32–33, 56
Muirson, George, 50
Muirson Label Company, 9, 39*fig.*, 50, 51*fig.*, 52*fig.*

narrative, 6–7, 14, 17, 19, 21, 24, 55, 56, 59, 126; historical, 18, 20, 22, 26–27, 30, 56; personal, 18, 20, 21, 22, 23, 25, 55; place, 20
National Heritage Area, 127
Native Americans, 28, 32–33, 56. *See also* indigenous peoples; Ohlone
non-place, 30, 115–19, 127
nostalgia, 24, 56, 79, 114, 125–27

office parks, 5, 6, 7, 10, 29, 110, 112, 115–17
Ohlone, 28, 29; Costanoan, 29; Muwekma, 29
Olson, Charlie, 1–2, 81, 104–6, 115, 121, 126, 130
Olson, Deborah, 8, 9, 101, 105–6, 115, 129
Olson, R. C., 101
open space, 98, 100, 110, 115, 120, 129
Orchard and Farm, 49
orchardists, 2, 23, 48, 53, 91, 94, 101, 106, 108, 114
orchards, 4, 7, 9, 39*fig.*, 42*fig.*, 43*fig.*, 52*fig.*; Andy's, 113–15, 130; beauty, 37–44, 51, 120; continuous, 40, 41, 55, 95; heritage, 125; largest, 2, 41; Olson's, 1–2, 101, 104–6, 130; productivity of, 6, 39, 44–45, 48, 58; removal, 5, 10, 30, 92, 104–8, 110–12, 120, 124; sense of place, 77–79, 83, 90; vista, 40–41, 51–53, 55; work, 59–70. *See also* fruit workers; labor
Out West magazine, 42, 43

Sunsweet, 49, 62, 70
syrup, 71, 72

taxes, 83, 95–96, 106, 129
Taylor, Bayard, 38
technology, 6, 7, 13, 29, 79, 117, 121. *See also*
    computer industry; electronics;
    mobility; Silicon Valley
Thompson, Albert R., 73
Thorp, Sam, 128
tourism, 15, 33
tourist(s), 22–23, 32, 33, 34, 36, 52, 55, 116;
    attraction, 36; discourse, 21, 22–23, 34,
    55, 66, 107
trays, 3–4, 62, 63–65, 64*fig.*, 66, 68, 84

urbanization, 5–6, 29–30, 99–102, 107, 120

Valley of Heart's Delight (film), 60, 110

Valley View (brand), 51–52
Veggielution Community Farm, 129

wages, 27, 80, 85
Williamson Act, 101
women, 66, 68, 70–71, 75, 77–79, 80, 121
Wool, Bruce, 106
Wool, Frederick, 57–58
Wool, Jane, 57–58
Wool, Jennifer, 74, 75, 78, 106, 108, 123
Wool family, 24, 36, 59
World War I, 3
World War II, 2, 5, 7, 10, 30, 82, 87–88, 91,
    114

Zavella, Patricia, 75, 77, 79
Zerbo, Anthony, 62, 63
Zetterquist, Jim, 9, 24, 59, 75, 78, 123, 125

Founded in 1893,
UNIVERSITY OF CALIFORNIA PRESS
publishes bold, progressive books and journals
on topics in the arts, humanities, social sciences,
and natural sciences—with a focus on social
justice issues—that inspire thought and action
among readers worldwide.

The UC PRESS FOUNDATION
raises funds to uphold the press's vital role
as an independent, nonprofit publisher, and
receives philanthropic support from a wide
range of individuals and institutions—and from
committed readers like you. To learn more, visit
ucpress.edu/supportus.

Milton Keynes UK
Ingram Content Group UK Ltd.
UKHW020413200524
442884UK00007B/428